THE ART AND SCIENCE OF CINEMA

ANWAR HUDA

ATLANTIC
ATLANTIC
PUBLISHERS & DISTRIBUTORS

Published by
ATLANTIC PUBLISHERS AND DISTRIBUTORS
B-2, Vishal Enclave, Opp. Rajouri Garden, New Delhi-110027
Phones : 25413460, 25429987, 25466842

Sales Office
7/22, Ansari Road, Darya Ganj, New Delhi-110002
Phones : 23273880, 23275880, 23280451
Fax : 91-11-23285873
web : www.atlanticbooks.com
e-mail : info@atlanticbooks.com

ISBN 81-269-0348-1

Printed in India at
Nice Printing Press, Delhi

PREFACE

> "Cinema is everything, literature, sculpture, music, painting, everything."
>
> —*Pier Paolo Pasolini*

We do not see any art so beautiful, so communicative as cinema. It is a harmonious blend of talent and technology. The cinema is like a horizon, where science and art meet. The filmmaking is a collective noun and, therefore, it cannot be compared with writing or painting. It is more like sculpture or music, where a team of talented human beings works to produce everlasting great classics.

This book is the outcome of the labour of love for cinema. It provides a clear and concise introduction to the exciting world of film. Today moviemaking is one of the fastest growing fields in the world, as more and more people realize its possibilities and potentials. "The Art and Science of Cinema" is a key to understand the basics of Cinema as well as a guide for film lovers.

Many books have been written on cinema, which were purely designed for film students, and hardly interest general lovers of cinema. I have purposely avoided too many technical things and tried my best to make the book informative and interesting. It is like the first book before you move to a more serious study. I am sure that I have provided all details about the medium that will be useful for both the film students as well as serious movie watchers.

Well, I hope, by the time you have read the whole book, you can enjoy and understand films better than before.

ANWAR HUDA

Acknowledgments

Many people from inside and outside the film industry made an invaluable contribution to the preparation of this research based book. I am highly indebted to them. And when I will make films, I will pay them handsomely. It is my promise and I am sure, this book will help me to get a producer to finance my first international film.

Chief Contributors

For the Great World Cinemas

T.G. Vaidyanathan
Pradeep Sebastian
Maithili Rao
Dinesh Raheja
Ajit Duara

For the World's Great Actors

Suresh Chabria
Pardeep Sebastian
Maithili Rao
Boman Desai
Siddhatha

For Films on Mental Illness

Nina Martyris

For the Most Underrated Films

Rashid Irani
Kiran David
Naman Ramchandran
Saibal Chatterjee
Anjum Rajabali
C.S. Venkiteswaran

For Movies Rewriting History

John Harlow
Nicholas Hellen

For Special Effects

Bertram D'costa

Bernd William

For Film Piracy

Amy Harmon

CONTENTS

Preface .... *iii*

Acknowledgments .... *v*

Chief Contributors .... *vii*

1. The Picture 1
   - Why Do We Watch Films 2
   - A Brief History of Cinema 8
   - The Great World Cinemas 10
2. The Audience 61
3. The Producer 64
4. The Filmmaker (Director) 66
   - World's Great Directors (Filmmakers) 72
5. The Cast 103
   - World's Great Actors 108
6. The Screenplay 125
7. The Budget 130
8. The Cinematography 133
9. The Editing 144
10. The Sound 149
11. The Art Direction 154
12. The Costume 157
13. The Make-Up 160

14. The Music 162

15. The Special Effects 165

16. The Stunts 173

17. The Play and the Film 176

18. The Documentary 178

19. Films on Mental Illness 181

20. The Most Underrated Films 184

21. The Bollywood 190

22. The Box Office 194

23. Movies Rewriting History 197

24. Film Piracy 200

25. IMAX Films and Theatre 203

26. War Films 205

27. Still Photography 208

28. OSCAR Trivia 219

29. The Interesting Little Facts 246

30. The Best Genre Films 253

31. Pre-Production Works 257

32. Glossary 260

33. Further Readings 264

34. Film Schools, Museums and Websites 267

1

THE PICTURE

> "The white eye of the screen need only reflect the light that is properly its own to blow up the universe."
>
> —*Luis Bunuel*

A picture is worth a thousand words. Let oceans be the ink and all trees be the pens, still they cannot write those emotions so beautiful, so touching what a picture does. The medium of cinema is a combo of millions of pictures. It is all about motion and emotions. Any filmmaker, who favours words over images, is actually manufacturing a play not a film. It is purely about the magic of moving images, other things must remain supportive only.

Many purists may not accept cinema as an art as it is the youngest art, we all know. An artist works on behalf of the community and for the community. An art entertains us, informs us and soothes our senses. If these are the criterias to establish something as an art, then cinema is an art. Better than all arts. More powerful than all arts. Because nothing communicates better than this. It connects our subconscious, reflects our values, customs, styles and life. And like other arts, it can be preserved too. This art is the real crowd puller. It informs us, entertains us and thins our emotions.

Nature has given us a perfect optical instrument — eyes. We can see all colours as they are. The camera works like our eyes. But it can also record the images. Each image received by our eyes, remains on the retina for a fraction of a second. And these very images, moving at the speed of about 14 per second, merge together to produce the illusion of movement. This effect is called "The persistence of vision." The cinema works on the persistence of vision and thus the movements are recorded and reproduced.

Everybody wonders about the movements on the screen. The invention of the cinema was like a miracle. In many remote areas, people ran away after watching walking human beings and animals on the screen. They feared that the characters might come out of the screen. How do we capture movements, is the real question. In cinema halls, a projector runs the film at the speed of 24 frames per second. Each frame looks like a negative of still camera. Both are of 35 mm gauge. The speed of 24 frames per second produces the effect of movements. The movie camera records the images at the same speed. One and half feet of the film travels per second through the projector and the movie camera. This 35 mm film has perphoration (Small Holes) at the both sides, which are attached to the claws of the projector.

The making of film involves great talents and big money. It is the world's highest risky and the most entertaining business. A film's primary purpose is to tell an interesting story. The stories, which were once used to be heard and imagined, are now preserved on the screen. The magic of the movies will continue to reduce our sense and to some extent overwhelm us. Because the characters do the things in a film, what we cannot. We identify with the characters and achieve the emotional catharsis at the end of the picture. And the technology is growing very fast. The power of special effects plays the wizards to make anything and everything possible on the screen. When we think of the dinosaurs, we do not imagine, we think "Jurassic Park." That is it. Long live cinema!

WHY DO WE WATCH FILMS

What an absurd question? Of course for entertainment. It is another truth that the American students learn more from watching films than reading books. But the films do not contain the whole fact and therefore its primary goal is always to entertain the masses as well as the classes. And Cinema has already been acknowledged as the most popular form of entertainment. The magic of audio-visuals carrying an interesting story always makes us spellbound. In early days of cinema, movie halls all over the world played to the packed houses and the audience of all races and creeds worshipped at the shrine of the film. It was a revolutionary invention, which filled everybody's mind with awe and curiosity. The only art in the history of the world, in which scientists and artists worked together and brought revolution in the field of communication and entertainment. The cinema halls have engulfed everything, circus, theatre, even reading, and everything. Apart from entertainment, a film is watched for other reasons. Few of them are :

1. Emotional attachment
2. New File (Information)
3. New Phobea (Fear)
4. Need to bond
5. Need to conflict
6. Need for a conclusion

A film's story is developed with the help of good, bad and the ugly characters. A larger group of audience develops an emotional attachment with the protagonist of the story. They cry and laugh with him. They even feel like him. For three hours, the viewers remain in the world of storyteller. This identification with the hero, help to bring the public to the theatres.

New information and the new fear are another factors, which make us watch films. We have long heard and read about the dinosaurs, but never seen them. So the curiosity to know how they looked like, behaved like, made us go to the cinema halls. We experienced the new fear by watching the film. The fear of space, the past and the danger of future are experienced by watching different kinds of films. Films are like books. The only difference is that films also contain things of imagination.

We, as human beings, need to bond with others like us. A film's story is largely based on our own lives. The same bond is seen between the film's characters. In Michael Mann's 'Heat', it was the same need to bond, which ultimately becomes the tragic flaw of the protagonist. Films are instruments of Communication. And all filmmakers are basically communicators of their ideas, thoughts and visions. Film is a mass communication.

Communication Theory : Communication is a social process by which expression of human needs takes place and people influence each other. All communications are social. We cannot communicate to an inanimate object. The effective communication always involves more than one person at a time. It is basically the science of sharing ideas, views, thoughts, and expressions through some medium. It makes individual interaction possible and comprehensible. Communication is the basis on which man is considered a social being and it makes him engage in art, science, literature and many other socially useful disciplines. Over the ages man has learnt to communicate his needs in many ways.

Communication is basically meant for fulfilling human needs. When his needs are not met, he faces deprivation.

Human Needs	Without This	If Fulfilled
1. Physiological Need	(a) Hunger (b) Thirst (c) Weakness (d) Sickness	(a) Food (b) Drink (c) Strength (d) Health
2. Safety & Security Need	(a) Threat (b) Insecurity (c) Anxiety (d) Fear	(a) Safety (b) Security (c) Peace of Mind (d) Assurance
3. Love and affection needs	(a) Loneliness (b) Lack of appreciation (c) Rejection (d) Dejection	(a) Companionship (b) Appreciation (c) Acceptance (d) Intimacy
4. Esteem needs	(a) Guilt (b) Failure (c) Inadequacy (d) Lack of recognition	(a) Forgiveness (b) Success (c) Achievement (d) Recognition
5. Self-actualization needs	(a) Frustration (b) Emptiness (c) Uselessness (d) Boredom	(a) Satisfaction (b) Completeness (c) Usefulness (d) Purpose

The basic tool of communication which relates individual to the social environment is language; but communication can also be performed through, pictures, gestures and artifacts. Over the ages, visual medium, be it 'stone age painting, photographs or todays motion picture', has always been the most effective instrument of communication. In a nutshell, the process of communication is "who said what to whom with what effects?"

Types of Communication

Communication can be broadly classified into four groups :

1. **Intrapersonal :** When someone communicates with himself, it is called intrapersonal communication. This could be reflection, contemplation, writing a diary, thinking or making a self-decision. Meditation or communion with the divine can also be considered intrapersonal.
2. **Interpersonal :** This is a Communication between two individuals. This is the most widely used Communication among the humans.
3. **Group Communication :** This refers to Communication between more than two individuals. When we refer to the group communication, we mean a selective communication within small groups. A school's class, talking among friends or a meeting can be termed as group communication.
4. **Mass Communication :** This is a communication on a large scale, where the information is sent through some medium to the masses. Mass communication includes newspapers, magazines, big public meetings or rallies, television, radio and cinema. In this communication audience are not known.

Communication Process

How does a person convey his idea? This is the crucial process of communication, which is made up of two stages — Encoding and Decoding.

Encoding : The idea is there in a person's mind but how can he make the others understand what he is trying to communicate for this he has to make use of some medium. The medium could be a language, a sign or a picture.

Decoding : Once the message has been received it is up to the receiver to separate the message from the language. The receiver has to interpret the coded message in his mind to get the idea. Encoding and decoding are seen in their most advanced forms in military and intelligence operations.

The Receiver/Audience

1. **Perception :** Receiver selects those bits of information which he perceives to be useful.
2. **Status of Receiver :** This refers to whether or not the receiver is someone who will adopt the message and then become the intermediary through whom it will spread to the whole group.
3. **Location of the receiver :** This refers to the physical location as well as location in time, space and culture.
4. Does the Communication process affect or change the attitude of the receiver in anyway?

Feedback

It is a crucial aspect of the communication process. Without feedback there will be no way of assessing the effectiveness of communication. Feedback can be done through surveys, questionnaire, dialogue, visible effects on life etc.

The Effective Communication

Communication is said to be effective, when there is a change in obedience of receiver. When the attitude, ideas of the receiver are influenced and thus change in some way, the communication is said to be effective. Most of the Communications are not effective at all.

Cinema is one of the strongest mediums of communication. The visual medium has always been a powerful instrument to change opinion, lifestyle and thoughts. During the stone age itself, man drew pictures to express his thoughts and ideas. Today the world of moving pictures play a unique role in communication. The reach and appeal of the world cinema is growing day by day and people in urban and rural areas alike are responding to the impact of the visual medium. The films express ideas, messages, information to the people irrespective of their race, creed or colour. Images are continuously expressing those truths, imaginations and ideas what languages labour to tell or write.

So the audience and the viewers are always at the receiving ends. But their Feedbacks cause the filmmakers to become more innovative and challenging. There are few more factors which work upon the public, to bring them to the cinema halls.

Time Pass : Many of us buy movie tickets to have a good timepass. What better medium can be found than cinema to kill time? This section of audience prefer light Comedies or romantic dramas or a Sci-fi film. A sad film might mar the factor called Timepass. This habit is very unhealthy for the quality of cinema. Film makers of India are victims of this phenomenon. As most of the Indian viewers watch movies to kill time and get a value for their money. They have grown up watching 'Nautankis' (a roadshow play with songs and dances), so they want films that are reformed forms of the 'Nautankis'. Songs and dances are integral parts of the Bollywood films. The Indian viewers hardly carry brains inside the moviehalls.

Overwhelming Factor : The formulae filmmakers know that either make them love their films or hate their films. But let them care, by any means possible. Human beings are limited to perform certain acts, but never forget to imagine about those acts. They want to fly, want magical power, invisible power, fight and win against an army. But they cannot do any such things. And when they watch superman films they identify with him and get overwhelmed by his power to do anything. Today, most of the Hollywood films become hit because they succeed in overwhelming the viewers.

Imagination and Curiosity : This is another factor which leads us to the shrines of the films. Every human being has the natural power of imagination and a sense of curiosity. They want to fulfil their imagination and want to see how a certain film has done justice to his imagination. The information about the new releases are continuously shown on Television. This lead to a sense of curiosity. We hear about the new film from our friends, read reviews in newspapers — all these things make us decide what to watch and what not to watch.

Soothing our Senses : Today's work ethics make us physically and mentally tired. We want an escape, escape to a fairyland, a land of no tension, no worries. The colours of the films soothe our tensed nerves. We get refreshed by entertaining ourselves. The cut throat competition in today's job market, financial insecurity and hectic lifestyle make us depressed and soars up anxiety. Even our smiles carry boredom. It is no more effortless. Films make us laugh and connect to our emotions and thus relieves us from day to day tension. It works like balm.

To study the Craft : Only film students and film folks watch films for this purpose of studying the craft, its shots, editing or auteurship. They go to watch "English Patient" (1996) again and again to study and admire John Seale's cinematography and "Schindler's List" (1993) to study the most perfected auteurship of Steven Spielberg.

Every country has its own customs, styles and values. It is films reflect those customs or values. But the film has no barrier, no languages, just emotions. A universal theme will always attract the people from all over the world irrespective of caste, colour or creed. A film becomes universal, if its emotion is universal. Love, hate, magic or battle are all universal themes. They will work again and again. It is better to ask ourselves, why do we watch films, and we will get answer from within ourselves.

A BRIEF HISTORY OF CINEMA

The moving picture — the thought of recording the movement or action in a kind of permanent form has been a dream of man since stone age. The caveman's painting of running animals, humans and birds, for instance, must have been seemed remarkably like what would be later a film show, when seen by flickering lights.

Over the centuries many attempts were made to capture the magic of movement in still picture. But they could not produce movements through the moving images. Even when

Thomas Edison established the mechanical basis of the first moving picture camera, he still lacked the medium, he needed to put his ideas into practice. This was a kind of flexible, ribbon like film.

Films were the result of a long quest, in which a number of great thinkers, scientists and artists took part. They provided the answer to a question that had for long challenged, baffled and mystified man how to record action in a permanent form. Where, when and how they started is difficult to say. But the early pioneers were Edison and Lumie're Brothers. They laid the foundation and gave the basic technology. This was later built by filmmakers like D.W. Griffith, Eisenstein and Von Stroheim. They created the basic stuffs of the picture. However it is impossible to date such events precisely and is difficult to chart its progress in details.

American inventor Edison, who demonstrated the 'Kinetoscope' in 1893, was a kind of one-man peep show. The French Lumie're Brothers brought out their own improved version known as 'cinematographe' in 1895. This contained camera, projector and printer all in one. For the first time, it also used claw to move the film strip. It was portable and easy to use. This machine brought revolution and popularity among both the professionals as well as amateur movie makers. Everything was new, everything was experimental and the results were equally unpredictable. And then the technology grew so rapidly inventing so many machines that the making of impossible cinema became easier. The realization of dreams, ideas, thoughts and imagination was made possible on a permanent form. Brains were preserved on films.

In 1923, George Eastman launched the 'cinekodak system' and later came 'the cinemascope' Eastman colour and other improved versions. This was how the medium of cinema progressed technically in the hands of scientists and visualizers. And the technology is still progressing at even greater speed exploring all possibilities to create the best kind of cinemas. Where can we find such a great life-like medium as cinema to preserve our past, stories, imaginations, legends and the great acting. The magic of the motion picture became universal, eternal and the great entertainer.

THE GREAT WORLD CINEMAS

More than a thousand great films were made in one hundred year of film history. Now taking upon myself the task of picking favourites, a mere few out of these numbers, is risking certain heart break. Everybody has his own list of favourites. No list is final and perfect because there is no such thing as an objective list. But then there are films, that are universally acknowledged as greats. A century that has produced these masterworks cannot have gone by in vain. Cinema has legitimate claims to be considered the most enduring and life sustaining art form of the 20th century.

HOLLYWOOD

Hollywood is the most holy place for filmmakers. The cinema is known by it. Think about those stars, genre movies, snappy dialogue and achieving that beautiful balance between art and entertainment, and you immediately switch to the world of vision. While in other countries, filmmakers failed to blend art and entertainment, they have marvellously succeeded in doing that. The special effects, the great acting and the great execution make us spellbound. They are ruthless, perfect and most organized. They spend and earn in millions. And the most important thing they do, is to maintain quality along with quantity of the films.

Annie Hall (1977)
Dir. : Woody Allen
Cast : Woody Allen, Diane Keaton.

More or less biographical, the film explores fragments of Allen and Keaton's real life relationship.

The film won four OSCARS. Allen, for the first time dropped his visual gags and one liners for a blend of the comic and serious and succeeded brilliantly. The film makes a survey of almost every issue that plagued his own life to the exploration of a love affair.

All the President's Men (1976)
Dir. : Alan J. Pakula.
Cast : Robert Redford, Dustin Hoffman.

One of the finest political thriller ever made. It was the watergate story broken by the Bob Woodward and Carl Bernstein that finally nailed a lying Nixon. Skilfully directed by Pakula from a meticulously researched, finely paired script by William Goldman. The film was made in a documentary style. Michael Small's eerie theme music effectively adds to the atmosphere of dread and paranoia. The film won 4 Oscars.

The Big Sleep (1946)
Dir. : Howard Hawks.
Cast : Humphrey Bogart, Lauren Bacall.

Summoned to the lavish mansion of General Sternwod, Marlowe, private detective, is hired to investigate a blackmailer, a Hollywood smart book dealer who has compromising photos of the General's daughter.

The unwieldly plot, scripted by William Faulkner, had even the original author, Raymond Chandler, baffled. Along with John Huston's 'Maltese Falcon', 'The Big Sleep' is now a big film noir classic.

Ben Hur (1959)
Dir. : William Wyler
Cast : Charlton Heston, Jack Hawkins, Stephen Boyd, Haya Harareet, Huge Griffith and Sam Jaffe.

The multiple Oscar winner (11) Ben Hur was made at the budget of $ 15 million. It was a majestic achievement in the history of cinema, representing a superb blending of the motion picture arts by master craftsmen. The drama was accomplished without sacrificing the impact of the spectacle elements. The famous chariot race represents some 40 minutes of the most hair raising excitement ever witnessed. The Roman epic successfully depicts family relationship, and the enmity along with deeply religious theme involving the birth and crucifixion of Christ. Many heavyweight writers worked to make the script worthy for an epic. The film took 10 months to complete at Rome's 300 built sets.

Ben Hur is a fitting climax to Zimbalist's career as a producer. He died of a heart attack before the film was complete.

Blade Runner (1982)
Dir. : Ridley Scott
Cast : Harrison Ford, Rutger Hauer, Sean young.

The director of "Black Hawk Down" (2001) created atmosphere, mood and heart stopping visuals in Blade Runner. We see Los Angeles of 21st century. Harrison Ford is Deckard, a hard boiled detective in the Bogart tradition, except in the future they are called 'Blade Runners'. This new assignment is to hunt down and kill five Replicants (robots with human body and human memory) who have begun to rebel, wanting to live longer. In this Ridley Scott's sci-fi, Los Angeles seems permanently drenched in fog and drizzle, bathed in neon, with a sky claustrophobically encircled by flying cars, towering sky scrappers and giant bill boards.

The Bridge On The River Kwai (1957)
Dir. : David Lean
Cast : Willian Holden, Alec Guinness.

The film picked up seven Oscars including best picture, best director and best actor. A masterful performance by Alec Guinness as the half mad Col. Nicholson, who has surrendered his regiment to the Japanese in Burma in World War II fires this all male picture to Oscar winning excellence. The film was shot not in Burma, but in Sri Lanka, on the understanding that the film would not be anti Japanese but merely anti-war. The bridge took 9 months to construct. The film is the kind of exciting intelligent spectacle that only David Lean can provide.

Bonnie And Clyde (1967)
Dir. : Arthur Penn
Cast : Warren Beatty, Faye Dunaway, Gene Hackman.

This film about the two gangsters of 1930s, struck a chord with the 1967 youth culture movement worldwide, because it treats the two depression era lovers as largely sympathetic non conformist. The story turned into legend, acquiring the status of a Folk ballad. Four cameras set at various speeds, send Bonnie and Clyde to their deaths in slow motion. It won 2 Oscar.

Casablanca (1943)
Dir. : Michael Curtiz
Cast : Humphrey Bogart, Ingrid Bergman.

The most romantic film ever made. It is apparently every body's favourite. The now familiar plot involves expatriate American, Rick Blaine (Bogart), a cynical night club owner in Casablanca who discovers that his former sweet heart, Ilsa Lund (Bergman) who abandoned him years before in Paris, has just arrived in war torn Casablanca with her husband. She begs Rick to give back letters. With each new viewing you grow fonder of this influential romantic drama which so perfectly evokes our own day dreams about "lost chances, lost loves and love versus honour." The film won Oscar for best picture and best director.

Chinatown (1974)
Dir. : Roman Polanski
Cast : Jack Nicholson, Faye Dunaway, John Huston.

Tough, hard-boiled film noir from the director who loves to chill the spines of his audience. LAPD officer Jack Gittes (Nicholson) sets out on what seems like on innocuous divorce case, gets involved with his client Evelyn Mulwray (Duna way), which leads him to unravel a sordid mystery involving scams, murder and tragedy. Chinatown becomes a metaphor for all that is unspeakably evil, the decadence of a corrupt moral, municipal and social system. Robert Towne's script is superb. Polanski was absolutely right to choose the tragic ending over Towne's happier one — because of it nobody, who sees 'Chinatown' ever forgets it. It won one Oscar for the best original screenplay.

Citizen Kane (1941)
Dir. : Orson Welles
Cost : Orson Welles, Joseph Cotton.

A film book cannot be written without mentioning 'Citizen Kane' on its pages. A lesson for the film students, a glory for the makers and a classic for the viewers, the film is arguably the greatest movie ever made. It was made by a 25-year old. It is a dramatisation of the life of American newspaper tycoon William Randolph Hearts (whose fictionalised biography the film really is) who did everything possible to suppress the film. Innovative techniques include the cameraman Greg Toland's use of deep focus lenses, in which both close and distant, objects remain in focus on the screen. Nominated for 9 academy awards and winner of only one for the screenplay by Mankiewicz and Orson Welles, the film has generated much attention than any other films in the history of cinema.

Dressed To Kill (1980)
Dir. : Brian De Palma
Cast : Michael Caine, Angie Dickinson.

Like Hitchcock, Brian De Palma is a poet of suspense film. But in Hollywood, to prove you are an artist, you have to move away from making thrillers and make something tasteful and serious. And that is what Spielberg had to do. But Hitchcock did not succumb to that tyranny. But Brian De Palma has and predictably made an unsatisfactory film like "The Bon-fire of the Vanities". Even "The Untouchables" was too tame and respectable for the likes of him. He is the best only when he handles suspense. The sequence of the film, where a man and a woman playing cat and mouse in New York's legendary Metropolitan museum is perhaps — in its narrative, fluidity, control and rhythm the most visually hypnotic sequence you can ever hope to see in a movie.

English Patient (1996)
Dir. : Anthony Minghella
Cast : Ralph Finennes, Kristin Scott Thomas, Juliette Binoche, William Dafoe.

With a clutch of Oscars including those for best picture, best director and best Cinematography under its belt, 'The English Patient' has every reason to feel exceedingly proud. The film is a proud achievement. In this for more complex and articulate film Minghella returns to the terrain of the memory in search of answers to the question of love and war and how the two affect the moral and emotional sensitivities of an individual. Adopted from the Booker Prize winner novel by Michael Ondaatje.

The 'English Patient' becomes one of the best adopted film ever. Minghella has done full Justice to the film. The technical sides, specially John Seale's cinematography is brilliant. The film is an effortless synthesis of a forbidden romance and the stressful war ambience. It is a poetic beauty.

E.T. (Extra Terrestrial) (1982)
Dir. : Steven Spielberg
Cast : Henry Thomas, Drew Barrymore.

The film has aged zingily. Even two decades later, Steven Spielberg's much adored sci-fi fantasy is surprisingly even more peppy and cool than it was in 1982.

Playfully fusing elements from "The Wizard of OZ", "Lassic," "Peter Pan" and Disney masterpiece "Pinnochio", here is a wonderous adventure which is a visually dazzling as it is emotionally stirring. With his patented child like glee, Spielberg narrates the story of an alien, who lands in America and a friendship is developed between a 10-year old boy (Thomas) and the alien. The kid's only aim is to keep him away from others and to reunite it with its mother spaceship for a safe passage home. A film of poetic texture and nuances, E.T. celebrates the magic of the imagination. The film was again released after 20 years in 2002 with digitally remastered and adding of minutes of new footage. The creature is a marvel in make up effects technique. The film won '4' Oscar including best special effects.

Forrest Gump (1994)
Dir. : Robert Zemeckis
Cast : Tom Hanks.

When author Winston Groom set out to chart the 'deep' waters of the boffin with a heart, Forrest Gump, little did he know that the book as well as the film would pull the hearts of the millions. Robert Zemeckis had no qualms to go back to the past to create this master piece. The film won 6 Oscars out of 13 nominations. The special effects made it possible for Tom Hanks to meet the then President JFK.

The Godfather Trilogy (1972-74-90)
Dir. : Francis ford Coppola
Cast : Marlon Brando, Al Pacino, Robert De Niro, Robert Duvall, James Caan.

Almost everyone's favourites, Godfather films are a tribute to what cinema could be as a medium. It is an example of the best in filmmaking. The narrative, the music, the performance and the cinematography are brilliant. The ambience of Italian Culture is depicted in such a way that one feels part of it. The stylisations of the characters are incredible. Can anyone forget the opening sequence, the Godfather meets people from his community, and helps sort out their problems; in return he says he may need their help one day. Or the shooting scenes where the Camera has taken the shots from behind the windscreen : The Godfather is a criminal but the character is depicted so well that he is real, human and dignified. The entire Italian ambience of 1930s was recreated. The film talks at your intelligence level. It is a great cinema because it appeals to the intellectuals as well as the masses. The films have overwhelmed us with so many unforgettable scenes, faces and lines and images. We seem to know Corleone family better than our own. But Ford's gangster/family epic's triumph also lies in what critic John Powers pointed out to "While the Corleones embodied the myth of the family they also revealed the capacity for madness in these idealized patriarchies — in the name of the family, Michael can kill his own brother. The Godfather trilogy elevates the American gangster movies to a peak of tragic irony so far unmatched by any other American film then and now." Al Pacino, once said that the "Godfather III" was a great mistake. It should not have been made. Nobody wants Godfather to repent and change. May be, he was right. As the film could not become as lovable and watchable as part I & II. The Godfather won 3 Oscar and Part II won six.

Glory (1989)
Dir. : Edward Zwick
Cast : Morgan Freeman, Mathew Broderick, Denzel Washington.

Exhilarating, lyrical, inspiring, "Glory" a film about the American civil war, reminds us why we go the movies; to be awed by sheer visuals, the kind of spectacle that is a feast for the senses. One, that only cinema — not literature, not drama — can furnish. But 'Glory' is more than mere spectacle. It is a moving, unforgettable story about courage; heroism and honour — the kind that makes a man want to lay down his life for another. 1863, the 54th Massachusetts Volunteer Infantry becomes the first black regiment to fight in the Civil War. Director Robert Zwick and the great British Cinematographer Freddie Francis turn a war film into intense, poetic drama. It is a fiery, spirit-stirring experience. It won 3 Oscar.

The Graduate (1967)
Dir. : Mike Nichols
Cast : Dustin Hoffman, Anne Bancroft and Katherine Ross.

The role, which made Dustin Hoffman, an overnight star was first offered to Robert Redford. The film's theme of youthful rebellion against a materialistic adult world and its portrayal of a budding generation gap reflected (and anticipated) the temper of the times. This hilarious, astute generation gap fable is without doubt a modern American masterpiece, which along with 'Easy Rider' and 'Bonnie and Clyde' influenced the style and content of American Movies for a whole decade. The film won the Best Director Oscar.

The Hustler (1961)
Dir. : Robert Rossen
Cast : Paul Newman, George C. Scott, Jackie Gleason and Piper Laurie.

'Fast' Eddie felson (Newman) is a pool Shark who hustles his way across the country to Ames Billiard parlor in New York, where he challenges and beats the hitherto unbeaten Minnesota Fats, leaving him penniless and lonely. Robert Rossen presents a stark, pitiless world well caught in Eugene

Shuften's Oscar winning black and white photography. The film won 2 Oscar.

Invasion of The Body Snatchers (1978)
Dir. : Philip Kaufman
Cast : Donald Sutherland, Brooke Adams, Jeff Goldblum and Leonard Nimoy.

Eerie, spooky, subtle, with Suspense so sharp it could cut your skin. The 1978 remake by Philip Kaufman of 1956 Don Siegel classic is probably the most thrilling Sci-fi horror movie ever made. Screenwriter W.D. Richter brilliantly updates Jack Finney's influential pulp Sci-fi novel by transplanting the horror to city — San Francisco. Aliens take over the earth in the shape of 'Cocoon-like' human sized pods, which suddenly appear everywhere, transplanting alien minds for human.

It Happened One Night (1934)
Dir. : Frank Capra
Cast : Clark Gable, Claudette Colbert, Walter Connolly and Roscoe Karns.

Peter (Gable) and Ellie (Colbert) define two characters in a certain type of male/female confrontation which was to become a staple of American films. Fate has thrown them together on the road. Peter is snappy and hearty and tough, Ellie, on the other hand, comes from so much money that her arrogance is really ignorance. They take each other down a peg so that they can fall in love, and when they do, after much contest, they are happily ever after. The film won Oscars for best film, director, actor and actress.

Indiana Jones And The Temple of Doom (1984)
Dir. : Steven Spielberg
Cast : Harrison Ford, Kate Capshaw, Philip Stone.

Prequel Indiana Jones finds dapper Harrison Ford as Indiana Jones in a Shanghai night club in 1935. He escapes from an enormous melee with the Chanteuse and oriental moppet key Huy Quan. They head by plane to the mountains of Asia where they are forced to jump out in an inflatable raft in an Indian village. Ford seems effortlessly to have picked up where he left off when Indiana Jones was last heard from. The film won Oscar for special effects.

Indiana Jones And The Last Crusade (1989)
Dir. : Steven Spielberg
Cast : Harrison Ford, Sean Connery, Denholm Elliott, Alison Doody.

More cerebral than other two Indiana Jones Films, this literate adventure entertains and enlightens kids and adults alike. Harrison Ford-Sean Connery father and son team gives 'Last Crusade' unexpected emotional depth reminding us that real film magic is not in special effects. Witty and laconic screenplay based on a story by George Lucus and Menno Meyjes, takes Ford and Connery on a quest for a prize bigger than the last Ark of the Covenant The Holy Grail. It won one Oscar for sound effects Editing.

Jaws (1975)
Dir. : Steven Spielberg
Cast : Roy Scheider, Richard Dreyfuss, Robert Shaw.

Jaws has genius, it was made by Spielberg as a novice relying entirely on instinct, guts and talents for a medium he was born to rule. Seeing Jaws today is just as nerve-jangling as when we first saw it. Based on Peter Benchley's best seller about a killer shark and a tourist beach town, is an $ 8 million film of consummate suspense, tension and terror. The creature is not even seen for about 82 minutes, and a subjective camera technique makes his earlier forays excruciatingly terrifying all the more for the invisibility. The film won 3 Oscar.

The Last Temptation of Christ (1988)
Dir. : Martin Scorsese
Cast : Willem Dafoe, Barbara Hershey, Harvey Keitel.

When first seen, its unorthodox poetic version of the life of Jesus enraged Fundamentalists but anybody who has seen it will testify that it is a profoundly religious work and Scorsese's masterpiece. It is the first biopic of Christ that tries to emphasise the human aspects of Jesus. It will remain one of the most intense and moving religious picture ever made.

L.A. Confidential (1997)
Dir. : Curtis Hanson
Cast : Russel Crowe, Kevin Spacey, Kim Bussinger.

The movie had managed to bag nine nominations (Oscar) ultimately winning two Oscars for best adopted screenplay and best supporting actress (Kim Bassinger). Set in early 1950s in Hollywood, it is a film noir. The movie showcases the rampant corruption in Los Angeles Police Department (LAPD) and the nexus between gangsters, prostitutes and the police force. It is also a technically brilliant film. Russel Crowe's great performance lives inside you and at the end, you cannot judge whether he is a good guy or a bad guy.

Midnight Cowboy (1969)
Dir. : John Schlesinger
Cast : Jon Voight, Dustin Hoffman.

Achingly sad, bitterly funny, here is the most sensitive film Hollywood ever made about loneliness, failure and friendship. John Voight is Joe Buck, a tall, handsome man who feels his calling is to be a stud, a gigolo. He goes to New York as he had heard that there are swarms of Rich, lonely sex-starved middle aged women who are looking out for a stud just like him. But in New York nobody even notices him. And when he meets Rasto Rizzo (Dustin Hoffman), a poor street-wise tramp, also down on his luck, both develop friendship. Midnight Cowboy's stud is not a loner like Robert De Nero in 'Taxi Driver' but he is lonely. The film won Oscar for the best picture, best director and best screenplay.

The Misfits (1961)
Dir. : John Huston
Cast : Clark Gable, Marilyn Monroe, Montgomery Clift, Eli Wallach.

Huston always chooses unusual material. The misfits fascinating subject : Now that the old west is dead, what do modern Cow-boys, who have lost their purpose of life, do with themselves? Gable and Monroe's last movie. He died 12 days after a retake of his final scene and she died the following year after a heavy overdose of drugs. Their scenes together (he was 59, she 35) are just unbearably sad.

Moonstruck (1987)
Dir. : Norman Jewison
Cast : Cher, Nicholos Cage, Olympia Dukakis.

A joy from start to finish. Simply the most romantic of romantic comedies to come out of Hollywood in years. The glorious lines, the fabulous acting and unforgettable characters leave us spell-bound. Cher is an independent widow, superstitious about marrying again but decides to give it one more chance and chooses to marry with an older man. But she is hexed all right, when she goes to invite her fiancé's brother (Nicholos Cage) for the wedding. Stanley's Oscar winning Screenplay evokes a whole ethnic Milieu — the Italian-American — humorously, vividly, enchantingly. The film won 3 Oscar.

My Darling Clementine (1946)
Dir. : John Ford
Cast : Henry Fonda, Victor Mature.

The best loved film about the legendary gunfight at OK Corral between Wyatt Earp (Fonda) and the Clanton brothers. Earp and his brothers have driven their cattle to the outskirts of Tombstone, Arizona. Earp rejects the cut-rate price, old man Clanton offers for the cattle. When Clanton kills Earp Jr., it is time for the Earps to strap on their guns and alongwith the alcoholic Doc Holliday (Mature) head for their revenge for historic gunfight at OK Corral.

Ninotchka (1939)
Dir. : Ernst Lubitsch
Cast : Greta Garbo, Melvyn Douglas.

Three Soviet envoys are sent to Paris to sell some jewellery to buy some farm machinery. When they start neglecting their duties to like the gay life of Paris, a stern female

"Comrade" Ninotchka (Garbo) is sent after them. She drops her stiff Russian manner once she meets the debonair Leon and all ends happily, in distant Constantinople. The divine Garbo reveals a Command of Comic inflection in this beautiful film.

Notorious (1946)
Dir. : Alfred Hitchcock
Cast : Cary Grant, Ingrid Bergman, Claude Rains.

This brilliant Hitchcock thriller combines romance, suspense and international intrigue with American agent Devlin (untrusting, passive and unsympathetic) in the coils of Alice Huberman (shady aggressive and alcoholic) the daughter of a convicted Nazy spy. Claude Rains' menacingly cool villainy is set off against his cigar-stomping mama's chilling authority.

On The Waterfront (1954)
Dir. : Elia Kazan
Cast : Marlon Brando, Rod Steiger, Eva Marie Saint, and Karl Malden.

The film gathers its force from the gradually unfolding moral consciousness of its hero Terry Malloy (Brando) who seems as touched by father Barry's water front priest as by remorse in having been a party to the death of Joey Doyle, the brother of the girl he has fallen in love with. The film is now a classic. The film won Oscars for the best picture, director, best actor, supporting actress, screenplay, art direction, cinematography and editing.

Oliver! (1968)
Dir. : Carol Reed
Cast : Mark Lester, Jackwild, Ron Moody, Shani Wallis.

Based on Charles Dickens' 'Oliver Twist', 'Oliver!' tells the story of little orphan boy who is trying to make the best of life on the streets of London. He moves from the orphanage to pickpockets den to a wealthy man's house. However, all those he encounters seem to be making plans to get him into a trap. He then realizes how wicked the world can be. Directed by Carol Reed, the film won '5' Oscars including best picture, best director.

One Flew Over The Cuckoo's Nest (1975)
Dir. : Milos Forman
Cast : Jack Nicholson, Louise Fletcher.

The film stars the most oscar nominated actor Jack Nicholson as an inmate of a mental asylum, playing a man faking madness. Though he was really a madman faking normal. His acting brilliantly suggested both. The film won five Oscar for best picture, director, actor, actress and screenplay.

Ordinary People (1980)
Dir. : Robert Redford
Cast : Donald Sutherland, Mary Tyler Moore, Judd Hirsch, Timothy Hutton, Scott Doebler.

Conrad Jarret Timothy, aged 17, may be having his second nervous breakdown. His first occurred after he and his brother Buck (Scott Doebler), the star of the family, were out boating and got caught in a sudden storm. Buck drowned and Conrad has never been able to forgive himself. Much of his present problem is that his mother Beth (Mary Moore) has never been able to forgive him either. His guilt at surviving is killing him. The only hope is a lovely girl who sings with him in school chorus. The film won Oscars for the best picture, best director, best supporting actor, and screenplay.

Picnic (1955)
Dir. : Joshua Logan
Cast : William Holden, Kim Novak.

Picnic is Logan's faithful screen adaptation of William Inge's Pulitzer prize winning play about life in a small town in America. Hal Carter (Holden) is a drifter come to a small Kansas town seeking out old college buddy, Alan, in the hope of landing a job with Alan's father — the richest man in the County. Veteran James Wong Howe's breathtaking photography is an unalloyed treat with that 1950s hit 'Moon glow' on the soundtrack. Truly a film for the young at heart. It won Oscar for editing and art direction.

Psycho (1960)
Dir. : Alfred Hitchcock
Cast : Anthony Perkins, Janet Leigh.

The now familiar plot of 'Psycho' concerns Norman Bates (Anthony), a neurasthenic motel proprietor who lives under the shadow of his domineering mother, who, apparently, does not move out of the forbidding Bates mansion. Janet Leigh, one of occupants, is seen chatting with Norman and is promptly butchered by Norman's mother in the now legendary shower sequence. Every subsequent horror movie is indebted to 'Psycho'. Berhard Herrmann's eerie score is unforgettable. The famous shower sequence took a week to film, which was made of 75 separate shots in 45 seconds. The blood was chocolate-Sauce, because that looked more authentic in black & white film. 'Psycho' has not dated a bit.

Pulp Fiction (1994)
Dir. : Quentin Tarantino
Cast : John Travolta, Samuel L. Jackson, Uma Thurman, Bruce Willis.

In 'Pulp Fiction' killing is not a sin, being uncool is. Quentin Tarantino's long, talky, tremendously entertaining gangster drama is all about hyper cool attitude, sassy backtalk and hipness. Tarantino and Roger Avary come up with some really mean dialogue to match it. In 'Pulp Fiction' words create and pop louder and faster than bullets. It won best screenplay Oscar.

Platoon (1986)
Dir. : Oliver Stone
Cast : Charlie Sheen, Tom Berenger, and Willem Dafoe.

Oliver Stone's controversial war saga set the tone for other Vietnam movies to follow. The Oscar winning film records horror of Vietnam conflict seen by a young Chris Taylor (Charlie Sheen). The blood, sweet and tears of war are brought out effectively in the gory, violent scenes. The film is ruthlessly perfect, also won Oscar for the best director, editing and sound.

Quest For Fire (1982)
Dir. : Jean-Jacques Annaud
Cast : Everett Mcgill, Rae Dawn Chong, Ron Perlman.

Despite four years of effort, a $ 12 million budget, gruelling location shooting in Kenya, Scotland, Iceland and Canada, hundreds of masks and costumes and a herd of difficult elephants (making their screen appearances as mammoths), Annaud and his collaborators have brought out a polished entertainment. This has never degenerated into a club and lion-skin spin off of 'Star Wars' and resolutely refuses to bludgeon the viewer with facile or gratuitous effects. Technical advisor Anthony Burgess invented special primitive jargons for the occasion. Gerard Brach's screenplay is loosely based on Jean-Henri Rosny the Elder's 'La guerre du Feu' (1911), a classic of French language popular literature. The film tells conflict between homosapiens and Neanderthals. Annaud wisely uses mimes, dancers, acrobats and stuntmen for many of the secondary and extra roles. Under the guidance of anthropologist Desmond Morris, they provide credible physical expression under their excellent masks and make up. The film won best make up Oscar.

Rosemary's Baby (1968)
Dir. : Roman Planski
Cast : Mia farrow, John Cassavetes, Ruth Gordon.

Not simply the most perfectly crafted suspense horror film, but one of the most perfectly crafted Hollywood films, Roman Polanski gets all the spooky nuances and the comic undertone of Ira Levin's great, influential supernatural thriller just right letting the audience spot the horror for themselves off at the side of the screen. Mia farrow is Rosemary, a pregnant housewife in a New York apartment, who begins to suspect that her neighbours, particularly an old couple, are modern day witches conspiring against her unborn baby. The film has you amused in a nervous, edgy sort of way, playing upon your innate feeling of urban paranoia skilfully.

Raiders of The Lost Ark (1981)
Dir. : Steven Spielberg
Cast : Harrison Ford, Karen Allen, Den Holm Elliott, Paul Freeman, Alfred Molina.

Steeped in a exotic atmosphere of lost civilizations, mystical talismans, gritty mercenary adventures, Nazi arch villains and ingenious death at every turn, the film is largely patterned on the serials of 1930s. Story by George Lucas and Philip Kaufman begins in 1936 as Indiana Jones (Ford), an archeologist and university professor who is not above a little mercenary activity on the side, plunders a South American jungle tomb. He secures of priceless golden Godhead, only to have it snatched away by longtime archeological rival Paul Freeman, now employed by the Nazi. Ford's mission is to beat the Germans to get ark. Director Steven Spielberg has deftly veiled proceedings in a sense of mystical wonder. The film won 5 Oscar including the best special effect.

Rebecca (1940)
Dir. : Alfred Hitchcock
Cast : Sir Laurence Olivier, Joan Fontaine, George Sanders.

The script of 'Rebecca' constantly designates shots to be made over the shoulders of the character, so that we are always invisibly in the scene, watching. We see through the eyes of Rebecca, whose presence, a year after her death in boating accident, still dominates the life of everyone who lives in the great English country house Manderly. The widower Maxim de Winter (Olivier), is given to moods of deep blackness, assumed to erupt from the devastating loss of the brilliant, beautiful Rebecca. Why maxim would want a wife who in every way seems inadequate to the splendours of his house and his lost love. The film won Oscar for the best picture.

Raging Bull (1980)
Dir. : Martin Scorsese
Cast : Robert De Niro.

"De Niro doesn't look at you, he considers you" says Martin Scorsese. Held in the power of that gaze you can expect anything next. He remarkably gained 60 pounds of extra weight to play the boxer Jake La Motta in 'Raging Bull'. He beats his head against a concrete wall for the jail scene to make it look authentic. The hero of Raging Bull is lonely and depressed. He turns his all depression and frustration in to power punches in the ring. Thus he is fighting both the opponent and his own depression. This great performance won De Niro Oscar for the best actor. It also won Oscar for best editing.

The Silence of The Lambs (1991)
Dir. : Jonathan Demme
Cast : Jodie Foster, Sir Anthony Hopkins.

Right from its opening credit sequence accomplished by Howard Shore's eerie yet haunting music score showing Jodie Foster running out of breath to its spooky end as Hannibal "the Cannibal" lecter is shown amiably stalking his 'dinner', Jonathan Demme's film has you on the edge of your seat with that combination of terror and pleasure only superb thriller can achieve. The plot is simple enough. A grotesque monster named Buffalo Bill has killed and flayed five women. Only Hannibal Lecter, another serial killer in custody, has all the answers. Hopkins plays Lecter with a fine cold relish. Demme, working from Thomas Harris suspenseful and scary novel, allows us to feel the slow process of envelopment and seduction. The film won 5 Oscar including the Best Picture and The best Director.

Singin In The Rain (1952)
Dir. : Gene Kelly, Stanley Donen
Cast : Gene Kelly, Debbie Reynolds, Jean Hagen, Donald O'Connor.

Gene Kelly, in the now Classic title number, dancing and tap-tapping his way through a rain-clogged street, swinging around a lamppost, splashing and jumping in joy because he has just fallen in love is the most joyous celebration of love, life and rain that has ever been put on screen. The setting is Hollywood in 1920s, making its transition to talkies. 'Singin' in the Rain; which has most mesmerizing choreography ever filmed, is easily Hollywood's best musical; it has great songs, great dances and a wonderful cast. A delight from start to finish.

A Soldier's Story (1984)
Dir. : Norman Jewison
Cast : Howard Rollins, Adolph Caesar, Denzel Washington.

Riveting, entertaining, probing examination of race issues that is part murder mystery, part sociological drama. Based on Charles Fuller's intriguing Pulitzer prize winning off-Broadway play and narrated superbly by director Norman Jewison, 'A Soldier's Story' uses (like Chinatown) a murder mystery to examine race issue from a very original standpoint. 'In the Head of The Night' is its inspiration, both have the same premise; noble, educated Negro from the liberal north solves a difficult mystery for conservative white southerners. Terrific jazz soundtrack by Herbie Hancock and a stunning ensemble performance from the black actors, 'A Soldier's Story' comes closer to any other Hollywood movie to being the exemplary thinking man's thriller.

Sunset Boulevard (1950)
Dir. : Billy Wilder
Cast : Gloria Swanson, William Holden, Eric Von Stroheim.

Ever wondered what life for retired movie stars must really be like? This classic noir movie has a chilling answer — that in their minds they have never really retired. A once famous actress, Norma Desmond, exquisitely and chillingly acted by Gloria Swanson, herself a former silent film star, is a multi millionaires holed up in her Hollywood mansion with no companion save her butter-chauffer Max Von Mayerling (Von Stroheim). Billy Wilder's 'Sunset Boulevard' is the best film Hollywood made on Hollywood. It won 3 Oscar.

Shakespeare In Love (1998)
Dir. : John Madden
Cast : Gwyneth Paltrow, Joseph Fiennes.

Forbidden romance, raffish show-biz comedy, literary pranksterism and class warfare jostle joyously in this intricately imagined, exuberantly acted, cunningly directed tale of how the young, distracted Bard gets in touch with the genius he does not know he possesses. The film won 7 Oscars for the best picture, best actress, best supporting actress, best original screenplay, best art direction and best original musical score.

Shine (1996)
Dir. : Scott Hicks
Cast : Geoffrey Rush, Armin Mueller Stahl, Sir John Gielgud Lynn Redgrave.

Shine is the story, inspired by the life of David Helfgott, the brilliant Australian pianist. The story centres on his relationship with his domineering father, who puts so much pressure on his genius son that he has nervous breakdown. It is an acting film. Geoffrey Rush, who played the character of David brilliantly, won Oscar for the best actor.

Schindler's List (1993)
Dir. : Steven Spielberg
Cast : Ralph Fiennes, Ben Kingsley, Liam Nesson.

After watching this epic, you come to know the real cinema and its power to move. Purposefully made in black and white, the film is Jews Holocaust drama, which is based on Thomas Keneally's Booker prize winning novel 'Schindler's Ark' (1982). The film was first offered to Martin Scorsese. But he declined the offer to direct because he believed he could not make as good a film as a Jewish director possibly could. And then Spielberg was called on. It is dark and depressing film, which tells the feelings of despair and no hope. Liam Nesson, a broker and a powerful businessman, who bought many Jews and thus saved the lives of hundreds of them from Nazi's attack. 'Schindler's List' is competent film, full of a studied craft that has been perfected over years by Steven Spielberg. The background score, cinematography, editing, direction and performances are brilliant. The film won 7 Oscar for the best picture, director, and screenplay, music, cinematography, and editing and art direction.

Saving Private Ryan (1998)
Dir. : Steven Spielberg
Cast : Tom Hanks, Matt Damon, and Edward J. Burns.

'Saving Private Ryan', Steven Spielberg's astonishing epic opens with what may be the most unforgettably brutal sequence in the history of war movies. Can any cause justify such carnage? That is the question the director of 'Schindler's List' poses here, and answers, without cliché, by dramatizing how honour can be wrested from absurdity by decency and dutifulness in the film. Spielberg does not glorify war but shows horrors of war more vividly than ever. For which he got top US civilian award as well as an Oscar for the best director. The film is encouraging a national dialogue about World War II, and the impact that the movie had on improving conversations in families about the contributions that veterans made. The most brutal war movie ever made, 'Saving Private Ryan' won 5 Oscars out of its 8 nominations.

Tender Mercies (1983)
Dir. : Bruce Beresford
Cast : Robert Duvall, Tess Harper.

Perhaps the most understated, spare, the subtle movie Hollywood ever made. Robert Duvall's ruthlessly restrained performance as a failure looking for redemption and a new start in life is one of the high points in the history of American acting. Southern writer Horton Foote and Australian director Bruce Beresford, both work from a minimalist perspective and style that is a far cry from the usual Hollywood hokum. It is that rare film that does not spell out everything and the best moments sneak up on you and work their magic quietly. It lingers in the mind long after it is over. It shows our lives; its love, grace, fate, faith and sin. It won 2 Oscar.

2001 : A Space Odyssey (1968)
Dir. : Stanley Kubrick
Cast : Keir Dullea, Gary Lockwood, Willim Sylvester.

'Star Wars' may look dated, but '2001 : A Space Odyssey' remains as awe-inspiring, fresh and hair raising as the day it was made. It is thanks to director Stanley Kubrick and writer

Arthur C. Clarke who insisted that the film not be watered down by explanations and remains a little mystical that makes the film seem fascinating and provocative even today. In a stark documentary fashion, the film depicts several encounters mankind has with never glimpsed aliens. The film contains some of the most powerful images ever to grace a Hollywood films, the bone turning into spaceship (The most famous cut in the film history), the mystical monoliths, HAL the almost human computer, ending that catapulted '2001' instantly into a cult film. And not to forget the film's now legendary "Thus Spoke Zarathrustra", theme music by Richard Strauss. The special effects add to the film's mystery. It won Oscar for the Best Special Effects.

Taxi Driver (1976)
Dir. : Martin Scorsese
Cast : Robert De Niro, Cybill Shepherd, Jodie Foster, Harvey Keitel.

'Taxi Driver' narrates the story of Travis Bickle (De Niro) an ex-marine, he is unable to sleep at nights, so he gets a job as a nighttime taxi driver. He dates to Bets (Cybill) but she parts her way soon. His increasing paranoia (by multiple causes) leads him to buy an arsenal of weapons. He meets a young prostitute Iris (Foster) and decides that his mission in life is to save her. He kills many including the pimp (Keitel). The end of the film shows that the media has treated him as hero because he saved Iris and returned her to her parents. He becomes loner again, drives off alone. The film is an example of restricted narration.

Titanic (1997)
Dir. : James Cameron
Cast : Leonardo De Caprio, Kate Winslet.

A professional and pictorial triumph for Hollywood, Titanic was most expensive film ($ 200 million). The director of "The Terminator" and "Terminator 2" James Cameron made this epic. This mammoth project took 6 months to be made and contained 550 computer-generated shots and while shooting many stuntmen broke their bones. This 3 hours 20 minutes saga of doomed love against the backdrop of ill-fated Titanic, which sank on its first voyage in Atlantic ocean in 1912, created box office record and equalled two films regarding Oscars. It was nominated for 14 Oscars, thus equaling "All About Eve" (1950) and won 11, equaling 'Ben Hur' (1959).

The Towering Inferno (1974)
Dir. : John Guillermin, Irwin Allen
Cast : Steve McQueen, Paul Newman, William Holden, Faye Dunaway, Robert Vaughn, and Richard Chamberlain.

'The Towering Inferno' is one of the greatest disaster pictures made, a personal and professional triumph for producer Irwin Allen. The $ 14 million cast has yielded a truly magnificent production. The 130 storey San Francisco building, that goes up in flames, is the simple plot of the film, which complements but does not at all overwhelm a thoughtful personal drama. It was nominated for the best picture Oscar, and won Oscar for editing and cinematography.

Vertigo (1958)
Dir. : Alfred Hitchcock
Cast : James Stewart, Kim Novak.

Mesmerizing, haunting, and seductive are blurbs freely floated around about a lot of movies with Hitchcock's dream-like 'Vertigo', it is not only true of how we in the audience experience it, it is also true of how James Stewart, the hero, experiences it in the film. He is a man suffering from spells of Vertigo, goes and falls headlong in love, experiencing a kind of vertigo of the heart. When you get to the end of film you want to start all over again to see how it was done : how you, like Stewart, were tricked.

White Heat (1949)
Dir. : Raoul Walsh
Cast : James Cagney, Virginio Mayo, and Edmond O'Brien.

The Great Swan Song of the 1930s gangster movie with a Freudian twist! Cagney plays a Psychopathic gangster. One of the toughest and brilliant crime films ever made, completely authentic, and Cagney's own character was based on notorious real-life gangster, Arthur 'Doc' Barker. The final image shot atop an actual oil refinery in Torance, California is chilling. With the refinery-searing inferno, Cagney mortally wounded calls out in triumph to his now dead mother; "I made it to the top of the world, ma!", simply unforgettable.

The French Connection (1971)
Dir. : William Friedkin
Cast : Gene Hackman, Fernando Ray, Roy Scheider, and Tony LoBianco.

So many changes have been made in Robin Moore's taut, factual reprise of one of the biggest narcotics hauls in New York police history that only the Skeleton remains but producer and screen writer have added enough Fictional flesh to provide director and his overall top notch cast with plenty of material, and they make the most of it. Shot almost entirely in and around New York, Owen Roizman's fluid colour camera explores most of Manhattan and much of Brooklyn without prettifying the backgrounds. The film won Oscars for the best picture, director and actor, screenplay, editing.

Lawrence Of Arabia (1962)
Dir. : David Lean
Cast : Peter O'Toole, Alec Guinness, Anthony Quinn, Jack Hawkins, and Omar Sharif.

Who can make this epic except David Lean, who always thought big, and did big, during the years of the first world war when Lawrence (Toole) was leading the Arabs in military campaigns against the Turks, he was confronted by his own General Allenby (Jack Hawkins). Lawrence begs him more guns, more money for Arabia. He unites mortal enemy tribes of Arabia and lead them. In the desert Lawrence comes alive so fully that he comes apart. The Arabs have made him first a prince and then a kind of prophet. He leads them on camels and horses, with guns and swords. They want to take Akaba, which was heavily guarded by Turks. The cinematography of the film is unparalleled. The film won Oscars for the best picture, best director, original score, art direction, cinematography, editing and sound.

Ten Commandments (1956)
Dir. : Cecil B. DeMille
Cast : Charlton Heston, Yul Bryner, and Anne Baxter.

This epic religious film, by the Grand old Man of Hollywood Cecil B. DeMille, has won hearts of millions all over the world over the years. Ramses I, the pharaoh is told that the 'Deliverer' of the Hebrews will soon be born and free his people. He commands that all newborn Jewish males be slaughtered. But Marthscott places her small son in a basket and sends him floating down the river Nile. The Pharaoh's sister finds the child and brings him up as her own son, naming him Moses. The film was nominated for 7 Oscars, including the best cinematography and special effect.

The Untouchables (1987)
Dir. : Brain De Palma
Cast : Kevin Costner, Sir Sean Connery, Andy Garcia.

In crime-laden 1920s Chicago, an honest day's work could get you killed, if you are on the hit-list of the most ruthless gangster the world has ever known. Eliot Ness, a federal agent, has come to Chicago with a mission — to put the ganglord Kingpin Capone out of business for good. Ness has to assemble his own group to take Capone down. They become the "Untouchables", fight tooth and nail to bring Capone down. With all costumes by Giorgio Armani, an Oscar winning cast, and director Brain De Palma at the helm, this grand gangster movie remains untouchable to this day. Sean Connery won the Best Supporting actor Oscar.

Jurassic Park (1993)
Dir. : Steven Spielberg
Cast : Sam Neill.

Based on the best seller by Michael Crichton, Jurassic Park was made by the magical hands of Steven Spielberg. He knows how to combine drama with special effects without sacrificing one for another. It broke all previous box office records, ruled the world with its life like special effects by recreating dinosaurs, which became extinct millions of years ago. The film won Oscars for the best special effect, sound effect and sound effect editing.

— Other must watch films —

Apocalypse Now (1979)
Dir. : Francis Ford Coppola
Cast : Marlon Brando, Robert Duvall, and Martin Sheen.

Coppola's epic retelling of Joseph Conrad's famous novel 'Heart of Darkness', uncovers the corruption of power amid the horrors of the Vietnam war. Winner of 2 Academy Awards, Coppola once said "It is not about Vietnam, it is Vietnam".

American Beauty (1999)
Dir. : Sam Mendes
Cast : Kevin Spacey, Annette Bening.

The film examines the special plight of suburban adolescents of America — the proverbial children on whom the sins of the fathers and mothers are visited. A dark comedy about family mayhem in suburbia, beautifully acted by Kevin Spacey as a father of the girl, who tries to seduce his daughter's classmate, is the winner of 5 Oscars including the best picture, director and actor. The cinematography and the background score are brilliant.

A Beautiful Mind (2001)
Dir. : Ron Howard
Cast : Russel Crowe, Jennifer Connelly, Ed Harris, Christopher Plummer.

Sylvia Nasar's 1998 biography of the eccentric mathematics genius John Forbes Nash Jr. turns out to be ideal material for director Ron Howard, whose films celebrate triumphs over adversity by love and human bonding. 'A Beautiful Mind' is as inspiring as it is excellently crafted. The sensitive screenplay by Akira Goldsman chronicles the life of Nash, beautifully played by Crowe, from his days as a shy student to 1994 when he won a Noble Prize for his trail blazing theory in the field of economics. The husband wife relationship which has spanned nearly five decades is the core of the film. Connelly as the devoted wife, Ed Harris as a nightmarish Federal agent and the veteran Christopher Plummer as the sympathetic psychiatrist are particularly impressive. Roger Deakin's Cinematography and James Horner's unobtrusive music score greatly benefit the overall impact of the film. The Academy Award winner Russel Crowe has effortlessly done the role of Dr. Nash. He is mesmerizing. The film won 4 Oscars including the best picture and the best director.

Gladiator (2000)
Dir. : Ridley Scott
Cast : Russel Crowe, Joaquin Phoenix, Oliver Reed, Djimon Hounsou, Derek Jacobi, Connie Nielsen, Richard Harris.

This Roman epic occupies a special place in the hearts of moviegoers. 'Ben-Hur', 'Spartacus' all were loved by the audience. The plot familiar from 1964 "The Fall of the Roman Empire" is set in 180 A.D., Emperor Marcus Aurelius (Harris) is ailing. He appoints his best general Maximus (Crowe), a caretaker of the Empire, whose motto is 'Strength And Honour'. But the emperor's son Commodus, whose lust for throne was well-known, kills his father, usurps the throne, orders maximum death, kills his boss, razes his house and his wife and son were defiled and slaughtered. Maximus has reason for revenge. He escapes and was sold into a troupe of gladiators. Their job is to fight and die. He makes a comeback in a new role. Screen writer David Franzoni, helped by John Logan and Willian Nicholson, had brought a well polished and entertaining script. Exuberant Oliver Reed gave a superbly performance as the leader of gladiators, but it was his last, as he died while filming his last scene. Russel Crowe was the perfect choice for the character of Maximus. He looked a real Roman. This $ 100 million film required arduous location shooting and elaborate computer effects. Director of 'Thelma And Louise', 'Blade Runner' and 'Alien' had done a remarkable job. The film won five Oscars out of its 12 nominations, including the best picture, best actor and best special effects.

Traffic (2000)

Dir. : Steven Soderbergh

Cast : Michael Douglas, Catherine Zeta Jones, Denis Quaid, Benicio Del Toro, Don Cheadle.

All Americans seem to be addicted to something that is bad for them, cigarettes, excessive getting and spending and drugs. Drugs kill and addle, they lie at the heart of a vast criminal enterprise and the feckless war against them costs billions of public dollar every year. 'Traffic' is the epic of our despair on this topic. The film is well made by Steven Soderbergh who handled his own camera and often edits in an artless, documentary style. The picture is full of strong, soberly realistic performances; its melodramatic beats are not too many and, in context, not particularly overstated. The film tells three different stories at the same time, all connected to the main plot. Michael Douglas, who is appointed by the president to be the new national drug czar only to discover that his own daughter, is an addict. Another story is about an honest Mexican drug-enforcement officer (Benicio Del Toro), mystified by the cruel omnipotence of Thomas Milian. The final story is of a San Diego material girl (Catherine Zeta Jones) whose lifestyle is threatened when her husband is arrested for high level trafficking. She proves to be a very tough nut when she takes over the family business. Stephen Gaghan's script, inspired by a British mini-series, jerks the audience's brains at many places. 'Traffic', a $ 50 million movie had earned $ 300 million world-wide. Soderbergh gave each story a distinct look in order to keep the audience oriented. He shot Washington in bleak and bluish colour and Mexico in grainy yellowish and slightly overexposed San Diego scenes to make the colours soft and blossoming. It was a nice contrast. The film won 4 Oscars including the best director, best editing and best screenplay.

The Longest Day (1962)

Dir. : Ken Annakin

Cast : Eddie Albert, Paul Anka, Richard Burton, Red Buttons, Sean Connery, Fabian, Peter Lawford, Roddy McDowell, Robert Mitchum, John Wayne.

This multi starer war epic tells the story of that fateful day that changed the world — when history held its breath and the world lost many of its beloved sons. D-Day, a day that would turn the tide of a war and change the face of history. This action classic demanded hundreds of thousands of soldiers and it got real soldiers from England, Germany, France and U.S., to work in the film. June 6, 1944, Omaha Beach — In what is the most publicised operation of world war II, the Allies launched a huge Combined operation to permanently dislodge a German army, the landing at the beach proved chaotic for the US 1st army under General Omar Bradley and the grim battle that followed, killed several American soldiers. Two more films; 'Dirty Dozen' and 'Saving Private Ryan' were made on this historical day, better known as D-Day. The Longest Day was nominated for 4 Academy Awards and won two including Best Special Effect.

Last Man Standing (1996)
Dir. : Walter Hill
Cast : Bruce Willis, Christopher Walken, Bruce Dern, David Patrick Kelly, Ned Eisenberg.

In this retelling of the Kurosawa classic 'Yojimbo' Jhon Smith (Willis) is the gun for hire who realizes he can play off two eternally warring gangs against each other. The Italian gang is led by Strozzi and the Irish one by Doyle. The two gangs have caused so much bloodshed in the town that the sheriff has abandoned all hope of restoring law and order. Strozzi recruits Willis to strengthen his position. But Willis exploits both gangs to finish them and at the end he is the only person who is seen standing. Walter Hill is an auteur of action whose narrative use of chase and confrontation have produced a gallery of highly commercial, critically acclaimed films like 'The Warriors', 'Red Heat', and 'Streets of Fire'. The writer, director has had an abiding interest in the American Western and was honoured with the prestigious Golden Boot and Western Heritage Award from the National Cowboy Hall of fame. The cinematography of 'Last Man Standing' is grainy, light sandy colour which beautifully suits the mood of the story. The action looks live and deathly. It is a heavy, powerful film, which appeals both the masses as well as the classes. One of the best gang war films made.

Braveheart (1995)
Dir. : Mel Gibson
Cast : Mel Gibson, Sophie Marceau, and Patrick McGoohan.

A 15th century Britain is well colorfully depicted in this epic full of love, battles and tragic moments. One of the best costume dramas and historical films. 'Braveheart' is Mel Gibson who leads Scottish army against Britain. The battles, shown in the film are unparalleled and unmatched. The multiple Oscar winner Braveheart remains a truly Braveheart film till today. It won 5 Oscar.

Other Classics

Gone with The Wind (Victor Fleming 1939), Dr. Zhivago (David Lean 1965), The Sound of Music (Robert Wise, 1965), Gandhi (Sir Richard Attenborough, 1982), Dances With The Wolves (Kevin Costner, 1990), Unforgiven (Client Eastwood, 1960), The Wizard of OZ (Victor Fleming, 1939), The Last Emperor (Bernardo Bertolucci 1987), Rain Man (1988), Out of Africa (1985), Amadeus (1984), Kramer Vs Kramer (1979), Cabaret (1972), Patton (1970), My Fair Lady (1964).

THE WORLD CINEMA

The history of world cinema is inscribed with names of such heroic pioneers. They are the enduring masters — Eisenstein (USSR), Jean Vigo (France), Luiz Bunuel (Spain), Carl Dreyer (Denmark), Fritz Lang and Murnau (Germany), Ozu and Mizoguchi (Japan) — whose seminal films are cinema's holy books. Unfortunately, many of the masterpieces are unavailable unless one belongs to a film society or has an access to a film archive. They are taken for granted classic without which one's film education is incomplete.

ARGENTINA

El Viage / The Journey (1992)

Dir. : Fernardo Solanas
Cast : Walter Quiroz, Fito Paez, Erivar El Kadri.

Solanas takes his protagonist, a teenaged boy, on a journey

from the extreme tip of South America north to Mexico, to search for his father as well as the roots of his ancient history. The stunning sweep of the Camera captures the entire history of Argentina and the threatened magnificence of a magical content.

Son of The Bride (2001)
Dir. : Juan Jose Campanella.

This Argentinian film by Juan Jose Campanella won the Audience Award at the Hawana Film Festival. It is about a successful restaurateur who shocks his family by announcing that he plans to remarry his ex-wife, now an Alzheimer's patient in a rest home. The film was nominated for Oscar in the best foreign film category.

Other film : The Official Story (1985).

AUSTRALIA

Picnic At Hanging Rock (1980)
Dir. : Peter Weir
Cast : Rachel Roberts, Dominic Guard, Helen Morse.

Like songs unheard being sweeter, an unsolved mystery in more haunting. It is about an ancient Forbidden land rebuking trespassers. There is punishment for sexual transgression. Three girls vanish never to be seen again. Weir uses haunting flute melody to complement a strong surrealism.

The Piano (1993)
Dir. : Jane Campion
Cast : Holly Hunter, Harvey Keitel, Sam Neill, Anna Paquin.

Jane Campion disproves a charge levelled against women director that they lack creative spatial ability, the imaginative vision to organize space for the Camera Frame. 'Piano' is dramatic story of a woman's repression and passion, revolt, and liberation. It is a minor masterpiece.

GREAT BRITAIN

Brief Encounter (1945)
Dir. : David Lean
Cast : Celia Johnson, Trevor Howard.

The early David Lean expressed all that is unique and best in England and caught the ineffable mood of post war melancholy. The bittersweet love story is told from Lara's point of view after the final parting of two conscience-stricken people who do not want to betray their families. Few shots of mute despairs are soul-searching.

A Matter Of Life And Death (1946)
Dir. : Michael Powell and Emeric Pressburger
Cast : David Niven, Roger Livesey, Marius Goring.

One is taken aback by the director's sheer bravado to even visualize this marvellously entertaining film about a RAF pilot who has to undergo a brain operation and then, because of a mis-trial in thoroughly bureaucratized Court somewhere up there, is sent back to earth. This was the time when Britain was counting the losses of its dead in the war! This film is the mother of all such fantasies about death and temporary resurrection of ordinary mortals.

Hamlet (1948)
Dir. : Sir Laurence Olivier
Cast : Sir Laurence Olivier, Jean Simmons, and Basil Sydney.

It is not matter of surprise that the most celebrated Shakespearean actor made the best 'Hamlet'. But it was more surprising, how he changed and compensated four pages text in two and a half. He compensated it with great visuals. Because he knew the superiority of show over tell in cinema. Olivier's 'Hamlet', which brings out all the facts of the doomed Prince of Denmark. The film won 4 Oscars — including best picture and best actor besides art direction and costumes — plus nominations for best director, best supporting actress for an 18 years old Jean Simmons playing Ophelia.

The Third Man (1949)
Dir. : Carol Reed
Cast : Orsen Welles, Joseph Cotten, Alida Valli.

Orsen Welles, plays that fascinating villain Harry Lime who appears halfway through the film. The Third Man is not merely one of the best thrillers ever made from a Graham Greene screen play but where many talents came together for a moment of cinematic felicity. The story is set in war-torn Vienna, where villain flogs watered down penicillin.

Other Noteworthy Films of U.K.

"The African Queen" (John Huston 1951), 'The Charge of The Light Brigade' (Tony Richardson 1968), The Count of the Monte Cristo (David Greene 1976), The Day of The Jackal (Fred Zinnemann 1973), Fear is the Key (Michael Tuchner 1973), The Four Feathers (Zoltan Korda 1939), Gold (Peter Hunt 1974), Guns At Batasi (John Guillermin 1964), Invanhoe (Richard Tharpe 1952), Khartoum (Basil Dearden 1966), The Sound Barrier (David Lean 1952), Zeppelin (Etienne Perier 1971), Zulu (CyEnfield 1964).

CHINA/HONG-KONG/TAIWAN

Dahong Denglong/ Raise the Red Lantern (1991)
Dir. : Zhang Yimou
Cast : Gong Li, Chen Zuoquion.

Few cinematographers have made such an assured passage to direction as Zhang yimou. The international success of Chen 'Kaige's Red Sorghum' and 'Yellow Earth' owes much to yimou's mastery of colour. 'Raise the Lantern' centres around the luminously beautiful Gong Li playing Songlian, the newest bride entering a fortress of house. The 18th century mansion of many courtyards is both a setting and a metaphor for a patriarchal system which condemns songlian to become "icon of Frozen desire". The custom of the house is for a red lantern to be lit in the courtyard of the wife whom the master favours for the night.

Ba wang Bie Ji/ Farewell, My concubine (1993)
Dir. : Chen Kaige
Cast : Leslie Cheung, Zhang Feng yi.

It required a Chinese director to present the corrective to Bertolucci's 'The Last Emperor' which endorsed China's official version of its recent history. The story of the two performers from harsh childhood when they are both apprenticed to the Peking Opera, to the denunciations of the Cultural Revolution, charts the vicissitudes of their friendship.

Crouching Tiger Hidden Dragon (2000)
Dir. : Ang Lee
Cast : Chow yun-Fat, Michelle yeoh, Li Mu Bai.

An epic account told through the tales of two women whose lives become entwined after the theft of the magically endowed green destiny sword. Gripping action and gravity defying martial art skills enthrall and overwhelm the audience. After making three English films, Ang Lee returned to Asia to make this film. 19th century China is well depicted. This was the first foreign film, which won 10 Oscar nominations, winning 4 including the best cinematography, art direction, background score. A tale of revenge and honour, thrillings and elegantly executed fight sequences and pleasurable classical story telling, became an instant hit world-wide. Yuen Wo-Ping choreographed the gravity defying actions of the film.

FRANCE

La Regle Du Jeu/ The Rules of the Game (1939)
Dir. : Jean Renior
Cast : Nora Gregor, Marcel Dalio, Roland Toutain, Jean Renoir.

His films do not overwhelm us. They absorb us. It is his most complex film with nine principle characters where the action moves from Paris to a country Chateau. His camera intuitively allowed his characters to be people in the theatre of life.

Journal D'un cure De Campagne/Diary of A Country Priest (1951)
Dir. : Robert Bresson
Cast : Claude Laydu.

The young priest of the film is wracked with pain and has to battle to gain the trust of a provincial town. The search for a state of grace—the quintessential Bresson theme climaxes with the death of the adversial countess but after the priest has battled for her soul. Underneath this spiritual quest, there is a subliminal and unresolved sexual context.

Lola Montes (1955)
Dir. : Max Ophuls
Cast : Peter Ustinov, Martine Carol, Anton Walbrook.

Lola Montes is a woman who is a prisoner of love and an exploitative social structure. A famous courtesan, she relives, her turbulent life in a series of complex flashbacks while touring with a circus. The film offers a fine example of Ophuls' signature camerawork. Style fuses with theme.

A Bout De Souffle/Breathless (1959)
Dir. : Jean Luc Godard
Cast : Jean Paul Belmondo, Jean Seber.

Godard always throws a hand grenade into the audience. Deliberate jump cuts, starting film from the middle of it and doing anything to be different, puts Godard into a different place. The film is a self-conscious tribute to the B grade action films and to Humphrey Bogart. 'Breathless' continues to be Godard's signature work.

Les Quartre cents coups/400 Blows (1959)
Dir. : Francois Truffaut
Cast : Jean Pierre Leaud, Albert Remy, Claire Maurier.

This film which comes from the heart and shows Truffaut's lifelong empathy not only for troubled children but all outsiders, is the most popular film made by him. Truffaut drew from his own painful adolescence to portray the rebellion of Antoine Doinelan emblematic figure in his oeuvre with compassion. The 13-year old Antoine's life is one of escape from unloving parents; a rigid school system.

Hiroshima Mon Amour (1959)
Dir. : Alain Resnais
Cast : Emmabuele Riva, Eijiokada.

Resnais' all films explore the themes of time and memory. This film weaves into its brief love affair between a French actress and a Japanese architect, her memory of another love affair with a German soldier when she was a young girl. She suffered at the hands of unforgiving compatriots because she loved the enemy during the war. The new love is also a war enemy but one who has suffered a nuclear holocaust, acts as catharsis as well as catalyst.

La Belle Noiseuse (1991)
Dir. : Jacques Rivette
Cast : Michel Piccoli, Jane Birkin, Emmanuele Beart.

Films about painters are invariably allegories for cinema. Rivettle paints his film with camera making it a modern masterpiece. Rivette confronts without evasions and apologies the theme of an ageing painter stricken by creative paralysis. Piccoli's unfinished work "Labelle Noiseuse", has been abandoned for nearly 10 years for which his wife had modelled. The new model is the luscious Emmanuele Beart, girlfriend of a young painter. The pain of creation is the supreme bliss of the film, but we never get to see the final painting, except in a flash.

Amelie (2001)
Dir. : Jean Pierre Jeunet.

This film has been a phenomenol critical success in Europe and the US. It was described as a detectable French Confection. It is about a naïve French girl who decides to change the lives of those around her. The film was nominated for 5 Oscars but lost all of them.

L' Atlante (1934)
Dir. : Jean Vigo.

Jean Vigo's L' Atlante has been consistently ranked among the top 10 films of all time by the sight and sound poll. David Thompson calls Vigo, the first young martyr to cinema. His lyrical surrealism blends beautiful with a documentarist's eye for the working class life in the simple story of a young skipper, his new bride and the orderman who works on the barge going past harshly industrialized town on the Seine. The chasm separating "L' Altante" from Titanic sums the distance between artistic unity and Hollywood hype.

Other noteworthy films : Monsieur Vincent (48). The walls of Malapaga (50), Forbidden Games (52), My Uncle (58), Black Orpheus (59), Indochina (92).

GERMANY

The Blue Angel (1930)
Dir. : Joseph von Sternberg
Cast : Emil Jannings, Marlene Dietrich.

Sternberg came back to Germany to make only one film, after years of flamboyant posing as the European artist working in Hollywood. The humour is totally absent in this remorseless tale of tawdry passion which destroys the prudent, puritanical old professor. The object of his hopeless passion is the cheap cabaret singer Lola Lola. 'The Blue Angel' is remarkable for its sexual honesty without recourse to nudity or graphic couplings.

Himmel Uber Berlin/Wings of Desire (1987)
Dir. : Wim Wenders
Cast : Bruno Ganz, Solveig Dommartic, Otto Sander.

The road movie director's signature work, 'Wings of Desire' is the story of two angels over Berlin with one of them falling in love with trapeze artist. Playful whimsy turns into metaphysical meditation and, paradoxically, crowded with memorable characters and engaging actions. Instead of a road movie, we have teeming street life.

Other films : The Tin Drum (79), Nowhere In Africa (2002).

Mephisto (1981)
Dir. : Istvan Szabo
Cast : Klaus Maria Brandaeur, Krystyna Janda.

The Mephistophelean bargain recurs in European literature and theatre time and again but not in cinema. That is, until Istvan came up with a brilliant script based on Klaus Mann's novel. The theme is the gradual corruption of a gifted actor who mortgages his integrity for a meteoric rise of Nazi Germany. The protagonist's Career is based on the life of a legendary actor, Gustav Grundgens (1899-1963) who was Germany's most famous actor, theatre director and impresario of his generation. But at the end after the prostitution of his talent and conscience, he is dismissed with contempt as a 'mere actor' by his Goblesian patron. The film won best foreign picture Oscar.

Other films of Hungary : "Two Half Times in Hell" (1961) by Zoltan Fabri, "Let's Love Each Other" (1996), "Gangster Film" (1998).

ITALY

Rome, Open City (1945)
Dir. : Roberto Rossellini
Cast : Anna Magnani, Aldo Fabrizi, Marcello Pagliero.

Roberto Rossellini, quite simply is one of the most underestimated stalwarts of world cinema. His films are as intellectually stimulating as they are down to earth. Rome, Open City is the harbinger of neo-realist movement. The film's primary concern was to create the cruelty and horror witnessed in Rome, during the German occupation. Rossellini originally intended to make a short documentary on a well-known priest who was shot by the Gestapo for abetting the partisans. But his sponsor, a wealthy old lady, insisted that Rossellini also make another short film about the heroism displayed by Rome's children against the Nazi forces. Rossellini fused the two short films and made Rome, Open City. This film was made under tremendous constraints. Raw stock was of substandard quality and even that had to be bought in the black market. Rossellini, filming largely in the actual homes of his cast and crew, also had to contend with fluctuating electricity. Funds were never sufficient. He sold his furniture and clothes to raise further finance. Rome, Open City (Roma, Citta Aperta) is now a classic. At the end, Rossellini commented "Ever since 'Roma, Citta Aperta,' I have maintained a conscious, determined endeavour to understand the world in which I live, in a spirit of humility and respect for the facts and for history".

Paisan/Paisa (1946)
Dir. : Roberto Rossellini
Cast : Carmela Sazio, Dots M. Johnson, Maria Michi, Harriet White, Bill Tubbs, Edmonds.

Once again improvisation, non-professional actors, and the narrative focus on partisan groups and ordinary people torn under by war, were of the essence. Rossellini points individual conflicts versus collective ones. The film is in episodes but the stories have a single-minded purpose to assert that finally it is the will that triumphs. The last, and most disturbing episodes of 'Paisan' describes the plight of the partisans and American soldiers who are hopelessly outnumbered and ultimately massacred by Germans. Rossellini's cinemas are immortal. A priceless legacy that has been bequeathed from one generation to the next and will continue, no doubt, in this millennium too.

The Bicycle Thief (1948)
Dir. : Vittorio de Sica
Cast : Lamberto Maggiorani, Enzo Staiola, Lianella Carell.

Vittorio de Sica's ode to the human spirit continues to be a must see at film society screenings and film appreciation courses. Despite occasional lapses into sentimentality, this black and white classic comes closest to the director's idea of transposing harsh reality to the realm of gut wrenching poetry. The sturdily structured screenplay by Cesare Zavattini, one of the neo-realism's leading theorists, portrays the disaster that results from the theft of a bicycle on which a man's livelihood depends. After searching too much, with his 10 years old son, the protagonist steals a bicycle but is caught redhanded. He is humiliated before his son. In the film's heart rending final sequence, little son, in a gesture of affection and solidarity clasps the hand of his emotionally devastated father. They walk off, melting facelessly into the crowd without any hope. The film shows poverty and unemployment which were rampant during World War II. It won best foreign picture Oscar.

Otto E Mezzo / Eight And A Half (1963)
Dir. : Frederico Fellini
Cast : Marcello Mastroianni, Anouk Aimee, Sandra Milo, Claudia Cardinale.

Fellini has the ability to make art and entertainment out of his unapologetic self-obsession. He makes his thoughts universal. Fellini's autobiographical exploration reaches a logical consummation in 'Eight and A Half', a title which sums up the 8 films and two shorts he has made up to this point. It is a director's block. He has no idea for the film. The film won best foreign picture Oscar.

Blow Up (1966)
Dir. : Michaelangelo Antonioni
Cast : David Hemmings, Vanessa Redgrave, Sarah Miles.

Some films become cult films for other filmmakers, quoted endlessly. Overtly, slyly, subversively and in a spirit of celebration. Blow-up, the most accessible film in Antonioni's bleak abstractions of reality as he saw it, has attained this status. The protagonist is Thomas, a fashion photographer and this affords the director to film models as stylized bodies carrying off shapes and colours. Blow-up does work like thriller. Blow-up can be enjoyed by moviegoers who never heard of Antonioni.

Novecento/ 1900 (1976)
Dir. : Bernardo Bertolucci
Cast : Robert De Niro, Gerard Depardieu, Donald Sutherland, Burt Lancaster, Laura Betti.

This is a post 'Last Tango in Paris' Bertolucci, almost arrogantly confident that he can encapsulate the early decades of 20th century in a 320-minute epic. The film begins with the birth of a new century and two births in two homes in his native Parma. Alfredo, the heir to the great mansion who grows up into Robert De Niro; Olmo, son of a worker on the estate who grows up into Depardieu. The boys are childhood friends but their circumstances, sensibility and destiny pits them across the class and political divide. The viewer becomes privy to the process of history. "1900" is the working political maturity and poetic expression. The result is true epic when there are far too few genuine epics. It is an ambitious idea, which works brilliantly most of the time. It is more true for Bertolucci who served his apprenticeship as a politically conscious filmmaker when he was still at college.

Cinema Paradiso (1988)
Dir. : Giuseppe Tornatore
Cast : Philippe Noiret, Jacques Perrin.

If anyone doubted the stamina of cinema in the age of Television, Tornatore's loving reaffirmation of faith in the power of movies to enchant and inspire is heart-warming. Tornatore pays a funny, affecting and affectionate tribute to the many stars and directors, the young boy devoured with such voracious appetite. The film won Oscar for Best Foreign film. Audiences and juries alike responded to the director's sheer love for cinema.

La Vita E Bella / Life is Beautiful (1998)
Dir. : Roberto Benigni
Cast : Roberto Benigni, Sergio Bustric, Giargio Cantarini Nicoletta Braschi, Durano.

An autobiographical film by one of the most famous comic actor-directors, Roberto Benigni's 'Life is Beautiful' created a wave among all types of audience's worldwide. Conjuring keys and hats out of thin air Guido (Benigni) a clever Jewish-Italian waiter, successfully courts Dora (Nicoletta Braschi), a beautiful local woman, in Fascist pre-World-War II Italy. His life, however, is turned upside down a few years later when he, Dora, and their young son, Giosu'c (Giorgio), are sent to Nazi concentration camp. Throughout it all, Guido determines to shield his son from this brutal reality by telling him comic stories. The film won 3 Oscars including the best foreign films, best actor. It was nominated for 7 Oscars.

Other Great Films of Italy : Shoeshine (1947), La Stranda (1956), The Nights of Cabiria (1957), Yesterday, Today & Tomorrow (1964), Mediterraneo (1991), Amarcord (1974).

IRAN

Khaneh-ye Dust Kojust? (Where is the friend's home?) (1987)
Dir. : Abbas Kiarostami
Cast : Babak Ahmadpour, Ahmad Ahmad Pour.

A little boy is about to do his homework when he discovers that he has taken his classmate's notebook by mistake, he sets off to go to the neighbouring village to return the notebook. But since he does not know where his friend lives, he is unable to find him. Finally he returns home and decides to do his friend's homework so that he would not get into trouble. 'Where Is My Friend's Home' is among classics of Iran. The transparent simplicity of his films makes an art of artlessness. What is most unique to his films is the spontaneous building up of a coherent, multi-layered narrative through small incidents told with episodic casualness.

Other great films of Iran : Gabbeh (Makhmalbaf), The Tree of Life (Meheranfar), and Life Goes On (Abbas Kiarostami), Under The Olive Tree (Abbas Kiarostami), 'Father' (Majid Majidi), 'Sara', 'Leela' (Daryush Mehrjui), Close Up (Abbas Kiarostami), The Last Act (Varuz Karim Masini), "Taste of Cherry" (Abbas Kiarostami), The White Balloon (Jafar Panahi), Children of Heaven (Majid Majidi), 'To Be Or Not To Be' (Keyanush Aiyari).

Note : "Children of Heaven" and "The White Balloon" were nominated for 'The Best Foreign Picture Oscar.'

INDIA

The Appu Trilogy (1955-56-59)
Dir. : Satyajit Ray
Cast : Kanu Banerjee, Karuna Banerjee, Chunnibala Devi, Pinaki Sen Gupta, Smaran Ghosal, Soumitra Chatterjee, Sharmila Tagore.

The Appu Trilogy (Pather Panchali, Aparajito, Apur Sagar) films, which, for the first time, exhibited the inherent powers of films medium as distinct from the make-believe world which till then dominated Indian cinema. It was after that Indian Cinema came into its own. Watching these films made a different experience. Pather Panchali (Song of the Little Road), based on a novel by Bibhuti Bhusan Bandopadhya, depicted the Indian Rural childhood. The film went on to win numerous prestigious international awards, many of them which were coming to India for the first time. Among these were the 'Best Human Document' award at Cannes. According to film historian Erik Barnouw, "'Appu Trilogy' formed an epic that moved the village to the city from the distant past to the recent past, from a structured rural life to an anarchic rural milieu and foreshadowed the scope of Ray's work in the decades to come". Satyajit Ray thought like a graphic artist with the intuition of a lyric poet and the vision of a realist. 'Pather Panchali' is full of the magic of childhood discoveries and the tragic inevitability of death amidst the genteel poverty of a priestly Brahmin's household in rural Bengal at the turn of the century. The central theme of 'Aparajito' is the growing distance between Appu and his mother, the thirst for education taking away the sensitive, intelligent boy to the wider world outside 'Aparajito' (The unvanquished) has its own organic unity 'Apur Sansar' (Appu's World) is alight with the beauty of love's down and darkens with the despair of death. The trilogy establishes Ray's mastery of the screenplay which sets a Renoir-like understanding of human psychology in a wider social perspective. He won special Oscar Award in 1992.

Ardh Satya (The Half Truth) (1983)

Dir. : Govind Nihlani

Cast : Om Puri, Smita Patil, Amrish Puri, Naseeruddin Shah, Sadashiv Amarapurkar.

The cop-hero in Indian cinema falls rather neatly into pre and post 'Ardh Satya' times. It is tempting to see a post-Emergency (after 1975) subtext in Nihlani's searing expose of the entire brutalizing process of the police system. Smita Patil, a civil Liberties activist, who falls in love with a violent cop who is thrusted into a system where success is measured by the individual's desensitization to violence and corruption.

Bhumika (The Role) (1976)
Dir. : Shyam Benegal
Cast : Smita Patil, Anant Nag, Amrish Puri, Naseeruddin Shah, Kulbhushan Kharbanda.

Like other glamour icon biopics (Frances, The Coal-miner's Daughter), it is a bleak stray about an actress need to search for and to assert her identity in a world that increasingly commodities her. Urvashi's (Patil) quest for happiness encompasses several broken relationships. Pushed into films, she sees Amol Palekar as her escape route. But she cannot escape paying the price for the freedom to follow her desires in a male dominated world of an actress.

Deewar (The Wall) (1975)
Dir. : Yash Chopra
Cast : Amitabh Bachchan, Shashi Kapoor, Nirupa Roy.

The socio-economic climate favoured Amitabh Bachchan's decision to vend violence at the marquee in the time of romance. Amitabh Bachchan displaced the then superstar romantic Rajesh Khanna with his young Angry Man's image. The best screenplay ever written in the history of Bollywood cinema, 'Deewar' is a story of two brothers, one is police, another is a gangster. How he becomes the angry gangster, is the essence of the script. The mother tears herself away from the gangster Amitabh, now for him, death is the only redemption.

Do Beegha Zameen (Two Acres Of Land — 1953)
Dir. : Bimal Roy
Cast : Balraj Sahni, Nirupa Roy, Rattan Kumar.

This is a survival story of almost Darwinian intensity. A farmer fights against all odds to preserve his two acres of farmland from a grasping landlord. Migrating to Calcutta, the farmer (Sahni) slaves in subhuman conditions as rickshaw-puller, has a near fatal accident, almost loses his wife — all in his struggle to find the memory to repay his loan and free his land. Italian film 'Bicycle Thief' inspired Bimal Roy to make a realistic film of human suffering and bonding. In the end the farmer fails to get his land back. This tragedy leaves an unforgettable experience upon the viewers.

Mother India (1957)
Dir. : Mehboob Khan
Cast : Nargis, Sunil Dutt, Raj Kumar, Rajendra Kumar.

One of the three Indian films nominated for the best foreign picture Oscar, Mother India became one of India's best known cultural artifacts. Like mother earth who feeds the world till she is parched but can also turn devastatingly ruthless, Mother India (Nargis) too is a form of earth goddess with a gun powder kick. When her husband leaves her, she single handedly brings up her two sons, but one son (Dutt) becomes a robber. Nargis in a blood-chilling climax shoots down her own rebellious son.

Lagaan (The Tax) (2001)
Dir. : Ashutosh Gowarikar
Cast : Amir Khan, Gracy Singh, Blackthorn.

The first crossover Indian film, nominated for the best Foreign picture Oscar, 'Lagaan' is triumph of will, where cricket-illiterate Indian farmers lead by Amir Khan have to form a team, train them and play a match with an English team to save themselves and other villages from paying triple Lagaan. It is tale of the ruled and the rulers. Though there is no battle of life and death, Amir Khan knew that only willpower could make them survive. They play and win. 'Lagaan' needed several English actors, and they were pursued to act on less wages. One and a half hour cricket match sustains the audience's interest. It is world-class film both technically as well as artistically.

Other Great Indian Films : Akaler Sandhney / In Search of Famine (Mrinal Sen 1980), Anantaram / Monologue (Adoor Gopalakrishnan 1987), Charulata (Satyajit Ray 1964), Garam Hawa/Warm Winds (Ms. Sathyu 1973), Guide (Vijay Anand 1965), Jaane Bhi do Yaaron / Who Played the Piper (Kundan Shah 1983), Jalsagar / The Music Room (Satyajit Ray 1948), Maya Miraga / The Mirage (Nirad Mohapatra 1983), Meghe Dhaka Tara / The Cloud Covered Star (Ritwik Ghatak 1960),

Nayakan / Hero (Mani Ratnam 1987), Piravi / Birth (Shaji N. Karun 1988), Pushpak / The Chariot (Singeetham Srinivas Rao 1987), Pyaasa / The Eternal Thirst (Guru Dutt 1957), Sant Tukaram (S. Fatehlal Damle 1936), Sholay / Embers (Ramesh Sippy 1975), Shri 420 (Raj Kapur 1955), Thampu / The Circus Tent (G. Aravindan 1978), 36 Chowringhee Lane (Aparna Sen 1981), Bandit Queen (Shekhar Kapoor 1995), Mughal-E-Azam / The Great Moghal Emperor (K. Asif 1960), Salaam Bombay / Goodbye Bombay (Mira Nair 1988), Kunku (V. Santaram 1937).

JAPAN

Rashomon (1951)
Dir. : Akira Kurosawa
Cast : Toshiro Mifune, Masayuki Mori, Machiko kyo.

This film has become a ready metaphor, an easy catch phrase, and a lazy short cut for us to express an idea as profound as the relative nature of all truth. In 1950, this film dazzled the world of cinema and opened the door into a different film making culture with its distinguished history, distinctive aesthetics and narrative codes. Rashomon is a series of flashbacks, a central anecdote — the rape of woman accompanying her nobleman husband in a forest by a bandit who is also accused of killing the husband — is presented four times by four different people. Kurosawa's bravura camerawork complements the stylized acting but he blurs the narration. It won best foreign picture Oscar.

Merry Christmas Mr. Lawrence (1982)
Dir. : Nagisa Oshima
Cast : David Bowie, Tom Conti, Ryuchi Sakamoto

Oshima breaks the Japanese silence about the Second World War. When the Japanese establishment refuses even today to acknowledge its less than admirable war record, Japan's angry man decided to confront the issue. In this film, he plunges into the treatment of British prisoners in a Java Camp in a familiar thematic framework of the relationship between authority and its victims. British soldiers want to be treated like soldiers. One of the Japanese officers see it in terms of patriotism and one of them finds nothing wrong with being brutal to the enemy in his power. Despite its flaws, the film is a powerful indictment of militarism.

Other Great Japanese Films : Throne of Blood (Akira Kurosawa), Seven Samurai (Akira Kwrosawa, Yojimbo (Akira Kurosawa), Tokyo Monogatari (Ozu 1953), Ugetsu Monogatari (Mizoguschi 1952), Gate of Hell (1954), Samurai, The Legends of Muschashi (1955).

POLAND

Czlowiekz Zelaza / Man Of Iron (1981)
Dir. : Andrzej Wajda
Cast : Jerzy Radziwillowicz, Krystyna Janda.

The younger Wajda gave the world a trilogy of films — 'Kanal', 'Ashes and Diamonds', 'Lotna' — which brought out the pain and confusion of post war Poland 'Man of Iron' took its young documentary filmmaker to Poland to find the famed bricklayer who had been a hero of the socialist labour in the Stalinist era. Wajda and his film alter ego return four years later to document the solidarity Revolution. The flow of fact through fiction through the use of archival photographs, tapes, eyewitness testimonies, posters, graffiti, street songs, gives this remarkable film its steely supple strength.

Everything for Sale
Dir. : Andrzej Wajda.

Zbigniew Cybulski was Wajda's favourite actor. He acted in his 'Ashes and Diamonds'. And when he died in a train accident, while making a film, he was replaced by another actor, Danial Olbrychski. Wajda made this movie on the incident, which talks about an actor going to a location and accidentally being killed and the repercussion on the unit and the search for a replacement. And the inevitable sort of heartlessness that involves to have to keep in mind the practical aspect. It tackles the theme of celebrity and work. And work is always more important. It must go. A terribly moving film.

POLAND / FRANCE / SWITZERLAND

Trois Colours : Bleu, Blanc, Rouge / Three Colours : Blue, White, Red (1993, 1994)
Dir. : Krzystof Kieslowski
Cast : (For Bleu) Juliet Binoche, Benoit Regent (For Rouge) : Irene Jacob, Jean-Louis Trintignant.

When Kieslowski died, the world mourned a master who died at the height of his creative power. It was the harshly chilling yet infinitely compassionate retelling of the Ten Commandments for our times in the 'Decalogue', which brought critical acclaim to this rigorous and reticent director. The final trilogy symbolizing three colours which stand for liberty, equality and fraternity, are for more lush but again, shot through with his signature themes of irony and elusive, refracted meanings. 'Blue' is a mournful on them to the ideal of a new, post cold war Europe. It probes the depths of despair. The film is complemented by a soaring beautiful score, which uses passages of silence to stunning effect. Kieslowski's mordant humour returns when Karol, the protagonist of 'white', returns to Poland. Paris has made him homeless, and penniless. 'Red' imposes a formal unity on the trilogy with the judicial intervention of a Prospero like retired judge. A young model and the old judge meet as adversaries initially but a curious bond develops between them. The films have dramatic intensity, formal beauty and epiphanies of irony.

Other Films of Switzerland : Journey of Hope (1990), Dangerous Moves (1984).

THE NETHERLANDS

Karakter/ Character (1997)
Dir. : Mike Van Diem
Cast : Fedja Van Huet, Jan Decleir, Betty Schuurman, Victor Low, Tamar Van Den Dop, and Hans Kestings.

Character is the feature debut of Mike Van Diem. It is set in the Dutch port of Rotterdam during the economic crisis of the Thirties. The protagonist Katadreuffe, and eager and ambitious young man who does everything he can to escape his narrow-minded surroundings. He is supported by his friend but thwarted by his dominant father. The father cannot come to terms with the fact that he was rejected by Jaba, Katadreuffe's mother, and takes out his anger and disappointment on his bastard son. The son prepared the final confrontation with his biological father. The film won Best Foreign Picture Oscar.

Other Films : Antonia's Line (1995), The Assault (1986).

BOSNIA AND HERZEGOVINA

No Man's Land (2001)
Dir. : Danis Tanovic.

'No Man's Land' is Danis Tanovic's anti-war film. It is about a Bosnian and a Serbian soldier caught in a French between enemy lines. It is deeply and painfully authentic. It has come from a country that does not make many movies due to wars and conflicts. The great effort, the fine acting and an emotional screenplay were finely knit into the film. 'No Man's Land' won the Best Foreign Picture Oscar.

RUSSIA

Prisoner of The Mountain (1996)
Dir. : Sergey Bodrov
Cast : Oleg Menshikov, Sergey Bodrov Jr., Susnna Mekhralieva.

This much acclaimed film — at many festivals — is a modern interpretation of a classic Tolstoy story. It is brilliant for the depth of its insight, the daring of its contemporaneity and devastating in its indictment of Russia's war against the fiercely independent Chechens. Tolstoy story of how the chief of mountain village takes two Russian soldiers hostage in the hope of exchanging them for his son by the Russians is unsparingly updated. The director is referring to Chechenya.

Other Films of Russia : Burnt By the Sun (1994), Moscow Does Not Believe in Tears (1980), Dersu Uzala (1975), War and Peace (1968).

SPAIN

Carmen (1983)
Dir. : Carlos Saura
Cast : Antonio Gades, Laura Del Sol.

Carmen places Bizet's opera in a theatre setting fades, a renowned dancer / choreographer plays the head of a dance company rehearsing the classic dramas. He falls hopelessly in love with the dancer playing Carmen with predictable irony; the fiery romance runs parallel to the classic story. The music is flamenco version of Bizet's beloved score and dancers, feet beating out complex rhythms, dazzle us with their flashing beauty.

Other Films : All About My Mother (1999), Belle Epoque (1993), Volver A Empezar (1982).

SWEDEN

Seventh Seal (1957)
Dir. : Ingmar Bergman
Cast : Max Von Sydow, Gunnar Bjornstrand, Beng Ekerot.

It is an allegory for man's confrontation with the ultimate reality of death. Bergman sets this deeply religious film — a film, which admits the validity of doubt as essential to faith — in a medieval Sweden stricken by plague. We are introduced to a variety of people. Among them is the mysterious figure of death. To delay the Death, the knight challenges Death to a game of chess. One of the great passages in the film, which is an allegorical journey into self and abstract truth, is the 'Dance of Death', described as Bergman's "Majestic Summation of medieval imagery" while Death leads his six victims to a fiercely merry dance, the powerful image soars to imaginative heights.

Other Films : Funny and Alexander (1983), Through A Glass Darkly (1961), The Virgin Spring (1960).

THAILAND

The Moonhunter (2001)
Dir. : Bhandit Rittakol
Cast : Chantha, Suwanno.

This film is based on the infamous October 14 Student Revolution 1973, when many of students were shot dead by the police for protesting against the military regime of that time. The film's director was an eyewitness to the actual killings, as he was then a reporter with the 'Nation' newspaper. Hence, he had the actual footage of the killings which he used in the film. Which became the chief bone of contention between him and the Censor. The film was finally passed without any cuts. Prime Minister Thaksin Shinawatra himself attended the premiere and seemed to approve the film. Because although the film is a study of Communism, the protagonists become totally disenchanted with its ideology at the end of the film. A lot of the film is set in the jungles of Laos, where Setsan interacted with Communist groups from Cambodia and China. Finally disillusioned with the Communism, he returns to his city. One of the most realistic films from Thailand.

OTHER GREAT WORLD FILMS

Battleship Potemkin (Russia, Eisenstein 1925), Ivan The Terrible Part II (Russia, Eisenstein 1945), L'Age D'or (Spain, Louis Bunuel 1930), The Discreet Charm of the Bourgeoisie (France Bunuel 1972), The Mabuse Trilogy (Germany, Fitz Lang 1922, 1932), Metropolis (Germany, Fitz Lang 1927), M (Germany Fitz 1931), Nosferatu (Germany, Murnau 1922), The Passion of Joan of Arc (Denmark Carl Dreyer 1928), Red Sorghum (China, Chen Kaige), Yellow Earth (China, Chen Kaige), Cabinet of Dr. Cligary (Germany, Robert Wiene), All that Jazz (Bob Fose), Elling (Norway 2001), Kolya (Czech Republic 1996), Barbett's Feast (Denmark 1987).

2

The Audience

Whatever directors, actors, writers speak through theirs films, they need acceptance by the audience/viewers. They are as much important as the film's scripts. Poor scripts attract poor number of the audience and great scripts attract great number of the audience. Everything comes behind the good scripts and a good number of the audience. As Elia Kazan has rightly said, "audience are like hounds, they smell a film." Yes, as long as the film's story is good, they will keep coming to the cinema halls. The film is a kingdom ruled by the two kings; script and the audience. All filmmakers want their films to be seen by as many people as possible. Those, who deliver well, survive, others become extinct. There is no such thing as the loyal audience — loyal to their favourite stars or filmmakers — now they are loyal to their money. They pay only when their senses are treated well either by being emotionally quenched, or being overwhelmed. Loyal audience have become shifting audience. Filmmakers cannot blame audience.

This survival of Darvinian intensity has made all filmmakers conscious, curious and true. Those, who don't change, are not heard off. Like all battles, few become victors, others are massacred at the box-office. The audiences are now more visually literate and can differentiate good films from the bad ones. They are invisible force causing motion among film-persons of emotions. They are more hungry, expect high and innovative films. They see films on its merit, not on its stars or any names. 'The Darwinian Audience' has become a truth, and a force too. It pass judgments on those who are fit to survive. The quest for something engaging and interesting makes all film gods not to smile much on their creations.

They cannot survive the fissioning of the bad atoms, good films or no films.

Films are unfinished if they do not get audience. Films, that satisfy only its makers and fail to bring the audience, are total waste of money, time and energy. Directors should try to make more and more films for the audience and only a few ones for themselves. Then they can make themselves creatively happy and can survive too. This audience factor creates tensions, arguments and fights among the producers and makers. The filmmakers want their creative freedom, but before they can get that, they have to be successful at the box-office. More the success more the creative freedom. Steven Spielberg had full creative-freedom while making 'Schindler's List' and 'Saving Private Ryan', but before these films he had proved himself as a successful filmmaker with his 'Jurassic Park', 'Jaws' and 'E.T.'

The genre audience have their own kinds of the films. A war film may not work well with the women, the same way a cartoon film finds only kids as their loyal watchers. These target audience films work best only with whom they are targeted. A romantic comedy can attract young couples in a large number but not serious movie watchers. Action films work well with the teens, which form the main bulk of the viewers. Any film, which handles dramas, action, adventure and romance in a uniquely well manner, becomes an instant hit with all kinds of audiences irrespective of their age, race or gender. 'Titanic' is one of such films. It is a beautiful blend of love, action and adventure. All of them turn into a tragedy, which brings emotional catharsis among the viewers. Everybody relates with the movie and its theme.

Bulk of the audience want to be overwhelmed by the film. Filmmakers know this human weakness and take the full advantage. All James Bond films follow this rule. The Rule of overwhelming the audience gave us films like 'Pearl Harbor' and 'Independence Day'. The audience wonders and find themselves intimidated by such films. All their imaginations are fulfilled. They feel like a part of the movie.

Those films with whom audience identify themselves, become huge hits. The lost love, The Tragic hero, the anti-hero — all of us identify with these and feel like we were the heroes, we lost the love and feel all those emotions which the protagonist of the film feels. This identification factor is the oldest and most powerful factor in the film history. We cry and laugh with the hero, we die with the hero, we fight with the hero. The distance between the screen and the seat of a single audience becomes zero and he feels more being on the screen rather than on the seat.

The power of the audience is so great that many of the Hollywood films are shown to campus audience prior to its release. If their reaction is not good, filmmakers reshoot and even change the basic story. Tragic ending becoming a happy ending is the outcome of this tradition. The audience will continue to keep on ruling, demanding and making judgments. And the filmmakers have to follow their verdict and change themselves without expecting any mercy from the Darwinian Audience. Because they are life-blood. Their participation is indirect but of extreme importance.

3

The Producer

He is neither below the line crew members nor above the line crew members. He is the king among the persons of the filmworld. Money rules everything. He is the lord of money. He is the great gambler, who runs the world's highest risky business, called filmmaking.

He puts his money where his mouth is. Once he has a great and saleable idea or story, he hires a director and then entire team to start his film. A budget is decided and film goes on floor. He remains on the set to supervise the whole production and to get the film made in decided budget and on time. Many producers battle with their directors on the issues of a budget and storychanges. This job is never over. At the end of the shooting, editing, he supervisor the film's publicity and release. A lukewarm response may bring a heart attack to its producer and he may turn pauper. Producer Zimbalist died of heart attack before the completion of his film "Ben Hur" with the budget going in millions. A film is produced by two-three producers. So the loss or profit becomes tolerable.

The producers are so powerful that they hardly give any creative freedom to their directors. Many of them are called 'Scissor hands', because the rights of final cut belongs to them. Keeping the business aspects in mind, they cut, re-edit, re-shoot, change story and do everything possible to make their films hit. Unless and until you are Steven Spielberg, you cannot interfere with their absolute power. These creatures are basically money hungry creatures, who also have a little showmanship in their blood.

Many big studios, like 20th Century Fox, Warner Bros., MGM and Disney, have made great films over the years. These film companies provide us great spectacles. They spend in millions, earn in billions and the business goes on and on. These are the places, where all technologists and artists work together to achieve miracles. The hugely popular films like 'Snowwhite', 'The lion king,' and 'The jungle book' were made by Disney and classics like 'Titanic' and 'Braveheart' were produced by 20th Century Fox.

When the director is the producer of the film, he has full controls and commands over a film. The budget becomes more flexible and accommodates more expenditures to achieve something worth watching. Star-produced or director-produced films always go overbudget. Because for them, vision matters more than money. They are the films that are close to their hearts. Many films suffer due to budget constraints. A good budget is always crucial for making a good film. Quality is compromised if the budget is less than desired. We need producers like Jerry Bruckheimer, whose much spoken line is "any doubt, throw more money".

4

The Filmmaker (Director)

Filmmakers are the creators of the possibilities. They are the restless souls, mad, crazy and impatient people, who want to change their ideas, visions and stories into images. They think in images not words. But only few of them are true visionaries. Rest of them do films as business. Great ones are known as auteurs and all others are just directors. They are popularly called as the captains of the ship.

Filmmaking is divided into two parts : creative and technicals. The creative one consists of director, actor and writer. A director has the power of imagination, visualisation and picturisation of video space in his mind. He sits at the top, his commands are followed by the technical persons. He is the highly paid and most respectable person among the film tribe and society. He is the person who initiates a film, develops the idea, works on budget, predesigns the settings, selects the locations, chooses the right actors and costumes, rehearses the performers, guides the production team and after the shooting is over, supervises editing and special effects. He is the one man show.

A person becomes a film director because he badly needs a medium to express himself. His all words are pictures. They creatively stimulate him to transfer those words into moving images so that the whole world can see what he saw in his mind. The true directors are very passionate about the medium and their visions. Some live cinema for cinema's sake others use it just as a larger than life medium. For them thoughts or matters are more important than the medium. This second group of filmmakers do not accept all films to direct. For them, money grossers are not important. They do not start a film until and unless they are creatively seized by them.

Here, like other arts, creativity is to achieve a tangible representation of what the mind's eye can see. The translation of ideas and impressions into words, pictures or dance forms. Through this the creator gains personal joy, satisfaction and perhaps ecstasy. And he also creates enjoyment for all those who see, read or hear it.

The journey of becoming a film director is full of struggle and strife. Those, who are not fortunate enough to be sons and daughters of filmgods, struggle and suffer endlessly to become directors. As the road of success is always under construction, only those having ambition as well as persistence, survive. Others fail and return. All assistant directors do not become directors, because they lack the power of imagination and the force of contact. Contact works in the film business. Some directors like Spielberg and Ron Howard started early in their life. They used 8 mm cameras and films to make shorts.

The most serious and dedicated directors are those who have survived the impossible. And they are doing, what they always wanted to do till the end of life. It is not the glamour or money, which drive them crazy. They work not for names, but for self-realisation. They want to make others feel what they feel. Films are emotions and motions. How can anybody make a film unless he is a sensitive human being. These very sensitive human beings who turn directors can recreate history, create future and project lives on the screen with the content of the powerful sense of feelings. Real filmmakers are born.

But above all every filmmaker is a communicator. Some are more effective, some less. They communicate their ideas, visions, thoughts and feelings. If a director's ideas, thoughts or visions get acceptance by a lager audience, he is called an effective communicator. Today, Steven Spielberg is called the most effective communicator, because his films 'Schindler's List' and 'Saving Private Ryan' have entered into our subconscious minds. While watching these films, we feel coldness, coldness of life, horror, tragedy and despair. And all our emotions are spent up.

A film director carries a tremendous load of responsibilities upon his shoulders. He is responsible for the society in which he lives, responsible for the good or bad work. Bad is questioned, good is praised. He is responsible from the beginning to the end. He must be an all rounder. He must have three eyes, for creative, technical and business. From choosing the right story, writer, actors and selecting the best studios and equipments, he has twelve hands and many brains to help him doing all those stuffs, which an ordinary human being cannot. Everyone waits for his commands. And he has to be quick in commanding. He is as much practical as dreamy. He should have knowledge of all departments of filmmaking. When he talks to his costume designer, it seems he does not know anything except costumes, and when he guides his cameraman, it seems he knows nothing but the camera and its possibilities. He is made of many personalities. Anybody would tempt to pluck his mind.

He always acts in a critical condition. This makes him furious on occasions. James Cameron, the director of 'Titanic' and 'Terminator' films is often accused of misbehaving. While shooting for 'Titanic' he said "When I am spending US $ 60,000 per hour and my head is under throttle, it's my job to be impatient, let the Crew go to hell. I must get what I want!" He is messianic and mad, messianic in terms of his vision and mad in terms of getting what he wants.

A film director is a strong observer, highly imaginative, innovative and charishmatic person. He has tremendous abilities and capabilities. Above all he is a simple human being. He is always Yes or No Sayer, the amplifier, the refiner, the particulariser and the final decision is always his. He has to ensure that a film must not be pompous, pretentious or overbearing and it must entertain. It should be as brilliant as 'Dr. Zhivago' as restrained as 'Tender Mercies'. A good director thinks more of the images, metaphor and reactions than about words. Creative manipulation is his weapon. He always, like a chess player, thinks his next move in advance. If a director allows his seam (technique) to show he is either careless, inexpert or wanting to show his brushwork rather than the whole statement.

They are often accused of being self-obsessed and egoists. But all artists are like that. It does not mean that they do not love humanity. There is so much to read, think and imagine that an artist hardly gets any time to socialize or make others happy. It is not his job, his is make his soul happy. It is often true that directors do not respect other's intelligence, but it is also true that they even do not respect their own. They are egoists but not fragile egoists. Work ego is necessary to achieve the desired results. There are so many egos involved at the time of filming, a director has to handle those egos too in addition to his own.

Another accusation which a director gets is that he treats actors as cattle or puppets. Hitchcock is the most fired director of this accusation. He himself said that all actors must be treated like cattle but they are not cattle. Film is a director's medium. Actors must remain true to their characters and follow their director's guide. It is another truth that sometimes actors give miraculous performance than what director has thought of. As director John Huston once said "In a given scene I have no idea of what should happen, but I do not tell the actors, instead I tell them go ahead and do it. Sometimes they do it better, sometimes they do something accidentally which is effective and true. I jump on the accident."

Another great quality of a director is that he should never favour words over images. As a film's artistic importance rests in what the viewers see, what they hear is underscoring. After all a film is a moving picture and a director who favours dialogues over images is actually manufacturing a play not a film. It is essential to engage the viewers. Though the creative quality of a film is the private affair of a filmmaker, but a film which pleases only its director and not the audience is a waste.

Making movies is a director's passion. It is a faculty which does not allow other jobs to grow. As Star Wars creator George Lucus once said "I love making movies because my fascination with the medium has driven everything. I love to work with it and explore the possibilities." A director continuously travels through the stages of restlessness for self-expression. He is a great learner. If his vision are not translated into actions, they become hallucinations. He must be demanding because when you are working with some one who is very demanding, you aught to be at your best.

He must have a clear idea of what he wants and how to get that. There is no room for the confusions or hesitations. Few great directors like Steven Spielberg, prepare storyboards (sketches of the shots on the papers) prior to the shooting. So the task becomes easier and only mechanical. Action sequences and ad films must be sketched on papers prior to shooting to avoid delay and confusion. There is no need for storyboards for character psychology films. Let them remain in your mind.

The director is the whole and soul of a film, he is the only person who has an idea in totality. In short, he is the process of the film. Today there are no good or bad directors but only flop or hit directors. Successful directors are always in demand. A director must change his taste, style and ideas to survive. He should handle actors with utmost care. Otherwise they will give miserable performance. A good director is down to earth, sincere and difficult, difficult because he cannot compromise. He has to put lots of sweat and homework into his career. For a director, an OK shot is as satisfying as an orgasm.

A director should not be a dictator. This ability lies in getting the work done, beautifully and timely. He arranges the forces at work. His talent lies in getting actors and the crews to use their talent to the optimum level. He cannot teach acting. Though it is another truth that sometimes directors perform so well that actors feel inadequate. The directors share hopes and intentions with his crews and the audience. Positive feedback from the audience raises his confidence.

There are two kinds of directors. One who comes from the technical fields and the other who migrates from the creative fields. Cinematographers, editors and other such technical masters turned directors belong to the first group. Actors, writers turned directors belong to the second group. The particular abilities and shortcomings differ from group to group. An editor turned director may capture wonderful shots with utmost technical clarity but he finds it difficult to extract those wonderful actings and the essence of the script. In the same way an actor turned director has all the power to achieve fine acting and the essence of the script but he may fail technically as a filmmaker. But those, who are born makers, have an all-rounding power. They know the character psychology and feel it like an actor and they also know about the right shots and lenses as much as a cinematographer do. But they are very rare. Only few on the planet. The first and the last truth is that everybody from the writer to the spot boy, wants to become the director. But can they really become the filmmaker?

So there are two types of director : 'the auteur', who manifests a consistency of style and theme across his films, and the 'metteurs-en-scene', who are merely technician. The great auteurs are Alfred Hitchcock, Steven Spielberg, Francis Ford Coppola, Michael Mann, Oliver Stone, Joel Schumacher and David Lean. They all have their unique style, theme and visions across all their films. The crowd of other directors belong to the "metteurs-en-scene" groups. They just record the story without any personal difference. You do not recognize the picture by any names.

Creative freedom is the most powerful tool in the director's hand. Without this he is a zero-power. Auteurs cannot work without the creative freedom. But first time directors have to sacrifice it. Producers cut the director's creative freedom to make the film saleable. But they do not interfere with those directors who have proved themselves as successful at the box-office. More the success more the creative freedom. First you have to make few big grosser, then you will have the taste of the full creative freedom. Or you can have it, if you are the producer of your film. A good budget is necessary for the creative freedom. Qualities are compromised if the budget suffers. Sometimes directors have to spend their own money to keep the film afloat. Steven Soderbergh spent his own $ 1,00,000 while making 'Traffic' (2000).

The directors have to die many times to keep the merciless market smiling. They do those films, they have no faith in, just for money. They make all sorts of compromises and even accepting those suggestions, which have no creative value. You have to create fake things, fake history, controversy and anything that can work. But then there are directors, who do not succumb. And they make the real films, which may not suit the taste of the general viewers, but they are critically acclaimed, like Michael Mann's "ALI". Many European filmmakers are still making those gritty, real, touching films, which affect our senses.

A film is a director's medium. So it becomes very important to know the great directors of the world and their hallmark films. Here is a list of these beautiful filmmakers who have enthralled us with their works. Some are always greater than others. But all are great in their own way.

WORLD'S GREAT DIRECTORS (FILMMAKERS)

Hollywood

Steven Spielberg

He is credited with rejuvenating American cinema. His films are imbued with a sense of wonder and celebrate the magic and mystery that imagination can reveal. The most well-known name in the history of cinema, Steven Spielberg made four of Hollywood's ten top grossing films. The description the most commercially successful filmmaker suites him more than anyone else. He was making 8 mm films when he was a boy. The winner of Oscars for his Holocaust epic 'Schindler's List' (1993), and 'Saving Private Ryan' (1998), is now the king indeed. He reached his pinnacle after creating dinosaurs on the screen with his 'Jurassic Park' (1993). Based on the best seller by Michael Chrichton, it broke all previous box office records. Like a true auteur, he remained true to his subjects. No love stories against the backdrops of Jewish Holocaust or World War II. Instead he believed in male bonding and humanity rather than a love between two persons. The most brutal war movie 'Saving Private Ryan' won him the highest Civilian Medal of the U.S. Army. Cinema is the medium, he was born to rule. He knows how to combine special effects with human drama without sacrificing one for another. He is the master of all — emotions, character psychology, actions, special effects and drama. He became a graduate in 2002. Though he was already awarded six honorary doctorates. Married to Kate Capshaw, they have seven children. Many hits of the years like 'Harry Potter' and 'Spiderman' were first offered to him, but he passed saying "Though it is fun to see those big grosser come in but they are no more creatively stimulating to me." Dream Works Studio belongs to him. His understanding of the craft is unmatched in the history of motion pictures.

His major Films : Duel (1971), Sugar Land Express (1973), Jaws (1975), Close Encounters of the Third Kind (1978), Raiders of The Lost Ark (1981), E.T. (Extra-Terrestrials 1983), The Colar Purple (1985), Indiana Jones And The Last Crusade (1989), 1941 (1979), Hook (1991), Schindler's List (1993), Jurassic Park (1993), The Lost World (1997), Amistad (1997), Saving Private Ryan (1998), A-I (Artificial Intelligence 2001), Minority Report (2002), Catch Me If You Can (2002).

Francis Ford Coppola

The poet of gangsters films, Coppola's 'Godfather Trilogy' is included in everybody's list of favourite films. Godfather films are a tribute to what cinema could be as a medium. It is an example of the best in filmmaking. He makes cinemas which appeal both the intellectuals as well as the masses. His slow narrative and the scene choreography are incredible and par-excellent. He belongs to a film family, whose most of the members have won Oscars in their respective fields including actor Walter Huston, director John Huston and Coppola's nephew Nicholac Cage. Coppola won Oscar for the best director for his film 'Godfather II' (1974). He and Mario Puzo, together wrote all Godfather films and won two Oscars for best adopted screenplays.

His other major film is 'Apolcalypse Now' and 'Peggy Sue Got Married' (1986).

David Lean

He was born in a Quaker family and not allowed to see movies. In future he would become the greatest master of epics. A chosen guru by many young filmmakers, David Lean could satisfy himself with only big films. His films are like lessons for all film students and the classics for us. He became famous for his epic films of grandiose effects, difficult location shooting and cultural and literary value. All his films demonstrate an obsessive cultivation of craft and fastidious concern with Production details. He won two best director Oscars for 'The Bridge on the River Kwai' (1957) and 'Lawrence of Arabia' (1962). His other greats are : 'Dr. Zivago' (1965),

'The Sound Barrier a Brief Encounter' (1945), 'Ryan's Daughter, Great Expectations' (1946), 'In Which We Serve', 'Oliver Twist' (1948).

Martin Scorsese

He is one of the most dedicated and perfectionist film-makers. After serious deliberations about entering the priesthood (he entered a seminary in 1956), Scorsese opted to channel his passions into film. He refused to direct 'Schindler's List' in 1980s because he believed he could not make as good a film as a Jewish director possibly could. He outraged some religious groups by attempting to portray human son of God in his film 'The Last Temptation of Christ'. Before returning to more familiar territory with the mafia in "Goodfellas", he also directed Michael Jackson's "Bad" music video.

Filmography : After Hours, Last Waltz, Taxi Driver (1976), Raging Bull (1980), Goodfellas (1990), Cape Fear (1991), The Age of Innocence (1993), Casino (1995), The Gangs of New York (2002).

Oliver Stone

Hollywood's most belligerent auteur Oliver Stone knows best; the visceral depiction of the strong bonds between men and arms. He is always in War-Zone making more overtly military movies. He also creates controversies with his movies and documentaries. He is the most controversial writer-director of Hollywood. His films are like locker room stuffs and if you do not like the smell of testosterone, then Stone's films may not be the perfect way to spend a Sunday. The unabashed enthusiasm for experimentation, the willingness to use jump cuts, side steps and non-linear interruptions make Oliver Stone different from others. He is known for recreating history and pulling out pages from the forgotten past. Nominated for ten Academy Awards, he won three Oscars, two for the best director (Born on the Fourth of July & Platoon) and one for writing 'Midnight Express'.

His major Films : The Doors, Seizure, Wall Street, Talk Radio, Nixon, Between Heaven And Earth, 'Salvadar' JFK, Any Given Sunday, Platoon, U-turn, Born on the Fourth of July, Alexander.

As a Writer : Conan the Barbarian, Scarface, Midnight Express (he wrote most of his films).

Michael Mann

Why Pacino is so right in Mann's films. Because Mann's Cinema is about professionalism and ruthlessness and it is always in the intense groove. His films are aggressively hypnotic, they grab you by the lapels and keep you there. Mann's films require your complete emotional commitment. In other words, they are overwhelming but claustrophobically true. In Mann's films the 'mise en scene' is controlled, so entrancingly framed and lit, it constantly threatens, to subsume or belittle the human action.

Don Simpson's biography mentions that Mann's films can be characterized as artificially perfected structures crafted on similar genre as real estate. "The Last of the Mohicans" after 'vice' had given him the financial muscle to be a totally independent auteur. "Mohicans" represents the moment when Mann's auteur becomes unassailable. It is a case of filmmaker becoming an organization.

His major Films : Thief (1981), Manhunter (1986), The Last of The Mohicans (1992), Heat (1995), The Insider (1999), Ali (2001).

Alfred Hitchcock

The poet of suspense and horror whose tombstone reads "I am in on a plot", Alfred Hitchcock suffered from mortal fear psychology in his childhood. He visited Hollywood in 1940, but was turned down by virtually all motion picture studios, because they thought, he could not make a Hollywood film. He was finally offered to direct "Rebecca" (1940) by producer David O Selznick. He churned out more than fifty films in about half a century. Most of them are thrillers full of suspense and gore. In the early days of his film career he worked in many departments of filmmaking. He even looked after accounts and production works. That was the reason he had too much experience and knowledge of all departments of filmmaking. His technical mastery enable him to attempt unusual camera angles in shooting different scenes. He was often accused of misbehaving with his actors, whom he treated like cattle. But he himself said 'Actors are like cattle but not

Cattle'. As an auteur, he tried to convince others that his films are his medium, not actor's. His emphasis was on visual impact. Some of his films have become classics and standard reference for the students of film art and science. Though he was nominated four times for the best Director Oscar, he never won it.

Filmography : The 39 Steps (1935), Rebecca (1940), Under Capricorn (1949), The Lady Vanishes (1938), Strangers on a Train (1951), Dial M for Murder (1954), Rear Window (1954), To Catch A Thief (1955), The Man Who Knew Too much (1956), Vertigo (1958), North By Northwest (1959), Psycho (1960), The Birds (1963).

Woody Allen

He is one of the most talented writer-director in Hollywood. Nominated for Oscar more than a dozen times, he wrote and directed 'Annie Hall' (1977), which won the 'Best Picture', 'Best director' and 'Best Screenplay' Oscar. He is known for his witty aphorisms and intellectual humour.

Major Films : Everyone Says I Love You, Take The Money And Run, The Purple Rose Of Cairo, Hannah And Her Sisters, Bullets over Broadway.

Michael Curtiz

He is the creator of "Casablanca" (1942), the most romantic film ever made. It is apparently everybody's favourite. Though some critics called it a 'Shallow masterpiece' but it is a 'Masterpiece'.

Other main Films : The Adventure of Robin Hood (1938), The Sea Hawk (1940), The Sea Wolf (1941), Captain Blood (1935), The Charge of the Light Brigade (1936), The Egyptian (1954).

George Lucus

For more than two decades, George Lucus and the technical wizards at ILM (Industrial Lights and Magic) have literally changed the face of movie making with their stunning, often unbelievable visual effects. Started in 1975 with 'Star Wars' George Lucus worked on a small budget and straining time constraint to create the wonderful world of Luke obi-wan, Derth the Vader and others. He used digital actors more than anybody. He is known for remaking, reinventing, improving and repolishing his star wars films. The new Chapters in star wars Saga, Star wars episode one : Phantom Menace (1999) and Star Wars : Attack of the Clones (2002), have broken all previous box office records. His films will interest those who love special effects and alien's worlds. Other may find these films boring. He runs two companies 'Lucus Digital' (special effects creator) and 'Lucus Films Ltd' (Production Company).

John Huston

He gave many hits. He had a great understanding of script, acting and execution. He won Oscar for the 'Best Director' for his film "The Treasure of The Sierra Madre" (1948). He belonged to the family, whose most of the members won Oscars. His father was famous actor Walter Huston.

Other Films : The African Queen (1951), The Man Who would Be King (1975), Moby Dick (1956), The Roots of Heaven (1958), Prizzi's Honour, The Maltese Falcon, The Misfits (1961), Wise Blood (79).

Ron Howard

Howard, once a child star, made his acting debut at four in a 1959 film "The Journey". He directed his first feature film at nine, an 8 mm effort starring his father as a hobo stealing a pie. He won the 'Best Director' Oscar for his film "A Beautiful Mind" (2001).

Other Films : Splash, Cocoon, Apollo 13, Ransom, Black Draft, Grand Theft Auto.

Willian Wyler

He is responsible for the creation of $ 15 million Roman epic 'Ben-Hur' (1959), which won 11 Oscars. Only 38 years later 'Titanic' could achieve this number of Oscars. William Wyler is the most nominated director for Oscar in the history of cinema, a record 12 times between 1936 to 1965. He won the 'Best Director' Oscar for three times for his films 'Mrs. Miniver' (1942), The Best years of our Lives (1946), and Ben-Hur (1959).

Other Films : The Storm (1930).

John Ford

He won the most number of the 'Best Director' Oscar, a record four times for his films, 'The Informer' (1935), The Grapes of Wrath (1940), How Green was my Valley (1941), and The Quiet Man (1952).

Other Films : The Black Watch (1929), Mogambo (1953), My Darling Clementine (1946), The Searcher, The Stage Coach.

Ridley Scott

He is the most influential and versatile filmmaker of our time. He is also a graphic designer, painter and an art-director. He started his career with "The Duelists", (1977) and then came a break through hit 'Alien' (1979). Nominated for the 'Best Director' Oscar twice for 'Gladiator (2000) and 'Black Hawk Down" (2001) but did not win it.

Other Films : Blade Runner (1982), Thelma and Louise, Hannibal (2001).

Cecil B. De Mille

The 'Grand Old Man' of Hollywood, Cecil made the most famous religious film "The Ten Commandments" (1956) that has won the hearts of millions all over the world over the years.

Major Films : "The Greatest Show on Earth" (1952) won the 'Best Picture' Oscar.

Other Hits : Four Frightened People (1934), Reap the Wild Wind (1942) Unconquered (1947).

Elia Kazan

Elia Kazan said "Audience are like hounds, they smell a film" one of the most prolific filmmakers, Elia Kazan won 2 'Best Director' Oscar for "Gentleman's Agreement" (1947) and "On The Waterfront" (1954). Other film is "Man of A Tightrope" (1953).

Peter Weir

His Major films are : "Picnic At Hanging Rock", "Witness", The Mosquito Coast (1986), The Year of Living Dangerously (1982).

Roman Polanski

His films have a certain magic that draws the audience to his films again and again. He cannot go to the U.S. without going to jail. He fled from there to France in 1978 as he was about to be sentenced to prison for raping a 13-year old girl.

Main Films : Chinatown (1974), Rosemary's Baby (1968), The Tragedy of Macbeth, Tess (1980), Pirates (1986), Repulsion, Death And The Maiden, The Pianist. He was nominated for the Best director three times, and won once for 'The Pianist' other nominations for 'Chinatown, & 'Tess' (1980).

Philip Kaufman

His film "Invasion of The Body Snatcher" (1978), a remake of 1956 Don Siegel Classic, is probably the most thrilling Sci-fi horror movie ever made.

Other Films : The White Dawn (1974), The Right Stuff (1983), Clear And Present Danger (1994).

Sir Richard Attenborough

Critics and Peers consider Sir Richard Attenborough the legitimate heir of that other British master of the historical epic, David Lean. Not many would have foreseen such accolades for the endearingly modest stage and screen actor who began his career in Lean's "In Which We Serve". An innate interest and cultivated ability to bring biographies to life, plus a life long passion to translate Gandhi's epochal life on to the screen, have made Attenborough a brand name for the grant bio-pic. "Gandhi" and multiple Oscars are synonymous. Elevated to Lord Attenborough in 1993, he devotes an amazing amount of time to extra cinematic cultural responsibilities.

Filmography : Oh! what A lovely War (1969), Young Winston (1972), A Bridge Too Far (1977), Magic (1978), Gandhi (1982), A Chorus Line (1985), Cry Freedom (1992), Chaplin (1992), Shadowlands (1994), In Love And War (1996).

Brian De Palma

Like Hitchcock, Brian De Palma is a poet of suspense films. He is the master filmmaker only when he is at those suspenseful, visually sensuous movies. "Dressed to Kill" (1980) is his best suspense film. He assembled an oscar winning cast, hired Giorgio Armani for all the costumes to create the grand gangster film "Untouchable" (1987).

Other Films : "The Bonefire of the Vanities", "Carlito's Way".

Orson Welles

At the age of 25 he made 'Citizen Kane' (1941), arguably the greatest film ever made. It was nominated for 9 Oscars, but won only one for the 'Best Screenplay'. It is a must watch film for the film students as well as common lovers of cinema.

Other Film : "Touch of Evil".

Stanley Kubrick

Even after his death (1999), he provokes extreme reaction and an unending curiosity. Controversy only adds to the enigmatic nature of his genius. He could not see the release of his last directed film 'Eyes Wide Shut' starring Tom Cruise and Nicole Kidman. He was the visionary auteur who had the courage of his convictions. The range of his subjects and treatments is more than ambitions. Horror, sexual fantasy, war, child abuse, the nuclear threat, space travel, eighteenth century morality each title has become a psychic milestone. With "Lolita", "Dr. Strangelove" and "2001 — A Space Odyssey", he ceased being Hollywood's expert young craftsman and transformed himself into the expatriate genius, the visionary auteur. Steven Spielberg declared him as his 'guru'. Both makers exchanged views and ideas. Spielberg directed Kubrick's "A-I" (Artificial Intelligence) (2001).

Filmography : Fear And Desire (1953), Killer's Kiss (1955), The Killing (1956), Paths of Glory (1957), Spartacus (1960), Lolita (1962), Dr. Strangelove, or How I learned to Stop Worrying And Love The Bomb (1963), 2001 : A Space Odyssey (1968), A Clockwork Orange (1971), Barry Lyndon (1975), The Shining (1980), Full Metal Jacket (1987), Eyes Wide Shut (1999).

Frank Capra

Three time winner of the 'Best Director' Oscar for his films 'It Happened One Night' (1934), 'Mr. Deeds Goes to Town' (1936), 'You can't Take it with you' (1938), Frank Capra was one of the leading figure in Hollywood at that time. He also won Oscar for his documentary "Prelude to War" (1942).

Other Films : 'Mr. Smith Goes to Washington' (1936), American Madness (1932), Lost Horizon (1937), Meet John Doe (1941).

Billy Wilder

Two time winner of the 'Best Director' Oscar for his films "The Last Weekend" (1945), and "The Apartment" (1960), Billy Wilder delivered other major hits like "Double Indemnity" Sunset Boulevard (1950), The Spirit of St. Louis (1957), Some Like It Hot (1959).

Joseph L. Mankiewicz

He is responsible for the creation of "All About Eve" (1950), the most beautiful film, which ran many weeks in many Cinema halls all-around the world and won a record number of 14 Oscar nominations. Only 47 years later "Titanic" could equal this number. Joseph won two 'Best Director' Oscar for "A Letter To Three Wires" (1949), and "All About Eve" (1950).

Other Film : Sleuth.

John Frankenheimer

He is known for his documentary style of filmmaking. Another poet of suspense and action.

Major Hits : The Manchurian Candidate (1962), Grand Prix (1966), The Gypsy Moths (1969), The Horseman (1971), French Connection II (1975).

Joel Schumacher

A true auteur, who maintains his particular theme and style throughout his films. He developed his own distinctive ways of structuring narratives, moving his camera and cutting scenes which become known to film goers and studio executives alike. His name can guarantee to the studio executive a certain style of film making and particularly in the distribution and marketing of his films. "Batman And Robin" (1997) is identified in its trailer as 'A Joel Schumacher Film'. He made a non-commercial film "Tiger Land (2000)" shot in a documentary style with natural lighting, hand held cameras and realistic dialogues. It was a Vietnam war film.

Other Films : 48 Hours, Bad Company.

James Cameron

He is a genius and a maniac, genius in terms of his vision and maniac in terms of getting what he wants. His films deal with the treachery of technology. He knows how to blend action with drama and special effect. He is an allrounder. Finally he got his Oscars for the 'Best Director' and the 'Best Editor' for his film "Titanic".

Other Films : Terminator I & II, Aliens (1986), The Abyss (1989), True Lies, Titanic (1997).

Peter Jackson

This New Zealander filmmaker had made his way into Hollywood with his "Heavenly Creatures" (1994) and "The Frighteners" (1997). And he became a global name as soon as the first part of "The Lord of The Rings" hit the theatres in December 2001. "The fellowship of The Ring" (2001) was nominated for 13 Oscars and won 4 including the Best Cinematography and "The Best Visual Effects". The other two parts "The Two Towers" (2002) and "The Return of the King" (2003) have also become major successes around the globe. JRR Tolkien's adventure fantasy novel, "The Lord of the Rings" was beautifully converted on to the screen. Peter Jackson has done a commendable job in tackling perhaps the most intimidating Fantasy classic by Tolkien. The playful spookiness of Peter Jackson's direction provides a lively and light touch. The trilogy is loved by all the people irrespective of their gender, age and race.

Neil Jordon

Neil Jordon is a novelist who came to films. And like his fiction, his films also won immediate recognition from critics. The widely acclaimed "The Crying Game" (1992) won him the Oscar for "Best Original Screenplay".

Filmography : Angel (1982), The Company of Wolves (1985), Mona Lisa (1986), High Spirits (1987), We're no Angels (1989), The Miracle (1991), The Crying Game (1992), Interview with The Vampire (1994), Michael Collins (1996), The End of the Affair (1999).

Walter Hill

Walter Hill is an auteur of action whose narrative use of chase and confrontation have produced a gallery of highly commercial, critically acclaimed films for over two decades. The writer-director has had an abiding interest in the American Western. He introduced Eddie Murphy to Hollywood.

Filmography : Hard Times (1975), The Driver (1979), The Warriors (1980), Southern Comfort (1982), 48 Hrs (1984), Streets of Fire (1985), Brewster's Millions (1986), Red Heat (1989), Geronimo (1993), Last Man Standing (1996).

Other good directors and their hallmark films

Douglas Sirk	Magnificent Obsession
John Madden	Shakespeare in Love (1998)
Jean Jacques Annuad	Quest For Fire (1981), Enemy At The Gates (2001)
Robert Zemeckis	Forrest Gump (1994)
Anthony Minghella	English Patient (1996)
Chris Columbus	Harry Potter And The Philosopher's Stone
Shekhar Kapur	Elizabeth (1998)
Vincente Minnelli	Gigi (1958)
Robert Redford	Ordinary People (1980)
M. Night Shyamalan	The Sixth Sense (1999)
Howard Hawks	The Big Sleep (1946)
Kevin Costner	Dances with The Wolves (1990)
Don Siegel	Invasion of the Body Snatcher (1956)
Curtis Hanson	L.A. Confidential (1997)
Quentin Tarantino	Pulp Fiction (1994), Reservior Dogs, Kill Bill (Two parts)
Scott Hicks	Shine (1996)
Victor Fleming	Gone with The Wind 1939, The Wizard of OZ (1939)
Edward Zwick	Glory (1989), The Last Samurai (2003)
Anthony Mann	EL CID (1961)
Milos Forman	One Flew Over The Cuckoo's Nest (1975), Amadens (1984)
Sir Carol Reed	Oliver! (1969)
Sam Mendes	American Beauty (1999), Road To Perdition (2002)

Robert Altman	Gosford Park (2001)
Steven Soderbergh	Traffic (2000), Erin Brockovich (2000)
Barry Lewinson	The Rain Man (1988)
Robert Wise	Kramer Vs Kramer (1979)
William Fredkien	The French Connection (1971)
Robert Wise	The Sound of The Music (1965)
Franklin J. Schaffner	Patton (1970), Papillon (1973)
Ronald Emmerich	Independence Day (1996)
Stephen Sommers	Mummy (1999), Mummy Returns (2001)
George Cukar	My Fair Lady (1964)
Mike Nichols	The Graduate (1967)
Alan J. Pakula	All The President's Men (1976)
Jonathan Demme	The Silence of The Lamb (1991)
John Schelesinger	The Midnight Cowboy (1969)
Norman Jewison	Moonstruck (1987), A Soldier's Story (1984)
David Lynch	Blue Velvet, Mulholland Drive (2001)
Client Eastwood	Unforgiven (1960)
Antonioni	L'Aventura
John Dahl	Kill me Again (1989), Red Rock West (1993)
Mary Brother	Duck Soup
Buster Keaton	The General
Sidney Lumet	Murder On The Orient Express (1974), Serpico
Henry Hathaway	Kiss of Death
Terrence Malick	The Thin Red Line (1998)
Robert Aldrich	Dirty Dozen (1967)
Baz Luhrman	Moulin Rough (2001)
Michael Bay	Pearl Harbor (2001)
John Woo	Face Off (1997), Windtalkers (2002)
Cameron Crowe	Jerry Maguire (1996), Almost Famous (2000)
Randal Wallace	We Were Soldiers (2002)
Brian G. Hutton	Where Eagles Dare (1968)
Ang Lee	Sense And Sensibility (1995), Crouching Tiger Hidden Dragon (2000), Hulk (2003)
John G. Avildsen	Rocky (1976)
Martin Brest	Scent of A Woman (1992)
Stephen Hopkins	The Ghost And The Darkness (1996)

Martin Campbell	Golden Eye (1995)
Luc Besson	Nikita (1990), Leon (1994), The Fifty Element (1996)
Tim Burton	Planet of the Apes (2001), Batman 2 (1992)
Mike Newell	Donnie Brasco (1996)
Robert Rodriguez	Desperado (1995)
Briyan Singer	Usual Suspects (1995)
David Fincher	Seven (1995)
Tim Robbins	Dead Man Walking (1995)
Mike Figgis	Leaving Los Vegas (1995)
Amy Heckerling	Clueless (1995)
Antoine Fuqua	Training Day (2001)
John Boorman	Excalibur (1981)
Joshua Logan	Camelot (1967)
Jerry Zucker	First Knight
Rob Marshall	Chicago (2002)
George Roy Hill	Sting (1973)
Bernardo Bertolucci	The Last Emperor (1987)
Otto Preminger	Exodus (1960)
Richard Fleischer	The Vikings (1958)
Cy Enfield	Zulu (1964)
Sydney Pollock	Out of Africa (1985)
James L. Brooks	Terms of Endearment (1983)
Warren Beatty	Reds (1981)
Michael Cimino	The Deerhunter (1978)
Bob Fosse	Cabaret (1972)
Fred Zinnemann	A Man For All Seasons (1966)
Tony Richardson	Tom Jones (1963)
George Stevens	Giant (195), A Place In The Sun (1951)
Delbert Mann	Marty (1955)
Leo MacCarey	The Awful Truth (1937), Going My Way (1944)
Frank Lloyd	The Divine Lady (1928), Cavalcade (1932)
Frank Borzage	Bad Girl 1931, Seventh Heaven (1927)
Norman Taurog	Skippy (1930)
Lewis Milestone	All Quiet on The Western Front (1929), Two Arabian Knights (1928)

George Seaton	Airport (1970)
Michael Chrichton	Coma (1978)
Tony Scott	Days of Thunder (1990), Top Gun (1986)
John Boorman	Deliverance (1972)
Mark Robson	Earthquake (1974)
Robert Aldrich	The Flight of the Phoenix (1965)
John Guillermin	Guns At Batasi (1964)
John Sturges	Ice station Zebra (1968)
Richard Thorpe	Ivanhoe (1952)
Basil Dearden	Khartoum (1966)
Henry King	King of the Khyber Rifles (1953)
David Butler	King Richard and the Crusader (1954)
King Vidor	Northwest Passage (1940)
Stanley Kramer	The Pride And the Passion (1957)
Kevin Reynolds	Robin Hood : The Prince of Thieves (1991)
Roland Joffe	The Mission (1986), The Killing Fields (1984)
Joel Coel	O Brother, Where Art Thou? (2000)
Nicholas Hytner	The Crucible (1996)
Stephen Daldry	Billy Elliot (2001), The Hours (2002)
David Russel	Three Kings (1999)
Sam Raimi	The Quick And the Dead (1995)

Russia

1. Eisenstein : The cinematic foundation, laid by such pioneers as Edison and Lumie're Brothers, was later built on by the filmmakers such as D.W. Griffith and Eisenstein. Eisenstein had shown the way to other filmmakers how to fuse a subversive sub-text into an apparently accurate historical narrative.

Films : Battleship Potemkin (1925), Ivan The Terrible Part II (1945), Strike (1924).

2. Sergey Bodrov : Bodrov's films are full of poignant warmth and piercing humour.

Main Film : Prizoners of The Mountain (1996).

3. Sergei Bondarchuk : Waterloo (1970), War And Peace.

4. Jurji Grymov : Mu Mu (1998).

Spain

1. Luis Bunuel : A towering genius, Bunuel is the Picasso and Cervantes of cinema. His terrifying surrealism opened our eyes to other ways of seeing. Exquisitely wrought images dissolve into another unexpected but deeply connected images at the subconscious level. With this arsenal Bunuel not only savages fascism and church hierarchy but mocks our bourgeois fetishes in the delightfully subversive "The Discreet Charm of the Bourgeoisie" (1972). Later Bunuel exiled himself first to Mexico and then to France which always been hospitable to the exiled artists. His other Film is "Robinson Crusoe".

2. Carlos Saura : "Carmen" (1983).

3. Pedro Almondovar : All About My Mother (1999), Talk to Her (2002).

Germany

1. Fitz Lang : A child of German expressionism and father of film noir fled to Hollywood. His films are chilling studies of criminality, which made cities into hellish nightmares. David Thomson points out that Lang's films go straight into the heart of our criminal corporate states.

Films : "Mabuse Trilogy" (1922, 32), "Metropolis" (1927), "M" (1931).

2. Murnau : He had imbued the Vampire's horror tales with a strange spiritual angst. All the special effects and a whole palette of colours have never been again recaptured the anguished cry of the tormented Soul.

Film : Nosferatu (1922).

3. Joseph von Sternberg	:	The Blue Angel (1930)
4. Wim Wenders	:	Himmel uber Berlin"/Wings of Desire (1987), Paris/Texas
5. Yilmaz Arslan	:	Yara (1998)
6. Cornelia Grunberg	:	Two In A Boat (1999)
7. Caroline Link	:	Beyond Silence
8. Wolfgang Beckar	:	Life Is All You Get (1997)
9. Robert Wiene	:	Cabinet of Dr. Caligary

Denmark

Carl Dreyer

His film 'The Passion of Joan Of Arc" (1928), describing the last day of the trial, is a symphony of images of intensity and intensively contained feelings revealed in all their purity in close-up. It is a textbook for all film makers to explore a character's interiority.

Japan

Ozu and Mizoguchi

They are the great zen masters of cinema whom the world discovered that too imperfectly only when Kurosawa, the Samurai, burst on the international film scene. In a way they are more innately Japanese in the tranquil, deeply meditative style they have perfected to tell beguilingly simply yet troublingly ambiguous stories about ordinary people with extraordinary rich interior lives. Sadly most of their films except Ozu's "Tokyo Monogatari" (1953) and Mizoguchi's "Ugetsu Monogatari" (1952), remain names in film history. Ozu's "An Autumn Afternoon" (1962) is a post-war Japanese Classic.

1. Akira Kurosawa : Way back in 1950 his "Rashomon" dazzled the filmmakers all over the world and opened the door into a different filmmaking culture with its distinguished history, aesthetics and narrative codes. Though Kurosawa faced the charge of being too western, yet he remained much Japanese and what he thought right, he did it. Donald Richie, the American Scholar who has interpreted Japanese cinema to the world, characterizes western aspect of Kurosawa as part of his western sensibility, akin to the abstract nature of modern art. Kurosawa is truly prodigious in the sheer range of his oeuvre. His "Throne of Blood" is the most original interpretation of Shakespeare's 'Macbeth' using 'Kabuki' the traditional interiors and the landscape to forge a cinematic equivalent of Shakespeare's language. Kurosawa is also the master of stirring action. His "Seven Samurai" was a period tribute to the American Western. When Hollywood made 'The Magnificent Seven' as a tribute to "Seven Samurai", the circle became complete. His "Yojimbo" is another film which inspired Walter Hill to make an American Western film, "The Last Man Standing".

His Films : Rashomon, Throne of Blood, Seven Samurai, Yojimbo. He won an Oscar as a lifetime achievement award.

2. Nagisha Oshima : Oshima's films are a study in cultural contrasts. He broke the Japanese silence about the Second World War. When Japanese establishment refuses even today to acknowledge its less than admirable war record, Japan's angry young man Oshima decided to confront the issue. Oshima's highly regarded earlier work "The Boy" had a passionate commitment to exposing the ugly underside of exploitation. In "Merry Christmas Mr. Laurence" (1982), he plunges into the treatment of British prisoners in a Java Camp in the familiar thematic framework of the relationship between authority and its victims.

Films : The Boy, Merry Christmas Mr. Lawrence (1982)

3. Masato Hara	:	20th Century Nostalgia (1997)
4. Hisashi saito	:	French Dressing (1997), Sunday Drive (1998)
5. Koji Wakamatsu	:	Ecstasy of Angels (1972)
6. Seijun Suzuki	:	Tokyodrifter (1966), Branded To Kill

France

1. Jean Vigo : His "L" Atlante (1934) has been consistently ranked among the top 10 films of all time by the 'Sight And Sound' Poll. David Thompson calls Vigo 'the first young martyr to cinema'. His lyrical surrealism blends beautifully with a documentarist's eye for the working class life in the simple story of a young skipper. It was a cinematic event and Vigo's tender, direct sensuousness of the images was rediscovered in all its potency. The chasm separating "L' Atlante" from "Titanic" sums up the distance between artistic purity and Hollywood hype.

2. Jean Renoir : If asked to name the greatest filmmaker of all time, Jean Renoir is the near unanimous choice of all filmmakers and almost all film critics. What is the reason for this rare unanimity in a field rife with contentious creeds and opposing ideologies of cinema? Renoir's films do not overwhelm us with mind boggling craftsmanship that demands our immediate attention. Rather it is a discovery of infinite shades and brush stores in a familiar beloved painting. This analogy is perhaps inheritable considerating Jean Renoir is the son of Auguste Renoir, the impressionist master. Jean Renoir's films delight in the play of natural light, illuminating the hearts and minds of the people he films with such humanistic sympathy. His remarkably beautiful, simple and real film are "La Regle Du Jeu / The Rules of the Game" (1939), "Grand Illusion" (1937).

3. Robert Bresson : He is an avowedly difficult filmmaker because he demands from the viewer the concentration to match the austere rigour of his films. But once you surrender to his unrelenting, agonizing search for faith, like the novice to his master, the result is deeply moving. Bresson stretches Dreyer's cinematic languages to its limits while stripping the narrative of all superfluities, of even acting as it is commonly understood. After a couple of early films, Bresson rejected the professional actor. His camera pokes the haunted, enigmatic faces of carefully choosen non-professional and long takes reveal the essence of the person.

Film : Journal D'un Cure De Campagne / Diary of A Country Priest (1951).

4. Max Ophuls : He was earlier dismissed as a sophisticated decorator (a true cosmopolitan who fled Nazi Germany to lead a peripatetic life in Russia, Italy, the US and finally France), obsessed with style over content. But like many neglected masters, Ophuls is enjoying a critical re-evaluation which places him among the greats. Central to Ophuls Oeuvre is the idea of the circularity of time as well as its tragic transience. And it is the women in his films who give themselves generously to time, to memory, to love and self-indulgence — even as they are made victims.

5. Jean-Luc Godard : Penelope Houston, the doyenne of English Critics and ex-editor of Sight and Sound compared Godard's films to "throwing a hand grenade into the audience". Time might have dulled the impact of the deliberate jump cuts and lost the freshness of "In" jokes meant for the filmmaker's cahiers due cinema coterie. Godard has gone on to make more radical, even abstruse, films but he will always be remembered as a youthful arrogant filmmaker, who broke all the laws of filmmaking.

Film : A Bout de Souffle / Breathless (1959).

6. Francois Truffaut : Of all the New wave directors Truffaut is the least political. But he enjoys the unique felicity of being loved by his peers who have other ideologies and audiences who may have never heard of the New Wave. It is because he is the true child of the Renoir heritage.

Films : "Jules et Jim", Les Quartre Cents Coups/400 Blows (1959).

7. Alain Resnais : Resnais is the loner who is part and yet not part of the New Wave. He is the most literary of the group, working in close collaboration with avant-garde writers like Marguerite Duras and yet, the most insistently cinematic in the centrality that editing plays his films. All his films explore the themes of time and memory.

Film : "Hiroshima Mon Amour" (1959).

Argentina

1. Fernardo Solanas : Magic realism is Latin America's greatest contribution to literature. But the varied and divergent film cultures of the continent have floundered in their attempt to translate the untranslatable collage of memory and myth, history and dailiness of everyday life, poetry and faith on to the screen. Fernardo Solanas comes closest to this challenge. His stunning sweep of the camera captures the threatened magnificence of a magical continent.

Film : El Viage / The Journey (1992).

2. Juna Jose Campanella : "Son Of The Bride" (2001).

Australia

Jane Campion

Jane Campion disproves a charge levelled against women directors that they lack 'Creative spatial ability' the imaginative vision to organize space for the camera frame. "The Piano" (1993), a minor masterpiece has reverberations beyond its perfectly realized period setting.

Films : The Piano (1993), The Portrait of A Lady (1996), Sweetie, Passionless Moments, Holy Smoke (1999).

Great Britain

1. Michael Powell : It is surprising that Powell did not become a cult figure but then as some-one said, most cults begin in France and Powell was too eccentrically English for the French.

Film : A Matter of Life And Death (1946).

2. Sir Lawrence Olivier : A celebrated Shakespearean actor and a screen superstar, Sir Olivier was also a reputed and polished filmmaker. He had the natural ability to differ and accommodate from stage to screen. Most of his films are based on Shakespearean plays. He fills his films with visual poetry, which wonderfully compensates many pages of the plays. He won the 'Best Actor' and 'Best Director' Oscar for his film "Hamlet".

Films : Henry V, Hamlet (1948).

Sir Richard Attenborough, Stanley Kubrick and David Lean, Sir Carol Reed are also British directors.

China / Hong Kong / Taiwan

1. Zhang Yimou : Few Cinematographers have made such an assured passage to direction as Zhang Yimou of China. The international success of Chen Kaige's "Red Shorghum' and "Yellow Earth", owes much to Yimou's mastery of colour. Like many new Chinese auteurs Yimou seeds his narrative with subtexts, which invite a reading of the changing political situation. Even when one is unfamiliar with intricacies of post-cultural Revolution China, Zhang Yimou offers pure cinematic pleasures, which recall the interiors of Ozu and Mizoguchi.

Film : Dahong Denglong / Raise The Red Lantern (1991).

2. Chen Kaige : It required a Chinese director to present the corrective to Bertolucci's "The Last Emperor" which endorsed China's official version of its recent history. Chen Kaige, who was noticed internationally for his more realistic and personal films, used the art and artifice of the Peking opera, the symbiotic relationship between art and performing artiste, to interpret the turbulent decades from 1925 onwards without pulling any punches. His "Ba Wang Bie Ji / Farewell,

My Concubine (1993) is the denunciations of the Cultural Revolution and charts the vicissitudes of the friendship.

Films : Red Shorghum, Yellow Earth, Farewell My Concubine.

3. Wong Kar-Wai : "As Tears Go By" (1988), Days of Being Wild (1990), Chungking Express (1994), Ashes of Time (1994), Fallen Angels (1995).

4. Peter Chan : Comrades : Almost A Love Story (1996).

5. John Woo : Before migrating to Hollywood and making "Hard Target", Broken Arrow, Face Off, and MI-2 (All of them are hardcore action films), he worked in Hong Kong film Industry, where he made few critically acclaimed films.

Films : The Killer, Hard Boiled, Bullet In The Head.

6. Ang Lee : After establishing his feet firmly in Hollywood with his films like 'Sense and Sensibility' (1995), Ang Lee went back to make a legendary film "Crouching Tiger Hidden Dragon" (2000), the only foreign picture nominated for 10 Oscars (won 4), which is a playful homage to the martial arts genre set in 19th Century China. His other major film is "Hulk" (2003).

7. Yon Fan : His films are about deep feelings, feelings of love and loss, obsession and rejection. This very sensitive of director, who felt like foreigner in his own filmworld, once said, "I love Hong Kong films. But do Hong Kong films love me?"

Films : A certain Romance (1984), Last Romance (1986), Immortal Story (1986), Double Fixation, Bishonen (1998), Peony Pavilion (2001).

Tsai Ming-Liang (ViveL'Amour), HouHsiao-Hsien and Edward Young are another three Taiwanese directors working today.

Hungary

Istvan Szabo : Though Mephistophelean bargain recurs in European literature and theatre time and again but not in Cinema. That is until Istvan Szabo came up with a brilliant script based on Klaus Mann's novel.

Films : Mephisto (1981), Taking Sides, Sunshine.

Other notable directors of Hungary are : Pal Sandar, Gyrorgy Szomjas, Karoly Makk, Niklos Janko and Fabri Zoltan.

Italy

Roberto Rossellini : Quite simply one of the most underestimated stalwarts of world cinema. His films are as intellectually stimulating as they are down to earth. He offers intellectual stimulation besides the documentary truth of neo-realism. His "Rome, Open City" (1945) defined not only the style but also the ethic of the neo-realist movement.

Films : Pasan (1946), Roma, Citta Aperta (1945).

Vittorio de Sica : His films are ode to the human spirit. They continue to be a must see at film societies and film courses. His simple, poetic, down to earth, gut-wrenching films just make us feel for the truth of life and history.

Major Films : Bicycle Thief (1951), Shoe-shine, Umberto D.

Frederico Fellini : He is a filmmaker whom you love passionately or hate with equal fervour. But you cannot be indifferent however much you deplore his excessive posturing. Because he has the ability to make art and entertainment out of his unapologetic self-obession. He conveys not only his passionate engagement and despairing disengagement with his art but subtly shifts gears and makes it universal. His "Nights of Cabiria" won the 'Best Foreign' picture Oscar.

Films : Otto E Mezzo / Eight and A Half (1963), Nights of Cabiria (1957), La Strada, La Dolce Vita, Juliet of The Spirit, Amaicord.

Michaelangelo Antonioni : His films have become cult movies for other filmmakers, quoted endlessly, overtly, slyly, subversively and in a spirit of celebration. Bleak abstractions of reality are present in his all films.

Films : Blow Up (1966), L'Aventura, The Night, Street Cleaners, The Cry, The Passenger.

Bernardo Bertolucci : He is the son of one of the greatest poets of Italy, Attilo Bertolucci. Bernardo wanted to become a poet but dropped the idea as he thought he could never excel his dad. And he became an assistant director of director Pier Paolo Pasolini. His first film "Before The Revolution" (1964), was described as a mixture of radical politics and raw emotion, is perceptibly autobiographical, exploring the father-son relationship and rise of Fascism in pre-war Italy. After his film "Last Tango In Paris" got into a serious trouble for being declared as obscene, he was not allowed to vote for five years. What put him into the Oscar class was, of course "The Last Emperor" (1987), an epic of regal splendour in its sets, sensitive handling of its characters and indeed history. It has won 9 Oscars including the 'Best Picture' and the 'Best Director'. His "Noecento"/1900 (1976) is one of the true genuine epics today. This is 320 minutes long. "Little Buddha" is another hallmark religious film by Bertolucci.

Giuseppe Tornatore : If anyone doubted the stamina of cinema in the age of television, Tornatore's loving reaffirmation of faith in the power of movies to enchant and inspire is heart warming. His film "Cinema Paradiso" (1980) won him an Oscar for the 'Best Foreign Picture'. Audiences and juries alike responded to the director's sheer love for cinema.

Roberto Benigni : Benigni is one of the world's most acclaimed comic filmmakers and entertainers. He has acted in many films. As a filmmaker, he has his own unique style and theme. He made "Johnny Stecchino", the most successful film in the history of Italian cinema. "Life Is Beautiful" (1998) finally ended his long drought. He directed and acted in this film. It won 3 Oscars out of its 7 nominations. Benigni walked away with the 'Best Actor' and 'Best Foreign Picture' Oscars besides one for the 'Best Dramatic Score'.

Films : The Little Devi, The Monster, Johnny Stecchino, Life Is Beautiful.

Other noteworthy filmmakers of Italy are : Tinto Brass (Caligula 1980), and Vanna Paoli (Along The River 1990/The Pink House 1995).

Iran

Abbas Kiarostami : He is one among the internationally acclaimed auteurs of Iran, Mohsen Makhmalbaf, Darius Mehrjui, Majid Majidi. Their sheer charm, consistent quality the poetic simplicity and gentle humanity can be vividly seen in their films. They have got their individual mark irrespective of various constraints. Abbas' films have won so many international awards that now he wants younger filmmakers to have a chance.

Films : Traveller (1974), Close-Up (1987), Where Is My Friend's Home? (1987), And The Life Goes On (1992), Under the Olive Tree (1994), Taste of Cherry (1997).

Kianush Ayari : His hard hitting films have met with critical acclaim at home and abroad and achieved popular success.

Films : The Master (1986), Spectre Of The Scorpion (1988), Beyond The Fire (1989), The Glorious Day (1991), Two Halves of An Apple (1992), Bull's Horn (1995), To Be Or Not To Be.

Abolfazl Jalini : Jalini is a prolific filmmaker who has made a number of documentary and short films. Nobody handles children better than him. His films are about lonely children.

Films : Don, Scabies, and Dance of The Dust.

Kiumars Poorahmad : As a youth he was an amateur film critic. Later he made many documentaries and features and has evolved his own style in making films centred round young people.

Films : The Singer (1977), In Order Of Height (1978), Goyar (1987), Bread And Poetry (1988).

Dariush Mehrjui : He has grown into one of Iran's leading filmmakers whose films have been acclaimed at home and abroad for their sensitive depiction of social reality and deep study of character.

Films : The Cow (1970), The Postman (1972), Shirak (1987), Sara (1993).

Other prolific filmmakers of Iran are : Makhmalbaf (Gabbeh), Meheran (The Tree Of Life), Majid Majidi (Father, 'The Children of Heaven'), Varuz Karim (The Last Act), Jafar Panahi (The White Balloon).

Poland

1. Andrzej Wajda : Iron-willed Wajda, who has stayed on through all the political turmoils and crippling deprivations of his country caught in the force of history. Wajda left to make a couple of films in Europe but always returned as if he could not cut unbiblical cord to his motherland. He brought out the pain and confusion of post-war Poland in his trilogy film, Kanal, Ashes And Diamonds, Lotna. Wajda's cinema of moral concern plunged him headlong into capturing the solidarity movement, risking the wrath of official censorship.

Films : Czlowiek Z Zelaza / Man of Iron (1981), Kanal, Ashes And Dimonds, Lotna, Everything For Sale.

2. Krzysztof Kieslowski : He died at the height of his creative power. His film 'Decalogue' brought critical acclaim to this rigorous and reticent director. His films mesmerize you with their formal beauty, dramatic intensity and epiphanies of irony.

Films : Decalogue, Trois Colours : Bleu, Blanc, Rouge, (1993/94).

3. Dorota Kedzierzawska : Crows (1994).

4. Wladyslaw Paskowski : Demons of War (1998).

Sweden

Ingmar Bergman : When Bergmanesque becomes the ultimate adjective to describe cinematic excellence, it is hard to choose a particular film. Even his small films are marked with a characteristic beauty which seems inseparable from the whole. The range of themes explored in narrow but disturbingly, hauntingly deep. His films deal with family strife, the probing of psychological wounds inflicted by those closest to us. He is acknowledged as a 'Great Master' of cinema.

Films : Smiles Of A Summer Night, Seventh Seal (1957), The Silence.

Czech Republic

Vera Chytilova : She is the first lady of Czech film. She is known as the leader of the New Czech film direction from the sixties. From the start, her career was daringly original with an ability to observe ordinary, everyday things in an unconventional way.

Films : The Ceiling (1962), Automate World (1964), The Apple Game (1977), The Inheritance (1992), Traps (1998).

Karel Kachyna : He is a unique phenomenon on the Czech cinematography scene. He wrote and directed many full-length feature films. His films demonstrate the highest professional excellence. Times that were not favourable to free artistic expression politically or socially, Kachyna searched for ways of "Surviving" as a filmmaker about children and intimate psychological stories.

Films : Long Live The Republic (1965), The Ear (1970), I'm Jumping over Puddles Again (1971), The High Wall (1964), The Death of A Fly (1976), The Clouds will Roll Away (1950), Everything Ends Tonight (1954), The Singer (1960), King of The Bohemian Forest (1959).

Jan Nemec : *The New York Times* listed his second film "A Report on the Party and the Guests" (1966), among the ten best films of 1966 and he was chosen one of the five best directors of the year by the International Film Guide. When Soviet tanks invaded Czechoslovakia, Nemec's camera captured the grim story which was used in the Oscar winning short "Czechoslovakia" (1968). Later he was exiled.

Films : Diamonds of Night (1964), Martyrs Of Love (1967), Metamorphosis (1974), The Flames of The Royal Love (1990).

Korea

Park Kwang-Su : He is now acclaimed as the leader of Korea's "New Cinema Movement". He founded the Seol Film Group, an important step in the development of Korean independent film movement — a significant oppositional voice in the days of military government. His films reflect the point of tension of Korean history.

Films : Chilsu and Mansu (1988), Black Republic (1990), Berlin Report (1991), A Single Spark (1995).

Lee Myung-Sae : He is regarded a master stylist of Korean cinema.

Films : Gagman (1988), My Love, My Bride (1990), First Love (1993).

Philippines

Tikoy Aguiluz : Tikoy is one of the leading figures in the alternative cinema movement in the Philippines. He came into the international limelight in 1976 with a documentary "Mount Banabaw, Holy Mountain". Controversial at home, his film "Boat man" was marked by a characteristic refusal to bow to censorship. He is a fine documentary maker.

Films : Boatman (1984), Bagong Bayant OCW (1995), Segurista (1996), Rizal in Dapitan (1997).

Sri Lanka

Gamini Fonseka : For four decades, Gamini has dominated Sri Lankan cinema as actor-director who has so far worked in 130 films in Sinhla, Tamil, English and Urdu. Groomed by David Lean and moulded by Lester James Pieres, Gamini has won innumerable Best Actor and Best Director Awards. "Nidhanya" a film in which he acted is the sole entry from Sri Lanka among the world's best 140 films compiled in commemoration of century of world cinema.

Films : Sagarayak Meda, Koti Valigya, Nomiyena Minisun.

Israel

Rafi Bukaee : The writer-director and producer Rafi Bukaee has made heartwarming feature films. Films about the conflicts of history.

Films : Avanti Popolo (1986), Marco-Polo (1996).

Shemi Zahrin : Zahrin has written several scripts, among them the successful feature 'Tel-Aviv Stories', has won many awards.

Films : Passover Fever, Dangerous Acts (1998).

Other Great filmmakers of Israel are : Shabi Gabison (Shuru), Hanna Azoulai (Sh'hur), Orna Ben Dor-Niv (The New Land), Michael Bat Adam (Aya — An Autobiography), David Ben Shitrit (Behind The Wall of Exile), Igal Bursztein (Everlasting Joy).

Brazil

1. **Paulo Thiago :** The veteran Brazil director Paulo Thiago cleverly manages to infuse his characters with a contagious optimism. His films have several impressionistic touches.

Film : The Portrait (1998).

2. **Eliane Caffe :** Kenoma (1998).

3. **Claudio MacDowell :** Flagrant Adultery (1974), Lights, Bed, Action! (1976), Now We Can Get it (1983), The Call of The Oboe (1998).

The Netherlands

Orlow Seunke : Orlow made a name with widely respected films 'The Taste Of Water' (1982) and 'Pervola' (1995).

Other Films : Siberia (1995), Tropic of Emerald (1997).

Mike Van Diem : He brought the Oscar to his country with internationally acclaimed film "Character" (1997) which was his debut feature film. This film tells the relationship between a father and his bastard son.

India

Satyajit Ray : The most acclaimed of Indian film directors of his generation, Satyajit Ray was a celluloid genius who opened up a whole new world into Indian cinema. After him, the world knew about the Indian cinema. The year 1992 saw him winning a special Oscar Award — and leaving the scene forever. He is often called a renaissance man. His films are notable for their realistic portrayal of everyday life and artistic composition of his camera-work. He introduced the realistic style of filmmaking into Indian cinema.

Films : Pather Panchali (1955), Aparajito (1958), Apur Sansar (1959), Charulata (1964), Agantuk.

Bimal Roy : Bimal Roy was one of the most thoughtful and realistic directors of the world. He was highly inspired by the Italian neo-realist movement. After watching Vittorio de Sica's 'Bicycle Thief', he decided to make "Do Beegha Zameen/ Two acres of Land" (1953), that would be considered the most brutally true Indian film. This master of the 'mise en-scene' created a fascinating tableaux of images to convey realism. Today, there is no one like Bimal Roy in India.

Films : Biraj Bahu (1955), Parineeta (1954), Devdas (1956), Sujata (1959), Madhumati (1958), Bandini (1963).

Govind Nihlani : Unlike Hollywood, art and entertainment are two separate elements in Indian cinema. They hardly meet. Govind Nihlani represents the so-called art cinema who failed as a popular filmmaker because he has no faith in unrealistic things. He and Shyam Benegal are the true children of Satyajit Ray's cinematic style.

Films : Ardh Satya (1983), Aakrosh (1980).

Shyam Benegal : He is the master of woman-oriented films. He has a great understanding of women's psychology. All of his films deal with the plight of Indian women, both urban and rural. Another art filmmaker, who could not identify himself with the popular Bollywood cinema.

Films : Bhumika (1976), Junoon (1979), Kalyug (1981).

Mehboob Khan : He worked like David Lean to create epics. Mehboob Khan always thought big and did big. He is the first Indian filmmaker, whose film "Mother India" (1957) was nominated for the "Best Foreign Picture" Oscar and it lost Oscar for a single vote.

Films : Son Of India (1962), Andaaz (1949), Mother India (1957).

K. Asif : His film "Mughal-E-Azam"/ Akbar The Great (1960), along with "Mother India" and "Sholay" forms the film triad which is guaranteed a wide viewership whenever it released. He was the god of Indian historical Cinema, to the status of India's Cecil B. DeMille for the ambitious scale of his vision.

Mira Nair : She is Jane Campion of Indian cinema. This internationally acclaimed filmmaker has her own unique style and theme. Her "Salaam Bombay" (1988) was nominated for "The Best Foreign Picture" Oscar. Another film "Monsoon Wedding" (2001) won many prestigious international awards.

Films : Salaam Bombay (1988), Kamasutra (1997), Mansoon Wedding (2001).

Shekhar Kapur : He always wanted to migrate to Hollywood for making his kind of cinema. Though he made few popular films in India, but never identified himself with Bollywood's "Chalta hai attitude/ anything works" and its picnic like films. His films "Elizabeth" (1998) was nominated for 7 Oscar but won only one for the 'Best Make-up'. This was his first English film. "Four Feathers" (2002) is the second. He is the best when he makes films on woman and children. A master of biographical films.

Films : Masoom (1983), Mr. India (1987), Bandit Queen (1995).

Ashutosh Gowarikar : He had made a tremendously entertaining and artful film "Lagaan / The Tax" (2001), which was nominated for the 'Best Picture' Oscar. Though we cannot ignore the great contribution of its star and producer Amir Khan, whose creative and financial contributions took "Lagaan" to the world's heights.

- Other old great Masters of Indian Cinema are : V. Shantaram (Do Aankhein Barah Hath 1957), Sohrab Modi (Kundan 1955), B.R. Chopra (Naya Daur 1957), Raj Kapur (Sangam 1964, Shri 420 1955), Vijay Anand (Guide 1965), Guru Dutt (Pyasa 1957), Hrishikesh Mukherjee (Anand 1970), S. Fatehlal Damle (Sant Tukaram 1936).
- Other Great working Directors of India are : Mrinal Sen (Akater Sandhaney 1980), Adoor Gopalkrishnan (Anant Ram 1987), Yash Chopra (Deewar 1975), M.S. Sathyu (Garam Hawa 1973), Nirad Mohapatra (Maya Mrigya 1983), Mani Ratnam (Nayakan 1987), Shaji N. Karun (Piravi 1988), Singeethan Srinivas Rao (Pushpak 1987), Ramesh Sippy (Sholay 1975 — the most successful film of India), G. Arvindam (Thampu 1978), Ram Gopan Verma (Satya 1998), Vidhu Vinod Chopra (Parinda 1989), Deepa Mehta (Fire 1998, Earth 1999), Ketan Mehta (Mirch Masala 1986).

5
The Cast

"Actors are like cattle, handle them with care."

—*Alfred Hitchcock*

When Hitchcock said the above line, he did not mean that actors are cattle. If not handled with care, they may give a miserable performance. A ham scene should be avoided. For that all actors have to surrender some freedom to their screen directors. They are the people, viewers are going to watch. So they must be handled with care.

A perfect casting means that the half battle is won. The casting director and the director have multiple choices. But they must be very careful and choose only those faces that can justify the character. A writer can immensely contribute in right casting. A screen test becomes necessary for the selection of actors. If the film is historical or personality based, the casting director's job becomes tough. Face, height, weight and acting should justify the character. Weight can be increased or reduced but the face must match. Different characters demand different kinds of acting. Any actor, who is physically and mentally capable, has to do a lot of homework and groundwork to become the character he is going to play. Hollywood actor Will Smith turned down the role of playing the legendary boxer Muhammad Ali for five years because he did not think he was ready. For one year, he devoted six hours daily; 3 in the gym and 3 in the ring, and increased 20 Kg. of body weight to match the 100 Kg. Weight of Muhammad Ali. He learned Muhammad Ali's kentuky accent and his hyperactive behaviour. The result was remarkably good. He was no more Will Smith. He was Muhammad Ali in Michael Mann's film "Ali" (2001) and won a nomination for the 'Best Actor' Oscar.

Essential Acting

For hundreds of years, scholars have striven to define what it is that sets actors above the common herd, why it is they need to 'Act', none of these learned scholars has come near to unravelling the mystery. In addition to Olympic fitness, supreme courage, phenomenal powers of concentration, the acceleration of a puma and an insatiable appetite for sheer bloody sweat and grind and plain old fashioned sheer bloody hard work, the actor also needs supernatural ability to transform himself into another person; 'to other be'. Not simply to 'pretend' to be someone else but actually to 'enter' that person.

The actor must know what it is like to be everything from a Moghal emperor to an Elderly passer-by, he must know how the Frenchman feels when the alarm clock goes off, he must know how the alarm clock feels, he must experience the pain of the carrot on the chopping board. 'Truth' to the actor is what paint is to the artist and what ink is to the writer.

Scripts for Actors

It is an actor who gives life to the script, without him it is just a bundle of papers. Some actors seem to have that "Oh-well-we-might-as-well-rehearse-it-a-bit and then-do-it-in front of cameras" attitude. Which is so silly because they are cheating themselves and their viewers by neglecting to carry out the vital, rich and rewarding work of studying and analyzing the text. There is no royal road to understanding a text. It is simply a question of old-fashioned sweat, pain and toil. Because acting is the supreme test of physical and mental courage. It is like climbing Everest single-handed in the dark. It is like being asleep on a helter-skelter with no pyjamas and a hangover.

Truths for Actors

→ Self-awareness is the very stone of the art and craft of acting.

→ Actors perform on behalf of community. So they must not cheat them by the false acting.

→ Voice and eyes are the biggest tools of an actor's trade.

→ Style should support the content, making it more effective. It has no other purpose. It is not what you say but the way you say that clichés.

→ Actors must be aggressive listeners, the more sensitively they listen, the more effective can be their speech.

→ Use 'Quiet Opportunities' to listen and watch people in public places, on road, on train...anywhere.

→ 'Pause' in speech makes sentence audible and intelligible, it increases its emotional impact.

→ Explore the 'Silence'. Sometimes silence says everything. Make it effective with true reactions.

→ Climax of speech contains series of ascending steps, ascending scale of pitch, increase in volume and ascending rate of delivery.

→ Your voice and speech habits are an integral part of your personality. It has taken you many years to achieve them. Do not try to change them overnight. It is that make you different other actors. Do not adopt features that are totally alien to you. Your pattern of speech is influenced by your social, cultural and familial background.

→ Let awareness and flexibility be your aims rather than any set pattern, no matter how ideal they are.

→ DO NOT COPY OTHER ACTORS. COPY REAL LIFE PEOPLE.

→ Read scripts many times to know the complete biography and psychology of the character. Only then you can enter into the character truthfully. Talk to the writer and the director. They can tell you more about the character.

→ You have to live many lives. So see the world and its people. Travel as much as possible.

→ Be yourself.

→ If you want to adopt another countryman's accent, the best way is to meet the people who naturally use the accent you wish to adopt. Vowel and rhythm patterns are the best possible training.

→ Economy of action and grace of execution are the stamp of a good actor.

→ Economy of action means good posture, correct breathing and the proper exercise of muscular tension and relaxation.

→ Grace of execution means performing reliably, flexibly and without efforts.

→ Some actors have mobile faces that have naturally a wide range of movement, facial expressions and gestures and some actors have stiff and still faces that can deliver narrow movements and expressions.

→ If your performance is to carry the stamp of truth, the character you create must be gripped by his body feel and his body image must reflect his inner spirit.

→ Actors and directors have much in common. They need imagination, perception, sensitivity and charishma. The differences are in attitude and process.

→ Actors must have capability to repeat their actions and dialogues in the same exact manner for as many times as the director wants.

→ JUST FEEL. And everything will be alright.

→ Do not cage yourself in an image. Be versatile.

→ Ask for the script in advance.

→ Rehearsal time is not a luxury but a guarantee of a rounded performance and efficient shooting.

→ 'Restraint' is the key of superior performance. Do not overplay.

→ Watch all those films, which have won nomination for the 'Best Actor' Oscar. Five actors are nominated in each year. They are lessons for you.

→ You cannot cheat the camera. Give right looks and reactions.

→ A little confusion can destroy the reality. Make everything clear before going to the camera.

→ Recharge your mental and physical batteries by sleeping and resting.

→ Exercise and a good diet are must for the actors.
→ The true stardom means smiles of your mom and dad. Seek their blessing.
→ Develop a protein body. Reduce fat.
→ Remain in the character till the dubbing is over.
→ Live the character. Do not kill it.
→ All artists are basically lazy persons. They rest when they do not perform their art. By this, they gather a tremendous reserve of energy to be used later.
→ All artists are aliens in this world. They like to remain among their tribe only. They cannot do anything except their art.
→ Nobody can understand an artist except an artist.
→ An artist is a crazy, mad, restless person. The power of creation keeps him high above all.
→ Meditation and Yoga help an actor to explore himself.
→ Accept positive criticism and improve. Avoid sychophants.

Actors, particularly more committed to their craft, are fascinating people. They live several "Lives" and in many ways, mirror the society. It is said that true and visionary actors often expose the best and worst of us. In the words of an American acting master Michael Butler, if we can accept an actor's perception, we can make the next step towards enlightenment.

Great actors are auteurs in their own right. A great director may occasionally draw a memorable performance from an average actor, but great actors often give additional meaning to even the most mundane of role. No scriptwriter, cinematographer or film editor, however gifted he or she may be, can lift a character like an actor can. Actors give the screen writer's words exciting depths and dimensions, bring ideas to life and convey the complexity and confusions of the characters they play out.

Different actors approach acting differently. Some believe in "Living" the roles in lines of naturalistic approaches to performance instituted by Russian director Konstantin

Stanislavsky and further perfected by legendary acting tutor Lee Strasberg. Popularly known as the Method, this style, which calls for the actor to internalize the character by drawing upon emotional reserves stockpiled in his subconscious, has been immortalized by famous practitioners like Marlon Brando, Rober De Niro and Indian actor Naseeruddin Shah. Alternatively, there is the anti-naturalistic styles developed by German Playwright Bertolt Brecht and French filmmaker Robert Bresson. The Brechtian actor does not attempt to inhabit the role but remains outside it, thus alienating the spectator from the character and drawing him into a more active viewing where he is able to analyse the characters in ideological terms instead of just sharing their emotions. But styles apart, what is universally accepted is that great acting is about seemingly doing less and being more effective.

WORLD'S GREAT ACTORS

Al Pacino : The young, tacturn, intense, brooding Al Pacino along with Rober De Niro embody the best that contemporary American acting has to offer, particularly the 'Method' school. Together they are America's acting treasure. The heat of their acting can be seen in Michael Mann's 'Heat' (1995), where they are appearing in the same scene. Pacino unlike De Niro is more accessible, likeable and beguiling. He creates sympathy ever while playing a Satan. At the end of 'Godfather II' his face looks like a monster's, the whole corruption finds a place in his soul. This method actor can charmingly play the darkest character. His first love is theatre. His documentary, "Looking for Richard" (1996), which he wrote and directed, is a witty, intelligent exploration of acting. Passionate, warm, energetic, charming Pacino is America's best-loved contemporary actor. He won the 'Best Actor' Oscar for playing a blind Colonel in the film "Scent of A Woman". He turned down 'Kramer Vs Kramer' (1979), 'Born on the Fourth of July' (1989), 'Apocalypse Now' (1979), 'Star Wars' and 'Crimson Tide' (1995).

Major Films : The Godfather (1972), Serpico (1973), The Godfather II (1974), Scarface (1983), The Godfather III (1990), Scent of A Woman (1992), Heat (1995), Donnie Brasco (1997), The Devil's Advocate (1997), The Insider (1999), Any Given Sunday (1999), The Recruit (2002).

Sir Anthony Hopkins : Nobody could play the role of Hannibal as chillingly and convincingly as Hopkins did in "The Silence of the Lamb" for that, he won the 'Best actor' Oscar. The stillness of his being is haunting. The consummate actor that he is, Hopkins is able to play contradiction. His stillness that is behind what is so frightening about his Hannibal the Cannibal (The Greatest villain in cinema history), you fear this Sociopath most when he is silent. The greatest Shakespearean actor Sir Olivier was amazed at Hopkins incredible acting talent. He can read a script 300 times to get in to the character.

Major Films : The Silence of The Lamb, The Remains of The Day, Shadow Lands, Howards End, The Elephant Man, The Edge.

Catherine Deneuve : Some actors are natural born aristocrats. Catherine Deneuve, the cool blonde, muted elegance and peerless poise, has an enviable record of working with the greatest names in European Cinema, Bunuel and Truffaut, Jacques Demy and Roman Polanski, plus a whole new generation of directors have seen in Deneuve the perfect woman to portray their totally different conceptions of the eternal feminine.

Major Films : Belle De Jour (1967), Repulsion, The Mississipi Mermaid, My Favourite Season (1993), Place Vendome (1997).

Daniel Day Lewis : An actor of astonishing range and power, there is a raw, elemental physicality to the way Day Lewis plays his characters. This physicality was put to astonishing effect in 'Last of The Mohicans' when he played the half-breed frontier tracker, Hawkeye. Hurtling through the forest, Day Lewis made for a terrific action hero — perhaps the best Hollywood has seen in ages. He is one of the best character-stars of Hollywood. He had been consistently good, consistently watchable. He won 'Best Actor Oscar' for "My Left Foot".

Major Films : A Room With A View, My Left Foot, The Last of the Mohicans, In The Name of the Father, The Boxer, The Age of Innocence, The Gangs of New York.

Denzel Washington : He always performs competently but routinely and self-consciously. He is as compelling as any great actor. His performance is as stylish as ever but there is also a truthful, sincere quality to it. In 'Soldier's Story' he is damn good. His most layered, complex performance is Malcolm A : in the span of few hours, we watch Malcolm the character and Denzel the actor change and grow right before our eyes. Finally this African-American actor won Oscar for the 'Best Actor' for the film 'Training Day' (2001).

Major Films : Philadelphia, The Pelican Brief, Courage Under Fire, Fallen, Soldier's Story, Devil In Blue Dress, The Siege, The Bone Collector, Hurricane, Training Day.

Dustin Hoffman : He is arguably the greatest American actor working today. His style became self-conscious, mannered, affected and along the way has gathered so many tics. He is the most actorly of actors. He is deeply dedicated to his craft. He did not sleep and eat for three days to make the character look real in "Marathon Man".

Major Films : Graduate, Midnight Cowboy, Straw Dogs, All the President's Men, Marathon Man, Straight Time, Kramer Vs Karmer, Rain Man, Wag The Dog, Out Break, Hero, Ishtar, Billy Bathgate, Dick Tracy, Hook, Papion, Little Big Man, Mad City, Joan of Arc.

→ He won Oscar twice for the 'Best Actor' for the films "Kramer Vs Kramer" (1979) and "Rain Man" (1988).

Emma Thompson : Emma Thomson is a Hollywood rarity : A British thespian reborn at 33 as a Hollywood star. She makes intelligence and good sense look seductive, sexy. Her characteristic roles are plain, modest, bookish woman in period films. But there is something of the subversive comedienne to her that few movies tap.

Major Films : The Tall Guy, Much Ado About Nothing, Sense And Sensibility, Impromptu, Primary Colours, Dead Again, The Remains of The Day, Howard's End.

Gene Hackman : Many times a mediocre, even a bad movie seemed worth watching because Hackman was in it. Anything he does is so watchable. His killer smile coupled with his repressed fury can make us wonder. Who can forget his role, as a FBI agent is 'Mississipi Burning'? Hackman too has been overexposed and so his style has become so familiar to us. His best role is of a paranoid electronic surveillance man in 'The Conversation'. He won the 'Best Actor' Oscar for 'The French Connection' (1971).

Major Films : Mississipi Burning, Unforgiven, The Conversation, Night Moves, Hoosiers, The Quick And The Dead, The French Connection, Enemy of The State, Uncommon Valour, The French Connection II.

Gerard Depardieu : The beauty of Depardieu as an actor is his intuitive playing of his formidable but undeniable plebian physique against the poetry of his voice that can boom like a fog horn and then sink into an insinuating whisper. Add the expressiveness of his eyes that can turn translucent with tenderness or opaque with contained rage actor who sums up an entire age. This French actor has disclaimed stardom and considers himself "More of a story-teller, a balladeer, a king of the Road." Depardieu's marvelously modulated voice made us hear the cadences of France's best love plays.

Major Films : Fort Sanganne, Moon In The Gutter, Under Satan's Sun, Police, Danton, 1900, Bogus, The Man In The Iron Mask.

Gong Li : Chinese Cinema's international impact is identified by its exquisitely beautiful icon Gong Li. She symbolizes the convoluted revolt of filmmakers, who came to be called the Fifth Generation, against communist China's official film policy. It was destined that such delicately sensuous beauty should be best revealed in film after film by a master cinematographer turned director Zhang Yimou. Gong Li's enormous talent had helped her survive the many upheavals in China.

Major Films : Red Shorghum, Shanghai Triad, Ju Dou, The Story of Qui Ju.

Gary Oldman : One of the best actors of America, Gary Oldman's talent lies in making you feel his style of execution. Only few can match his menacing performance as a Russian terrorist in "Air force One". The cruelty can be seen on his face, his body language and in his words. One of the best character artists after Morgan Freeman, his body language is remarkably awesome, and face is terrorizing.

Must Watch : Airforce One, Lost In Space, Fifth Element, Leon, Chatahoochi, Sid And Nancy.

Holly Hunter : She is the most famous rule breaker in Hollywood. She does what a woman may or may not do on screen. Holly Hunter's raspy voice purs with pure animal relish in disembowelling the propriety of any given work. Holly Hunter has made a virtue of mocking at everything Hollywood holds sacred-glamour, safe star vehicles and conformism to any unwritten rules. She won the 'Best Actress' Oscar for "The Piano".

Films : The Piano, Miss Firecracker, Broadcast News.

Isabelle Huppert : Her fragile child-like beauty was perfect for the virginal shyness that ends in suicide in claude Goretta's "The Lacemaker". She has played unsympathetic roles in her early career. She was an upstart who uses the selfish upper middle class world for her own ends. This hint of the dark, amoral side to the delicate, almost bland prettiness that earned her the nickname Matchstick Girl made her Filmmaker Chabrol's favourite over the years. There is a fearless capacity in her for exploring the full complexity of being a woman and which makes her a favourite of woman directors.

Films : The Lacemaker, Violette Noziere, The Tront, Un affairs de Femmes, A Judgment In Stone, Couple de Foudre, Madam Bovary, Swindle, Heaven's Gate.

Johnny Depp : When you come to the end of Depp's performance you realize that he is subtly registered all the shades and nuances of the character he is playing. He is one of the America's greatest young actors. Another Brando in the making. Depp's beautiful almost angelic face is so still. When he acts you keep waiting for the firework, which do not come. Depp not Leonardo is Hollywood's acting future.

Films : Cry Baby, Fear And Loathing In Las Vegas, Gilbert Grape, Benny and Jaon, Edward Scissorhands, Edwood, Donnie Brasco, From Hell, Chocolate, The Pirates of Carribian : Curse of the Black Pearl.

Jodie Foster : She is about clear intelligence, cool rationality and calculated daring. Foster proved Hollywood history wrong when it came to a child star failing the adult test. At 13 she played Iris, the drug addicted teenage whore in 'Taxi Driver'.

The emotions he had to understand and portray is something no child should be asked to. Foster won two 'Best Actress' Oscar for her films "The Accused" (1988) and "The Silence of The Lamb" (1991). She started her acting career at the age of two and won two Oscars before she was 30.

Films : Napoleon and Samantha (1972), Kansas City Bomber (1972), Tom Sawyer (1973), Taxi Driver (1976), Maverick (1994), Contact (1997), Anna And The King (1999), The Panic Room (2002).

Jack Nicholson : He rose from 'B' class movies playing more villains and victims than heroes. While most actors specially Method actors are ready to bleed their performances dry of persona, Nicholson projected his persona. His acting style does not fit in with Method actors Jams Dean, Brando, Pacino, De Niro and he is not anything like the order actors Newman, Redford, Duvall, Hackman and Hoffman. He stands by himself. Nicholson is not an actor, he is an institution of acting. The most Oscar nominated actor (12) Jack Nicholson has won 3 Oscars including two 'Best Actor' Oscars for "One Flew Over The Cuckoo's Nest" (1975) and "As Good As It Gets" (1997).

Films : Chinatown, The Shining, Batman, Wolf, One Flew Over the Cuckoo's Nest, As Good As It Gets, The Pledge, About Schmidt, The Passenger, Easy Rider.

Meryl Streep : She is Hollywood's first choice when it come to playing a woman with an accent. She has a passion and purity that is normally only the gift of poetry, not mere professional expertise. It is difficult to imagine anyone else as "The French Lieutenant's Woman". The teasing, erotic mystery of the Victorian outcast who mantles herself in self-indulgent tragedy is a revelation from an actor known for her meticulous restraint. She is one of the two actresses, who has received the most number of Oscar nomination, 12 each. The other actress is Katharine Hepburn. Meryl Streep won two Oscar for "Kramer Vs Kramer" and "Sophie's Choice".

Films : The French Lieutenant's Woman, Plenty, She Devil, Death Becomes Her, Falling In Love, Bridges On Madison County, Silk Wood, Out of Africa, Post Cards From the Edge, Music of The Heart, Adaptation.

Michelle Pfeiffer : An actress of beauty and melancholy, Michelle Pfeiffer still lands leading roles. She made her debut as a bimbo in 'Grease' and 'Scar Face' but played it with certain toughness. Better parts came her way and she found the range to play them intelligently, all the time staying beautiful, glamourous, appealing, vulnerable.

Films : Grease, Scarface, The Fabulous Baker Boys, Tequila Sunrise, One Fine Day, Married To The Mob, Frankie and Jhonny, The Witches of Eastwick, Batman Returns, Wolf, The Age of Innocence, Love Field, The Deep End of The Ocean.

Morgan Freeman : The greatest character actor, Morgan Freeman gets his grace and energy from being a trained dancer, and his discipline from the theatre. He is perhaps only American actor who never overdoes his role, the only one who keeps in character — never doing anything more or less than what is required of his character. He can actually make you forget his acting. He does not make even a single false move. He is consistently accurate, subtle, restrained and taut. He has the mastery of exact posture, voice control, and precise gesture. Sometimes watching Freeman act can almost be a spiritual experience. He has been nominated twice — once for the best actor in 'Driving Miss Daisy' and for the best Supporting Actor in 'Street Smart', but he never won it.

Films : Street Smart, Seven, Driving Miss Daisy, Glory, Brubaker, The Shawshank Redemption, Lean on Me, The Unforgiven, Outbreak, Chain Reaction, Hard Rain, Deep Impact.

Marlon Brando : The Godfather of Hollywood films, Marlon Brando is the master of the 'Method' school of acting. His slow and lazy speech and movements have their own power and impact. He is the scene carrier. The eyes simply cannot turn away from him. Think American movies and you think acting, great looks, screen presence, charishma, talent as personified by Marlon Brando. He is the real special effect. Marlon Brando refused his 'Best Actor' Oscar for 'The Godfather' in 1972, because he objected to the film industry's treatment of Native Americans. He won another 'Best Actor' Oscar for "On The Waterfront" (1954).

Films : The Godfather, On the Waterfront, Apocalypse Now, A Street Car Named Desire, The Wild One, Burn!

Nicholas Cage : This intense, passionate, brooding actor, with wolf like eyes takes his craft so seriously that he swallowed six live cockroaches to make the scene really shock in "Vampire's Kiss" (1988), had two teeth removed without pain killers for "Birdy" and actually slashed his arm for "Racing The Moon". The most devoted actor Nicholas Cage is Francis Ford Coppola's nephew. His natural charishma and strong screen presence burn the screen. He is very passionate about acting. The dark roles always inspire Cage to be the best. He won the 'Best Actor' Oscar for "Leaving Las Vegas' (1995).

Films : Moonstruck, Racing The Moon, Birdy, Vampire's Kiss, Leaving Las Vegas, Con-Air, Face-Off, The City of Angel, Adaptation.

Paul Newman : Husky voiced, blue-eyed Paul Newman is one of a kind, a rarity anywhere, not just in Hollywood. He played the risky roles and dark characters. He can play the good guy, bad guy and an ugly guy with equal ease and perfection. His greatest role can be found in "Verdict" where he plays a troubled lawyer looking for redemption. Defying the star system and working against his own pretty boy image, Newman seems to have desperately reached out to play dark, troubled characters. He won the 'Best Actor' Oscar for "The Colour of Money" (1986).

Films : The Verdict, Blaze, The Hudsucker Proxy, Nobody's Fool, Twilight, The Colour of Money, The Life and Time of Judge Roy Bean, Hombre, Butch Cassidy And The Sundance Kid, Road To Perdition.

Robert De Niro : For Robert De Niro, acting is living different lives without risking real life consequences. Another great 'Method' actor De Niro does not look at you, he considers you. Held in the power of that gaze you can expect anything next : a bullet, an embrace, or your head bashed with a baseball bat. Cocking his head to one side, listening with his eyes going completely still, a thick silence that says so much. He does not want to be liked. He plays terrible people, monsters sometimes. Who can forget his shaking body in "The Mission". He has two kinds of acting styles — the fast-talking, fast gesturing manic roles and the considered, thoughtful restrained characters. He always says, "An actor must do less".

Another devoted actor, De Niro lost 30 pounds weight to play Travis Bickle in 'Taxi Diver' and gained 60 pounds when playing a boxer in 'Raging Bull'. He won the 'Best Actor' Oscar for "Raging Bull" and the Best Supporting Actor Oscar for "Godfather Part II".

Films : The Mission, Mean Street, Taxi Driver, King of Comedy, New York-New York, Cape Fear, Night and The City, The Untouchables, Awakenings, Analyse This, The Godfather II, True Concessions, Falling In Love, Guilty By Suspicion, Heat, Ronin, We are No Angels, Analyze That.

Russel Crowe : This New Zealand born Australian Hollywood actor struggled a great deal to reach among the top league of actors. He plays his characters by becoming the characters. He can loose, gain weight, change himself totally to fit the characters. At the end of "LA confidential" (1997) you cannot judge whether he was a good guy or bad guy. He makes you feel the character he is playing. Finally he won the 'Best Actor' Oscar for playing a Roman fighter in "Gladiator" (2000). He was also nominated for the 'Best Actor' Oscar twice for "The Insider" (1999) and 'A Beautiful Mind' (2001). His mesmerizing portrayal a Nobel Prize winner John Nash Jr. (He goes more than 40 years with amazing conviction) is a stamp of the truthful acting.

Films : L.A. Confidential, Gladiator, A Beautiful Mind, The Insider, The Quick and The Dead.

Sean Penn : He is a natural born actor. But he always says he is bored of acting and wants to quit. He dazzles with his chameleon-like transformations. He never seeks attention to his persona. His character becomes the persona. He can do so many different roles with so much truth. We can simply never forget his Academy Award nominated roles in "Sweet And Low Down" (1999) and "I am Sam" (2001).

Films : Dead Man Walking, Fast Times at Ridgemont High, Carlito's Way, The Thin Red Line, Sweet And Lowdown, I am Sam.

Susan Sarandon : She got her break playing the same irresistible, raunchy older woman in "Bull Durham and White Palace". Her big break came with "Thelma and Louise". Her greatest performance is to be found in Lorenzo's "Oil". She is so great here that even without acting in other films, she would have found a place among the greats. She won the 'Best Actress' Oscar for 'Dead Man Walking'.

Films : Bull Durham and White Palace, Thelma and Louise, Dead Man Walking, Oil, Stepmom.

Robert Duvall : His one film "Tender Mercies" can sum up his great acting talent. The strength of Duvall's acting is in what he does not do, in his holding back. His spareness, his economy, brings a meditative resonance to acting that is rare in American cinema. If anybody was born to play the role of Tom Hagen in "The Godfather" movies, it is Duvall. He won the 'Best Actor' Oscar for "Tender Mercies" (1983).

Films : The Apostle, The Godfather films, Tender Mercies.

Tom Hanks : He was best known for a string of roles in low budget comedies with names such as "Bachelor's Party" and "Turner & Hooch". He made an amiable light leading man, but nobody would have predicted, he would finish the 1900s as America's favourite hero, or become the first back-to-back Best Actor Oscar winner since Spencer Tracy. He himself says, "I'm not a chameleon. I don't disappear in any of the roles". His persona of an ordinary man in extraordinary circumstances is always visible. He won two consecutive Oscars for the Best Actor for his film "Philadelphia" (1993) and "Forrest Gump" (1994). His role as John Miller, the shell socked infantry captain in "Saving Private Ryan" (1998), will be remembered for longer.

Films : You have Got Mail, Saving Private Ryan, Cast Away, Philadelphia, Forrest Gump, Bachelor's Party, The Green Mile, Punchline, Big, Apollo 13, Volunteers, Road to Perdition, Catch Me If you Can!

Willem Dafoe : Anybody who has seen his films will agree that he is a tremendous actor. Eyes that bore into you and wide mouth with a toothy, dangerous, smile that could mean anything. His magnetism leaps at you in 'Mississippi Burning', as the spectacled by the books FBI agent he rivets you. You feel compelled to watch him. Dafoe was mesmerizing as Jesus in 'The Last Temptation of Christ'. He is magnetic and unsetting. But he has very few films as the lead actor.

Films : Mississippi Burning, The Last Temptation of Christ, Light Sleeper, English Patient, Speed 2, Saigon.

Will Smith : His one film 'ALI' (2001) can sum up the huge acting talent of this African American actor. Will Smith never leaves his exclusive power of electricism. Tremendous energy always seems to explode into a magnetic laugh or a deep-rooted anger. A singer of many hit albums Wills Smith was mesmerizing even in his early films like 'Six Degrees of Separation' and 'Bad Boys'. He became a cult figure with 'Independence Day' and ' Men In Black' (MIB). He is simply a versatile actor. He was nominated for the best Actor Oscar for playing the personality of the legendary boxer Muhammad Ali in Michael Mann's ALI.

Films : Six Degrees of Separation, Bad Boys, Independence Day, Men In Black, Men In Black 2, ALI, Bad Boys 2.

Robin Williams : In the early days of his career, critics called his performance lightweight and wondered if Williams had the discipline or complexity to achieve a rounded performance. And 1987 saw Robin Williams won an Academy Award nomination for his performance as wise cracking disc jockey in 'Good Morning Vietnam'. The role allowed him to use his humour and gift for improvisation while portraying a man struggling with the pain and loss of war. His performance became more restraint and rounded. He was tackling serious roles with poise and maturity. But he will always be remembered as a beautiful Comic actor.

In 1997, he won The Best Supporting Actor Oscar for a small film, 'Good Will Hunting'. Williams had been nominated three times before. After accepting the Oscar, he raised the statuette and declared "My father told me I should always have a back up profession like welding".

Films : Goodwill Hunting, Aladin, Jumanji, The Birdcage, Mrs. Doubt Fire, Good Morning Vietnam, Popeye, The World According To Garp, Patch Adams, The Father, The Flubber.

Ben Kingsley : "The stage demands acting. The camera explores behaviour", he said. Ben Kingsley understands this difference which is why he has had the best of two worlds. For how many actors can start with amateur theatre group, go on to bit roles in major plays, graduate to important roles with directors like Peter Brooks, become indispensable to the Royal Shakespeare Company, have the stage all to himself in solo shows, play Hamlet and Othello? How many can hit the screen with a portrayal of Gandhi under a director like Sir Richard Attenborough, bag roles with Steven Spielberg and Roman Polanski, John Slazenger and Barry Levinson? He had half Gujarati blood. And he played Gandhi. But that was an extraordinary coincidence, not the reason for the choice. To play Gandhi, he had lost much weight, tanned his skin, done yoga, read biographies and Gandhi's own writings which was in 23 volumes! He had come to New Delhi before six months of shooting, wall papered his room with Gandhi's photographs, listened to recordings of his voice. He did play many personalities like Lenin (The Train) and Shostakovich (Testimony). His best play is Harold Pinter's "Betrayal". He won the Best Actor Oscar for "Gandhi" (1982).

Films : Schindler's List, Gandhi, The Train, Testimony, Death And The Maiden, Sweeny Todd, Mission, Species.

Other great actors and their must watch films

Geoffrey Rush	Shine, Elizabeth, Shakespeare In Love
Cuba Gooding Jr.	Jerry Maguire
Michael Douglas	Wall Street, A Perfect Murder, The Ghost And the Darkness, Disclosure, Basic Instinct, The American President, Romancing the Stone
Jeremy Irons	Reversal of Fortune
William Hurt	The Kiss of the Spider Woman
F. Murray Abraham	Amadeus
Henry Fonda	On Golden Pond
Jon Voight	Coming Home, ALI, Midnight Cowboy
John Wayne	True Girl
Charlton Heston	Ben Hur, EI-CID, The Greatest show on Earth
Yul Bryner	The King And I, Ten Commandments
Sir Laurence Olivier	Hamlet
James Cagny	Yankee Doodle Dandy, The White Heat
Spencer Tracy	Boys Town, Captains Courageous

Kevin Spacey	American Beauty, Seven, L.A. Confidential
Roberto Benigni (Italy)	Life Is Beautiful, Down By Law, Night on Earth, So Close, Asterix
Mel Gibson	Braveheart, Ransom
Gary Sinise	Ransom, Snake's Eye, The Green Mile
Charles Chaplin	The Tramp, The Kid, The Gold Rush, City Lights, The Great Dictator, Limelight
Gwyneth Paltrow	A Perfect Murder, Shakespeare In Love, Shallow Hall
Ralph Fiennes	The English Patient, Schindler's List, The End of the Affair
Juliette Binoche	The English Patient, Chocolate, Three Colours : Blue, White, Red.
Harrison Ford	Indiana Jones Films, Blade Runner
Cate Blanchet	Elizabeth
Helen Hunt	As Good As It Gets, Cast Away
Matt Damon	Goodwill Hunting, Saving Private Ryan
Diane Lane	Unfaithful
Salma Hayek	Frida
Richard Burton	The Robe, Who is Afraid of Virginia Wolf.
Julianne Moore	The End of the Affair, Far From Heaven
Jude Law	The Talented Mr. Ripley, Enemy At the Gates, AI (Artificial Intelligence)
Kate Winslet	Sense and Sensibility, Titanic
Kathy Bates	Misery, Primary Colours, About Schmidt
Glenda Jackson	Woman In Love, A Touch of Class
Diane Keaton	Annie Hall
Jane Fonda	Klute, Coming Home
Katherine Hepburn	Guess Who's Coming to Dinner, The Lion In Winter, Morning Glory, On Golden Pond.
Elizabeth Taylor	Butterfield, Who is Afraid of Viginia Wolf?
Vivien Leigh	Gone With the Wind, A Streetcar named desire
Sophia Loren	Two Women, Judith
Sissy Spacek	Coal Miner's Daughter
Humphrey Bogart	The African Queen, Maltese Falcon
Toshiro Mifune (Japan)	Roshomon

Client Eastwood	The Good, the Bad and the Ugly, A Fistful of Dollars, The Bridges of Madison County
Greta Garbo	Mata Hari, Ninotchka
Orson Welles	Citizen Kane
Cary Grant	His Girl Friday
James Stewart	Mr. Smith Goes to Washington, The Philadelphia Story
Gary Cooper	High Noon
James Mason	Lolita
Samuel L. Jackson	Pulp Fiction, The Negotiator, Jackie Brown, Unbreakable
Bette Davis	All about Eve
Cher	Moonstruck
Ingrid Bergman	Casablanca
James Dean	Rebel without A cause
Anthony Perkins	Psycho
Nick Nolte	Affliction
Michael Caine	The Quiet American
Adrien Brody	The Pianist (2002)
Walter Brennan	Come And Get it, Kentucky, The Westerner
Liam Nesson	Rob Roy, Schindler's List
Glenn Close	Fatal Attraction, Dangerous Liaisons
Debra Winger	An Officer and Gentleman, Terms of Endearment, Black Widow, Shadow Lands
Kevin Kline	A Fish called Wanda, Cry Freedom, The Ice Storm, Sophie's Choice, In And Out
Kristin Scott Thomas	The English Patient, Angels and Insects
Harvey Keitel	Bad Lieutenant, The Last Temptation of Christ
Donald Sutherland	Ordinary People, Invasion of the Body Snatcher
Woody Allen	Annie Hall
Alec Guinness	The Bridge on the River Kwai
Rod Steiger	In the Heat of Night, On the Waterfront
William Holden	Picnic, Sunset Boulevard
Leslie Cheung (China)	Farewell My Concubine
Marcello Mastroianni (Italy)	Eight And a Half

PeterUstinor (France)	Lola Montes
Zbigniew Cybulski (Poland)	Ashes And Diamonds
John Molkovich	The Man In the Iron Mask, Con Air
Julia Robert	Erin Brockovich, Pretty Woman
Richard Gere	Primal Fear, Pretty Woman
Halle Berry	Monster's Ball
George Clooney	O Brother, Where Art Thou? Three Kings, The Peace Maker
Hilary Swank	Boys Don't Cry
Whoopi Goldberg	The Color Purple, The Associate, Bogus
Angelina Jolie	Girl Interrupted
Alicia Silverstone	Clueless
Anthony Quinn	The Message, Viva Zapata, Zorba, Lust For Life
Ed Harris	Border Line, Enemy At The Gates, A Beautiful Mind, The Right Stuff
Peter O' Toole	The Lawrence of Arabia, Lord Jim, The Stuntman, My Favourite Year, The Hating Class
Kevin Costner	Robin Hood Prince of Thieves, Bodyguard, Dances with The Wolves, The Untouchables
Jennifer Jason Leigh	The Best Little Girl In the World, Last Exit To Brooklyn

GREAT ACTORS OF INDIA

Indian actors are often blamed for loud and over acting. Why do they overdo their roles. Too many dialogues and less reactions are the hallmarks of Indian films. Indian films and actings are loud, because if we know the culture, customs and social life of India; they are basically loud. And the films and acting reflect the same loudness that is inherent in Indian social life. NSD (National School of Drama) New Delhi, has produced many great acting talents like Naseeruddin Shah and Om Puri, who became the master of restrained and method acting. The Indian actors can be divided into three categories, stars, star-actors and actors. Few Best Star-actors and their noteworthy Films are :

Amitabh Bachchan : BBC Polls has declared him the star of The Millenium ahead of Sir Olivier Lawrence. His noteworthy films are : Deewar (1975), Sharabi (1980), Mohabbatein (2000).

Amir Khan : The hero and the producer of the internationally acclaimed Oscar nominated 'Lagaan' (2001) is one of the most adorable Star-actor of India.

***Major films* :** 'Raakh', Rangeela, Sarfarosh, Lagaan.

Kamal Haasan : He is the Robert De Niro of India. Most famous for changing appearances. He has won the most number of acting trophies in India.

***Noteworthy films* :** Nayakan, Appu Raja, Hindustani, Pushpak.

Mammooty : Mathilukal, Vadakkan Veera Ratha, The Truth.

Tabbu (Actress) : Kalapani, Maachis, Virasat, Astitva, Chandni Bar.

Mohan Lal : Kireedam, His Highness Abdulla, Kalapani, Vaana Prastham, Balagopalan M.A.

Soumitra Chatterjee : Apur Sansar, Charulata, Devi, Ghare Baire.

Shobana (Actress) : Dolapathi, Manichitrathazhu, Rareeram.

Mamta Shankar (Actress) : Agantuk, Shakha Paro Shakha.

Shabana Azmi (Actress) : Fire, Godmother, Paar, Arth.

Dilip Kumar : Real name is Yusuf Khan, he is called the Marlon Brando of India.

***Films* :** Daag (1953), Azad (1955), Devdas (1956), Naya Daur (1957), Kohinoor (1960), Leader (1964), Ram Aur Shyam (1967), Shakti (1982).

Nargis (Actress) Mother India (1957).

Meena Kumari (Actress) : Sahib Biwi Aur Ghulam (1962), Pakeezah.

Nutan (Actress) : Bandini, Mai Tulsi Tere Aangan Ki, Milan.

Smita Patil (Actress) : Ardh Satya, Bhumika, Nishant, Chakra.

Sanjeev Kumar : Sholay, Trishul, Aandhi, Pati Patni Aur Woh.

Shahrukh Khan : The most Charishmatic & Stylised Star-actor of India.

Noteworthy films : Darr, DDLJ, Devdas.

The great Indian Character actors are :

Naseeruddin Shah : The most acclaimed method actor of India, Shah can be truly called Al Pacino of India. He is the god among Indian actors. Famous for his loathing of Bollywood films for its mediocrity. Finally his long drought of playing in an international film ended with getting a major role with Sir Sean Connery in "The League of Extraordinary Gentlemen" (2003).

His major films : Masoom, Aakrosh, Sarfarosh, Chakra, Ardha Satya, Bhumika, Mirch Masala.

Om Puri : Internationally well-known Indian actor, Om Puri has acted in several European and Hollywood productions.

His major films : Ardh Satya, Aakrosh, Sam and Me, City of Joy, East Is East.

Balraj Sahni : Do Beegha Zameen, Garam Coat, Hakeekat.

Amrish Puri : Mr. India, Virasat, Kala-Pani, Indiana Jones and The Temple of Doom.

Nana Patekar : Parinda, Angaar, Khamoshi, Krantiveer, Prahar.

6

The Screenplay

"You cannot start a film unless you have a dazzling story to Tell."

—*Producer Doug Wick*

Movie-making is both an art and a Science. The skills and complexities have to be practised and mastered but imagination and ideas are just as important. These ideas and imaginations are given a worldly and filmable shape in papers called screenplay.

The subject : How a writer or a director gets an idea for his films, is a matter of speculation. The sources of finding ideas are endless. Everything you see in your World can serve as a source. Some of the Common Sources of Ideas are imagination, observation, experience, people, reading, current events, past, future and even audience reactions. As soon as a writer gets an idea, many questions follow — Does it inform, who is the audience, will it be entertaining, what can be the budget etc.?

There are two groups of film subjects. First is a group of themes which have inherent filmic quality, the second group contains subjects which demand filmmaker's skill to make them work once they reach the screen. Subjects without an internal structure are obviously much more difficult to bring to the screen. A story is filled with dramatic situations to make it worth watching.

Telling a Story

Filmmaking is totally a psychological process. It contains thought, imagination, emotion and language. All filmmakers are basically story-tellers. Every story has a beginning, middle and end. This three way structures are orderly or inorderly presented onto the screen. Characterisation, dialogues and setting are other aspects to be looked upon while writing a screenplay. A screenplay is not the final documents. It always exists to be interpreted, altered and accommodated.

The Structure

The most important aspect of screenplay is its well-built structure. It is the structure which binds the various elements of the story into a concrete whole, a format which carries the logical and emotional progress of the story clearly and expressively. The most common structure used in films is 'Restorative Three Act Structure'. It was derived from Aristotlean notion that all dramas have a beginning, a middle and an end. These parts are joined coherently to tell a story. They are an extension of each other. Middle is an extension of the beginning and is followed by the end, which completes the story initiated by the beginning. Neither of these can exist without the others.

The beginning or the first act contains exposition, (establishing the characters or the tone of the story). The middle part is the largest and the thickest. Plots and sub plots become more complexed. And the end culminates into the climax making the story complete. The conflict started in the beginning, develops into confrontations between characters or situations. This conflict is resolved in the end, where we get a logical and clear denouement.

Plot Points

There are two plot points in a story. The first plot point happens when the character gets a turning point in his life. The second plot point portrays the Big gloom, when the protagonist is the far away from his goal.

Screenplays

The screenplays are the written materials by the professionals. They communicate to the crew what the writer and the director want from them. They are written in different formats — Shooting script, A/V Script and Story Boards.

Sample of a Normal film Screenplay :

67. INT. George Pell's study room. Night.

Close on George as he thinks about the meetings. Sarah, a tall girl who makes an effort not to risk being a distraction by dressing down her good looks, enters the study.

George

I am going out. Something I wasn't expecting.

Sarah

I'm sorry. But please don't go. I have to say something.

(He walks out of the room hurriedly, Camera on Sarah's gloomy face.)

-Cut-

All screenplays consist of master scene and each master scene begins with a Slug-line, which indicates whether the scene is situated inside or outside, its location and time. It is always written in uppercase letter. All details are written in present tense only. Special properties or sound must be mentioned in uppercase letter.

Shooting Script

It is a kind of technical script. Director's selection of shots, camera placing, its height, movements are clearly mentioned in the shooting scripts. A scene is broken into many shots. Directors make their own shooting scripts and give them to their cameramen. Cameramen's job becomes easier. Actor's movements, dress are also mentioned in the shooting script. It is a technical way of execution.

Sample :

22. INT LIVING ROOM NIGHT
Close up of Bongo Player
Beating the drums. He is
Wearing blue Jeans, red
T. Shirt and Sandals.

23. Angle on Meg
Sitting by the open window
Her head is bent. She is
Brooding over her split with

Barbara. She walks over to the
Bongo Player.

Sample of A/V Script (Primarily used in non-fictions)

Shot	Visual	Audio	SFX
1.	Close of Bongo player. The Camera tilts down to the player's feet meg is speaking to Joe.	Sound of Bongo. Meg "He is very clever and shrewd you know."	Light sound
2.	The Camera on Bongo, reveals player's hands beating it softly.		Sound of Bongo

Storyboard

Story boards are the most sophisticated and systematic way of executing scenes. They are primarily used in shooting of ads and action sequences of a film. Some great auteur like Spielberg and Satyajit Ray used storyboard for their films. The whole look of the shots is drawn into pictures by the professionals. It is like a cartoon book. Once the storyboard is complete; the shooting becomes only a mechanical exercise for the director.

Original Screenplay

The original screenplay is one which is directly written for the screen, and was not published before. The Academy of Motion Picture gives two Oscars for Original and adapted screenplay.

Adapted Screenplay

Adapted screenplays are based on materials, previously written in any form. They are primarily based on novel, play, or other piece of Fiction or biographies. Translating a book into visuals is the most difficult task for a writer. Most of them fail to justify the books. The changes are bound to happen. English Patient (1996) is one of the best Adapted Screenplays. It is a beautiful translation of words into images. When words are changed into another medium, they loose the power of emotion. Time duration is another factor which kills the real magical effect of reading. It is very difficult for a two and half hour film to bring the magic of many pages of literature. Few directors succeed to maintain the magic, others fail totally.

Few best screenplays and their writers :

Annie Hall (Woody Allen 1977), Lawrence of Arabia (Robert Bolt 1962), Citizen Kane (Herman J. Mankiewics and Orson Welles 1941), Casablanca (Julius J. Epstein, Philip G. Epstein 1943), All About Eve (Joseph L. Mankiewicz 1950), On the Water Front (Budd Schulberg 1954), Midnight Cowboy (Waldo Salt 1969), Chinatown (Robert Towne 1974), Ordinary People (Alvin Sargent 1980), Rebecca (Robert E. Sherwood 1940), Gone with the Wind (Sidney Howard 1939), Godfather Films (Mario Puzo, Francis Ford Coppola), English Patient (Anthony Minghella 1996), The Pianist (2002).

7

THE BUDGET

If the cinema is acknowledged as the most popular artistic medium, it is the most risky business too. Filmmaking is an art, science and the business. It involves too many people with too many different faculties. But they all have one thing in common — blood of a little showman. Today the cost of a very modest film would keep an American family in comfort for a lifetime. Financiers and producers who put their money into films, would like to retrieve their investments along with as much profit as their money would earn while sitting in a bank.

MGM's 'Cutthroat Island' (1995) cost more than $ 100 million to produce, promote and distribute. By May 1996 it had reportedly earned back just $ 11 million. This is the biggest loss in movie history. Kevin Costner's 'Water World' (1995) is another big loss. As it was the most expensive film till 'Titanic' (1997) broke its record. But 'Titanic' also became the highest earner in the film history just like 'Gone with the Wind' (1939). This game of numbers suggest one thing that the big money spenders are just like big gamblers. Loosing and winning are the two sides of the same coin.

The budget is the most important aspect in the process of filmmaking. As soon as the story and settings are finalized, they decide the budget. A good budget can increase the production value of a film and a poor budget causes so many compromises, that mar the beauty of the film. Reasonable budget offers tremendous creative freedom to the director. Producer Jerry Bruckheimer's favourite line is 'Any Doubt, Throw More Money'. But it is the director who uses the large sum of money to create wonder. Another king of risks is

British Producer Graham King who is steadily making inroads into the big-budget, risky Hollywood ventures. His films include like Michael Mann's 'ALI', Steven Soderbergh's 'Traffic' and Martin Scorsese's 'Gangs of New York'. 'Traffic,' a US $ 53 million film had so far earned more than $ 300 million world wide. Graham King, who left London in 1982 with a backpack, is now one of the most powerful Britons in Hollywood.

Filmmaking involves creative and technical manpowers. And their fees are sky-high. Actor like Tom Cruise, Bruce Willis and Tom Hanks Charge $ 20 million per film. It is very difficult to make a Hollywood film in less than 50 million. There are other technical people and crew to be paid well. It is the story, cast and settings, that decide the budget. The money is spent on following things :

Research : Includes visiting locations, meeting people, searching and going to libraries, museums etc.

Story : Producers have to pay for the rights of the adapted book and to the screenplay writers.

Raw Stock : Film negative.

Camera Department : Cameraman, director of photography.

Lights : Lights on hire, Light men, Light director.

Editor : Editing studio, editor, assistant editors.

Make up : Make up man, Asst. make up men.

Costume Design : Chief Costume designer, Asst. Costume designer and Costumes etc.

Art Direction : Art director, Set director, Asst. Art and Set directors, cost of building sets etc.

Fights : Stunt Coordinator, Action Manager, Asst. Action Master, materials used in actions.

Choreography : Dance Choreographer, dancers.

Sound : Sound Engineer, Sound effects engineers and sound effects editors and studio and effect charges.

Still Photographer : He has to remain on the sets all the time. His photographs help in removing continuity faults.

Production : Production manager, Spot-boys, Public Relation Officer etc.

Other charges include daily expenditures, lunch, conveyance, office expenditure, legal charges, censor fee, printing, show prints, distribution, promotion, publicity, miscellaneous expenditures and unforeseen expenditures etc. Promotion of a film is very crucial for the big opening. Film 'Godzilla' was promoted heavily by spending $ 50 million.

Hollywood films are becoming very expensive. An average budget of a modest Hollywood film falls between $ 60 million to $ 80 million. If the film becomes a huge money grosser, everybody, connected to the film, become in demand. Another risk is going over budget. Sometimes director has to spend from his own pocket to complete a film. Michael Bay, the director of the big budget film 'Pearl Harbor' (2001) was frankly told by its producers that if the film runs over budget, he has to pay. Michael Bay had plenty to put on Screen while filming 'Pearl Harbor'. The intricate battle sequences, that lasted for full 45 minutes, involved blowing up 17 ships, vintage planes screaming over panicked soldiers and in one chaotic scene on battleship 'Row' 350 bombs exploding in Seven Seconds. Luckily nothing went wrong except the blowing of huge money. Another fine example of big and well spent budget films is 'Ben Hur' (1959), the 11 Oscar winner Roman epic took ten months to complete at Rome's many studios. The building of 300 sets are the highlights of the film. The giant project was the climax to producer Zimbalist's career, but he died of a heart attack in Rome when the film was near completion.

The budget factor is affected from the kinds of producers. If the film's star is himself the producer of his film, it will certainly go over budget. Fine examples of this sort are John Travolta's 'Battlefield Earth' and Kevin Costner's 'Water World'. None of them could even manage to retrieve their costs. In this highly risky business if a film becomes a hit, it can make up a dozen flops. Like perfect casting, a perfect budget is also crucial. But it must be utilized to bring the magic not mania.

8

The Cinematography

For a long time, it has been a matter of debate that who is more important — man or the machine. If we praise the outstanding cinematography of 'English Patient' and 'Lawrence of Arabia' whom are we praising. Of course the men who created the brilliance of photography onto the screen. But it is never good to underestimate the power of machine. It is better to assume that man and machine are complementary to each other. An advanced technology will surely help to bring the magic. And a man with the vision and creativity will always try to bring that magic on to the screen. Film 'English Patient' is a rich visual experience. The desert looked like a woman's body, the sands of Sahara dissolve into the crumpled sheets that covered the disfigured Almasy's bed. There is a grandeur in every shot. John Seale's cinematography can stand upto comparison with Freddy Young's on 'Lawrence of Arabia'.

Every genre demands different type of filming to bring the psychological impact. Cinematographer Januz Kaminski employed two totally different ways of filming for 'Schindler's List' and 'Saving Private Ryan'. The former was shot in Black & White to tell the horrors of holocaust more vividly than ever, while 'Saving Private Ryan' another same period film, was shot in broken grains of colour and sepia tone with lots of jerky camera movements to show the horrors of World War II in a brutal way. He won Oscar for both of his films.

Cinematography is a motion photography. Photography is writing with light. Whatever is lit is captured by the lenses. The movie camera works on the rule of 'persistence of vision'. When our eyes see something, it remains 1/14 parts of a second on retina. And if the same image is moved at the speed of more than 20 per second, we get the illusion of motion. The movie camera exploits that illusion by running 24 frames of film negative per second through the gates of its lenses.

Lights

Lighting : Lighting is the most important aspect of cinematography. It helps to create the desired mood, and the psychology of the character. Wrong lighting kills the magic of the visuals. It is the light which make the picture. So it should be given Supreme importance. Different stories demand different lighting styles. Basic lights are :

Flood light : It has one built in reflector which can throw light into one direction. It is a medium hard-soft light. It is primarily used in news coverage. Not for creative use.

Multi 10 or 20 : This light is most frequently used in video. 10 stands for 1000 watts. It has standard illumination the only advantage is that it can be focused. Primarily used for interviews.

Solar : Normally used in both video and film, solar and baby solar (1000 watt) have got sun's effect in creation of shadows and illumination. Indoor filming may need 2 K.V. while outdoor has larger demands. It has a parabolic reflector which beams the light. The reflector and the bulb can move backward and forward. It has a lens called 'Fresnel lens'. The color of light is yellowish.

Spot light : Primarily used for stage shows. As it is a very hard and focused. A dancer is followed by the same light.

Effect projector : While other types of lights illuminate the object, effect projector projects source patterns like window etc.

HMI : The most advanced light, which have colour temperature of 5600 Kelvin, just like sun. It is mercury medium arc iodine. Mercury is burnt instead of oxygen. That's why it is not hazardous and consumes less power but gives sun-like light used in Films.

Lighting Styles

Filmmakers use different styles of lighting for shooting different scenes. A high-key picture is when an overall picture looks very bright. A low key picture means that only the object is in sharp focus while other things remain in dark. Graduated light is flat light. A high contrast happens when the difference between light and shadow is more while the low contrast is just opposite of that.

Quality of light : There are two qualities of light, hard and soft. Hard lights create hard edged shadows. Candle, spot light and sun are hard lights. Soft lights produce soft edges such as umbrella bounced light. It creates beauty, grandeur and glamour.

Three point formulae : The basic way of placing lights around the object. It consists of three lights : key light, fill light and back light. Key light illuminates the Frontal portion of an object and creates a shadow. Normally of 1000 watt. Fill light removes the shadow created by key light. If the key light is of 1000 watt, fill light would be of 2000 watt. It is placed just opposite of key light. Back light creates depth in the picture (500 watt).

Practical lights : Practical lights are those which are visible in the frame, such as candles, torch, moon, sun etc.

The Lighting Setup

Front lit : It is a simple way of lighting primarily used in news coverage. The only advantage is that you do not get any shadow. It just falls behind the illuminated object. But the picture looks flat. Not for creative use.

Broad light set-up : It consists more than one light, primarily used in shooting interviews and talk shows.

Narrow lit : In this style of lighting only the edges or the half face is visible. The background remains in dark. It is a low-key illumination, where practical lights make greater impact. Like a shining knife in total darkness.

Composition

Composition is the arrangement of pictorial elements to form a unified, harmonious whole. Since the movie watching is an emotional experience, everything should make this experience unforgettable. A still photograph deals in space only while motion picture is composed in both space and time. The composition should be meaningful to achieve the favourable viewer's reactions. The good composition demands artistic taste, aesthetics emotional awareness of the individual cameraman. Motion picture is a Combo of thousands of the pictures, so it is difficult to achieve a harmonious whole throughout all the pictures. But it is not impossible too if the director and his cameraman have little artistic sense.

Composition is made of Lines, Forms, Masses and movements.

Lines : Lines have their own significance and meaning in Composition. There are Z-line, S-line and diagonal-line composition. A Moving train, Army, Caravan or herds can be shown in S-line or diagonal line composition. S-line and Z-line are called Line of Beauty. They look so beautiful on the big screen.

Forms : Forms fill the frame in a meaningful way. A culprit is shown sitting on the chair while two cops interrogate him. Both the cops are placed standing at both sides of the culprit. If one cop is removed, forms will weaken. The culprit is subdued by this form of composition. This cop-culprit shot has a triangle form.

Masses : Mass is the pictorial weight of an object, an area, a figure or a group. A large mass captures viewer's attention by the power of its heavy pictorial weight. As our eyes follow the saccadic pattern (from left to right) so right side of frame should have heavy objects. It is a rule of Third, where we break the screen into three parts and our eyes centre on the left. So an object should be placed on either side of the screen, not on centre. The principle of Steelyard, which tells in details about the placing of an object in the frame, tells us how to keep big object in the foreground and small ones in the background to create the meaningful composition. For the filming of sky-land, the ratio of one-third should be maintained. The sky should be given more visual weight than land.

Movements : In still photography we can only suggest the movements while in motion picture we can show it. It is depicted in transitional lines, where viewer's eyes can follow a subject or go from left to right screen. Horizontal movement suggest travel, momentum, displacement. Ascending vertical movement can suggest freedom, aspiration, growth while descending vertical movement suggests crushing power, fall, danger or doom. Dynamic composition always enthralls the viewers. When both the objects and camera move it is called extreme dynamic composition.

Depth of the field : Depth of field can be simply achieved by placing main object between foreground and the background. Uneven lighting, practical lights, in the frame and wide angles are instrumental in creating the depth of the field.

Basic Shots

A scene is broken into many shots by the directors. An action scene may need several shots while a dramatic scene needs few shots. At each shot, camera placement changes. A good director has a clear idea of how many and what type of shots are required for filming a scene. All shots are later combined in a logical order by editing to tell the story in a beautiful way. Basic shots are :

ECU - Extreme Close-up (of knife, gun, eyes etc.)

VCU - Very Close-up (Face shot, from mid forehead to above the chin)

BCU - Big Close-up (Tight close-up, Full head)

Chinese Dolly — A complex traveling shot combining the pulling back of the camera with a sweeping pan.

CU	Close-up (just above head to upper chest).
MCU	Medium close-up (Cuts body at lower chest).
Knee shot	Three quarter length shot (cuts just below knees).
MLS	Medium Long Shot (Entire body plus short distance above and below).
LS	Long Shot (Person occupies ¾ to 1/3 of screen height).
ELS	Extreme Long Shot (of desert, river, sea).
Two Shot	Two Persons in the frame.
Three Shot	Three persons in the frame.
Crowd Shot	To Show the whole crowd.
OS Shot	Over the Shoulder Shot (when players talk back and forth to each other).

Reaction Shot	No dialogue, just face.
Cut Away Shot	Not from the main happening, taken from other location and pasted into the main.
Cut-In Shot	A shot of anything from the main happening.
Establishing Shot	A wide shot of a location at the beginning of a scene.
Freeze Shot	A visual effect, in which the moving picture appears to stop its motion in the mid of a shot.
Static Shot	A shot in which there is no camera movement.
Aerial Shot	A shot taken from the air. Also called 'Bird's Eye View'.
Reverse Shot	A shot made from the reverse direction of the previous shot.
Head on Shot	When an object moves towards the camera.
Tail Away Shot	When an object moves away from the camera.
Insert Short	Insert shots are non-life objects that are later pasted into the main.
Steady Cam Shot	A special wearable device, the camera moves with the character.
Technical Shot	Shots of the machines, space-ships, its mechanisms and devices etc. used in Sci-fi films.
Protection Shots	Safety shots, that are preserved and used in emergency.

Crane Shot, Trolly Shot, Zoom-in, Zoom-out, Dolly-in, Dolly-out and Track Shot.

Camera Angles

Camera angles are decided by the director. Each shot requires different angles to give meaning to the composition. It can be objective, subjective and point of view. A high angle can suggest poverty, depression, despair and lowness while a low angle suggests authority, boldness, fearlessness and attacking power. Psychological camera angling is the most powerful tool in the hands of a director. And he must exploit it to gain optimum effects. Most of the shots are taken by the audience's point of view.

But when a character sees something, the camera cuts to reveal that thing. It becomes subjective. Subjective angling has also viewer's participation along with player's interest.

OS shots are basically point of view shots but of players not viewers. An objective camera angle is of audience's point of view. A shot of constructions field or desert or sea is always objective. A Towering building will look more beautiful by low angle or three quarter angle. In this way its height, width and depth will be recorded.

Dutch or Russian angle produces impressionistic view. This is an unusual treatment suitable for montage sequence. Such scenes should be filmed with opposing tilts for editor's choice. Dutch tilt angle may be used to film a distraught player or a catastrophe scene.

All these angles are employed at different places to shoot different shots differently for greater psychological impact, where viewers are emotionally affected. All angles should be chosen carefully and according to the demand of the story or a particular scene.

Things To Remember

- Fore-knowledge of editing requirements is the director's best guide as to what shots are needed.
- The sun moves every minute and weather changes. It is only skilled use of lighting that can give the illusion that the edited scene took place in same time.
- Avoid 'just point and shoot' philosophy.
- The director should tell his cameraman about the purpose of each shot and the cameraman needs to know the effects required.
- It is always dangerous to reduce filmmaking to a series of rules and formulae. But before you break the rules, learn them first.
- A director must decide three things prior to any shot :
  1. Position of Camera
  2. Height of Camera
  3. Focal Length
- Never use Zoom. It is a compromise. Use block lenses and dolly shots.

- Eye level camera positioning is not always impressive, except shooting close-ups.
- With the exception of 50 mm lens (Normal human eye view), all lenses distort the images. But they are accepted.
- In dramas cinematographers have to be more concerned about the faces and the lines. In comedy, aside from the jokes, you have to be concerned with body language and facial expressions.
- Cinematographer should be a mood-maker. Cinematography is both a science and an art. But if you are not a good craftsman, it would be very difficult to be a true artist.
- Do not use too many close-ups. It mars the beauty of the film. T.V. is a medium of close-up.
- A series of shorter shots, each offering less but more digestive material is good if it sustains viewer's interest at peak level.
- Directors should try to make story board for at least filming action sequences.
- Mise-en-scene is the choreography of a scene.
- Mise-en-shot includes camera position, camera movement, shot scale, the duration of a single shot and the pace of editing.

Continuity

The director and the cameraman must maintain the continuity throughout all shots of a single scene. As shots are taken in freedom of space and time but the audience should never be able to tell the difference. Whenever the camera position changes, the things are likely to go out of frame. As soon as the camera stops, a break occurs. One of the biggest movie faults is to let this show in the finished films.

Directional continuity must be maintained at all costs.

If a player exists the shot from the right of the screen, he should enter the next shot from the left of the screen. Directional continuity is also about maintaining screen direction. Time and space continuity are another area to be looked upon.

Dynamic screen direction consists three types of direction : constant, contrasting and the neutral. Constant is either left to right or right to left. Contrasting is both left to right and right to left while neutral is towards or away from the camera.

Line of Axis : The thought of crossing the line panics even many well experienced directors. This line of axis must never be crossed. It result in transposition of the scene. The player on the left will suddenly appear on the right. Looks must be matched.

Zoom and Dolly

Zoom lens has variable focal length. It has so many lenses in one lens. But most of the directors prefer dolly over zoom. Zooms are very useful for wild like, sport photography. While dolly is used in video and film productions. Zoom lens is a compromise. Block lens is expensive and time consuming. But great results are achieved by using block lenses. In zoom, we loose the perspective while in dolly (track in) we get large perspective. In dolly a focus puller is required. To get the rich visuals, dolly and block lenses are preferred.

Head room : Head room is the screen portion above the player. To avoid heads being chopped, maintain head room. But it is not always necessary to do that.

Looking room : A player should be placed on either side of the frame to maintain the looking room.

Camera Movement

Pan : (Pan left/Pan right) Pan is the horizontal movement of the camera on its axis. Pan is basically searching. A shot must not be cut while panning. Blur pan, Swiss pan and Whip pan are other forms of panning.

Tilt : (tilt up/tilt down) Tilt is the vertical movement of the camera on its axis. Pan and tilt can be used simultaneously.

Reframing : Whenever a player gets-up or moves, the cameraman refrains him by panning, tilting or tracking the camera.

Clap Board

Clap board has tremendous value in shooting a film. The matching of sound, identification of shots, takes and scenes are done with the help of clapboard. An editor searches OK/NG shots with the help of clap. Assistant director show the Clapboard prior to every take. A shot may have one or many takes. Following things are written on a clapboard :

"Titanic" 26-7-96

Scene	Shot	Take
23	5	2

Continuity Sheets : Assistant directors prepare log sheet and dress continuity.

Log Sheet

Production Name			Date-		
Film-			Page-		
Location-			Director-		
Scene	Shot	Take	OK/NG	Dialogue	Remarks

Dress Continuity Sheet

Production Name			Date-		
Film-			Place-		
			Page		
Scene	actors	dress	Dialogue	Ornaments	Remarks

Movie Camera

Magazine : Movie cameras use film, which is placed in case called magazine. Arri Flex and panavision cameras have a built in feed and take up mechanism and are available as either 200 ft. or 400 ft. The 400 ft. magazine unlike 200 one, is designed for forward and reverse running and automatically adjusts itself to the direction in which camera is moving.

Three Lense Turret : The Three lens turret is designed to take three interchangeable lenses with a mounting diameter of 41 mm. The turret can be rotated easily by means of three grips until a click stop indicates the desired lens is in shooting position.

View finder : View finder is the cameraman's eye. Through it he sees a bright 6½ X magnified image upon the ground glass. All view finders are monochrome (Black & white) because black & white image has high resolution and the focusing becomes easier. However due to the large frame format of 35 mm film, the view finder image is slightly cut at the edges.

Motors : The motor's work is to run the Film at 24 frames per second through the gates. The speed can be fastened or slowed down to get the desired effects of slow or fast motion. A 17 frames per second will provide the effect of fast motion and more than 30 frames per second will result in slow motion. The motor is attached to the camera by means of Four Screw. It also serves as a grip for the operator's left hands.

Few Examples of the best Cinematography :

Lawrence of Arabia	(1962)
English Patient	(1996)
Saving Private Ryan	(1998)
Crouching Tiger Hidden Dragon	(2000)
Last Man Standing	(1996)
Schindler's List	(1993)
The Lord of the Rings Films	(2001, 02, 03)
Braveheart	(1995)
Titanic	(1997)
Ten Commandments	(1956)
Ben Hur	(1959)
Citizen Kane	(1941)
The Bridge On the River Kwai	(1957)
Gone with The Wind	(1939)
Dr. Zivago	(1965)
Traffic	(2000)
Cabaret	(1972)
Close Encounter of the Third kind	(1977)
Reds	(1981)
Gandhi	(1982)
Out of Africa	(1988)
The Last Emperor	(1987)
Glory	(1989)
JFK	(1991)
Dances with The Wolves	(1990)
Road To Perdition	(2002)

9

The Editing

Editing comes in a category somewhere between brain surgery at one extreme and tiling the bathroom at other.

A film is saved as well as destroyed in the editing room. A fine editor can surely uplift the overall look of the film. Film editing is all, cutting, pasting, joining, decorating and doing everything to make a film worth watching. Unedited film is like a waste. Nobody knows how to get the complete picture until an editor walks in. Dramatic emphasis, rhythm and pace are the three elements of fine editing. An editor should have complete knowledge of machine, aesthetics and a remarkable speed.

Though the first requirement of all editing is that shot 'A' should cut smoothly to shot 'B', yet many more things are done to get the finished print. Editing is the toughest job to master. Editing is the brain of filmmaking. Those directors, who were once editors, prove to be the finest directors. As they know what they want and how to get that without any fault or confusion. It is a truth that director's conceptual skills save the film at the editing time, otherwise careless and confused directors may cause the film to live in cutting room for much longer time. Bad editor may chop the film to death. And those few who try for miracle in the cutting room, are always in demand.

Editing is the force of filmic reality. A director puts immense trust upon his editor. Both of them work long and hard to come at final cut. To avoid extreme or desperate measures, a director should keep editing requirements in his mind while shooting his film.

Developing The Film

Once the shooting is over, the exposed negative of sound and picture are sent to the lab for processing.

1. Develop picture negative and print it on positive. It is called "Rush Print" (Rushes). If there is problem in rush print, re-shooting becomes necessary.
2. Sound is transferred on optical. Sound negative is always black and white. It is a separate raw stock. Matching of picture and sound is done by the sound of clapboard. If the picture negative is 200 ft., sound negative will also be 200 ft. after printing both we get synchronized picture negative.
3. Edit — Cut picture negative, sound negative and picture positive. Make rolls of all three. Today editing is first done on avid computers, where film is transferred on beta cassettes and then digitized on the hard disc. Then the film negative is cut according to the numbers given by avid system.
4. Print — Print Picture negative and sound negative. It is called married print. It has only dialogue and picture.
5. Dub dialogue, fill with music and effects.
6. Print edited picture negative and final sound negative and develop them. You get the first release print. It is sent for censor board approval.

→ **Colour correction :** Colour correction is necessary to make all frames look alike in colour and density. In early days lily shots were used for colour correction where a colour corrector looked after YMCD (Yellow Metallic Colour Density) of each frame. Now colour correction is done on computer, where each frame of the film is digitally scanned at full 2k. Resolution with colour depth of 16 bit per channel. It is then digitally graded which enriches and takes the colour and texture of the film to a greater height where optical grading cant reach and then corrected images are recorded back on the fine grain film.

7. Now we get the first corrected print. Now print original negative and sound negative on master positive.
8. Corrected master negative is printed onto internegative (Additional Negative).
9. Internegative is used to make required number of show prints. Show print go the cinema halls.
10. Master negative is kept safe for years.

Why we Edit : There are three reasons to edit a film :

(i) To Explain
(ii) To Create Illusion
(iii) To Create Effect

(i) To explain : (Cut) A number of cuts are executed and films are later joined logically to give life to the story as it was conceived and written. In simple continuity cutting shot 'A' is followed by shot 'B'. It is also relational cutting where next shot shows the relation to the previous shot. Dynamic cutting is used for action sequences. The cutting rate differs from scenes to scenes. A dramatic scene may have less cuts than an action scene.

(ii) To create illusion : It is the power of editing which defies the rule of space and time. The director shoots different shots at different location and times, but at the time of editing they are joined together to show a scene or a story in its entirety. The viewers are kept under illusion.

(iii) To create effect : There are a number of effects, generated by the computer wizards and later pasted on films to overwhelm the audience. Some basic effects are frequently used to tell the story with the desired psychological effect.

(A) *Dissolve* : It is a smooth and restful transition from one shot to the next without cutting the previous shot. Long journey, march or memory, nostalgia are shown by using this effect.

(B) *Fade in fade out* : It happens when a scene ends you see the screen going black (Fade Out) and the next scene opens (Fade In).

Apart from these two frequently used effects, there are effects like mosaic, painting, strobe, wipe, slow motion, fast motion, freeze etc.

Log sheet : An editor requires log sheet prepared by an assistant director. In this sheet scene number, shot number, take number, OK / NG shots, dialogue and other remarks are clearly mentioned. This sheet immensely helps an editor to search the wanted shots. The shots of clapboard are another help for the editor.

Continuity editing : An editor looks the eye line match, point of view cutting, the match on action cut and directional continuity. In the eye line match a player in one shot glances something off screen and a cut reveals that object. So the cut becomes meaningful. Point of view is just like eye match but in this, the object is seen through the character's eye. In action cut, shot A should match shot B creating coherence and orientation. In directional continuity if a player exits the shots from the right of the screen, he should enter the next shot from the left of the screen.

Non linear film editing : Now with the advent of sophisticated computer, old cutting rooms with movieolas, (Film preview screen), synchronizers, trimbins stuffed with picture and magnetic film have disappeared. The modern editor gets his rush print synced up at the lab and transfers it into the beta cassettes. Then the cassettes are digitized on the harddisc of Avid Computer. The sound is transferred from the location DAT on to the Beta cassettes and sync is achieved by an audiphile machine, which marries the time code at each clapboard on the picture with that at each bang on the DAT. All old machines have gone into the technical history. On the completion of the editing, machine prints out a negative cutting list, instant roll numbers and key numbers. Then the negative is conventionally cut according to that numbers.

Few Best Edited Films

Black Hawk Down	(2001)
English Patient	(1996)
Schindler's List	(1993)
Saving Private Ryan	(1998)

Traffic	(2000)
Titanic	(1997)
Dances with the Wolves	(1990)
JFK	(1991)
Chicago	(2002)
Unforgiven	(1992)
Forrest Gump	(1994)
Apollo 13	(1995)
Matrix	(1999)
The Last Emperor	(1987)
Gandhi	(1982)
Raiders of the Lost Ark	(1981)
The French Connection	(1971)
Chicago	(2002)

10

THE SOUND

Light can travel in vacuum, sound cannot. It needs some medium to reach its end. Its frequency is measured in hertz. Normal audible frequency is 20 to 20,000 hertz. Beyond this we cannot hear. But as we age, we loose the power of hearing high frequencies. Only 15 years old humans can hear sound which has frequency of 20,000 hertz. A 50-year-old human can hear only upto 14000 hertz of frequency. Any machine, which provides sound frequency of 20 to 20,000 hertz, is called hi-fi (High Fidelity). Animals like dogs and cats can hear very high frequency upto 50,000 hertz. The lowest frequency we can tolerate is 20 hertz. A drums sound is always of low frequency while other minute sounds are of high frequency.

Mono sound : Mono sound is that originates from a single point or source, without any sense of direction.

Stereo sound : Sound having the effects of direction (Left to Right). To achieve the stereo effect, speakers should be kept at a minimum distance of 6 feet from each other.

Simulated stereo : This is a device which can convert old mono sound into stereo sound.

Surround sound : The sound effects that come from all directions. If a car enters from the left of the screen we hear the noise from the left speakers and when it exits from the right of the screen, we hear from the right side speakers.

Digital sound : Digital sound is a great achievement. In real life whatever we hear are digital sounds. Sounds without any loss of power. In analogue system the power of the sound is lost in travelling and transferring but this does not happen with digital sound. Digital is accurate sound. Now we can hear the thunder of the clouds in cinema halls as clear and loud as we hear in normal life. Dolby is the company that has devoted itself in inventing digital sound technologies.

Acoustic : Acoustic is the study of the behaviour of sound in an enclosed room. The behaviour of sound changes according to the materials available inside the enclosed room. If the room is filled with thermacoal, the sound will be absorbed and there will be no echo or reverb. Dead studios and soundproof studios are specially designed by filling their walls, ceilings and floors with sound absorbing materials. No sound goes outside, no sound comes inside.

Echo : We all have real life experience of echo. You say something and it returns to you. The minimum distance needed for echo is 55 feet. There are two sounds in echo, original and the new.

Reverb : It is a hallow sound, produced by fans, lawn-movers etc. If affects the sound recording and so should be stopped.

Dead studio / Sound proof studio : A specially designed and constructed building which does not reflect any sound and absorbs all sounds. There is no echo or reverb. The acoustic specialist are hired to design those kind of studios and cinema halls. A cinema hall should have enough of thick curtains, cushions, carpets and grassy walls. So that the audience can enjoy true sound. Now most of the cinema halls are equipped with DTS surround sound.

Pitch control : This is a technical device that can alter human's voice into animal's and get the effect of the telephonic voice.

Bass boost : Bass boost is used to boost up human's voice, give it an extra importance over others. The voice of the god or an angel can be achieved by this device.

The importance of the true sound can be understood by the fact that the Academy awards two Oscars for the best sound and the best sound effects editing. The importance of the sound is much more in the context of horror and war films. If their sound is weak, viewers are not impressed. It is much easier to deceive the viewers by a false visual continuity but it is very hard to fool them by a bad sound continuity. If a master shot has the sound of traffic, it must remain the same in the close-ups of the individual players. Our brain is able to filter lots of unnecessary sounds but the film machines cannot. They must be filtered at the time of recording. Technically illiterate directors do not care about the quality and quantity of sounds. They heavily rely on technical people. But the auteurs know what kind of sound they want and when it should start and end. Listen the films like 'Titanic' and 'Saving Private Ryan' and see the magic. In 'Saving Private Ryan' you do not see the tank, you hear it first and the sound is so dangerous, it sends signals of the doom. In 'Titanic' when the keys fall in the water, actor Leonardo dips inside to get it. The sound of the keys inside the water is different and as soon as it is brought out, its sound changes. That things win oscars. The sounds of the films like 'Jurassic Park', 'The Lost World' and 'Twister' are overwhelming and take the films to a greater height.

Boom or Fish pole : The sound recordist is always tense. His ears are very sharp. The boom mike is good while recording many players on the set. The problem arises when the players move. There is a danger of boom's shadow in the shot. It should be kept up. To avoid any inconvenience, the sound recordist should rehearse with the boom prior to the shooting. The wide shots always present discomfort to the boomman. The danger is that the boom can cast and in-vision shadow and wider the shot the higher the mircrophone has to be above the top of the frame. To deal with this kind of situations, the actors who are standing far away in the background should be given their personal radio phones.

Sync sound and dubbing : The film camera make too much noise, so the dialogues and background sounds are not perfectly recorded. The dubbing of all dialogues and effects become essential. The dubbing has its own advantages and disadvantages.

The actors have to remain inside their characters till the dubbing is over. They have to re-emote, retell every line. And the other major problem with dubbing is no lip sync. Only few expert actors can give full lip sync and the effects of the breathing and other minute sounds. The sounds of sea, doors and other non-life objects hardly match the visuals. Though the sound editor and engineer mix the real time recordings of the effects with library sound effects, yet it is impossible to match the reality.

The sync sound is better than dubbing. It is recorded at the time of shooting. Actors are given mikes and they record their dialogues at the time of shooting. So the dramatic effect, lip sync and breathings are outstanding and very natural. The camera is covered with a blimp. The blimp checks camera's noise and keeps it quiet. The sync sound is a laborious job, but wherever there is labour, the result is always good.

Premix and final mix : As soon as premixes of all effects, music and dialogues are over, the editor starts his job for the final mix. He decides about what should be more or less louder than others. The director guides him about the beginning and ending of a certain sound or music. It is usually necessary to do several premixes first and then combine them into one at finalmix. The director should choose the best studio to achieve the best sound. Many dubbing theatres provide different kinds of quality services. Never hire a poorly equipped studio and cheap editors and engineers. It would be miserable business.

Sound effects editing : The sound people provide sounds for the all scenes, but it should be edited according to the need of the shots. A director should know where a sound should start, pause and end. He should be well-versed about the sound splits. He should hire the best sound effect editors to get the maximum results. The sound effects editing is as much important as the sound itself.

Things To Remember

→ Always try to choose such locations that are less noisy.

→ Costume and historical dramas must be given ultra treatment for the filtration of modern sounds.

→ Airport and railways lines are the bane of all filming. Avoid locations near them.

→ Some noises can be silenced by simply bribing the people causing those noises.

→ If the dialogue is clear, certain amount of background noises can be tolerated provided that the source is obvious to the viewers.

→ Always record wild tracks while shooting, that can be used at the time of mixing.

Few examples of the best sound : Saving Private Ryan (1998), Black Hawk Down (2001), Titanic (1997), Jurassic Park (1993), Twister (1996), Gladiator (2000), The Insider (1999), ALI (2001), The Thin Red Line (1998), Enemy At the Gates (2001), Patton (1970), Cabaret (1972), The Exorcist (1973), Earthquake (1974), Raiders of the Lost Ark (1981).

Few examples of the best sound effects editing : Saving Private Ryan (1998), Titanic (1997), U571 (2000), Pearl Harbor (2001), The Ghost And the Darkness (1996), Jurassic Park (1993), Raiders of the Lost Ark (1981), E.T. : Extraterrestrial (1982), Matrix (1999), Braveheart (1995), Speed (1994), Terminator-2 Judgment Day (1991), The Lord of the Rings, The Two Towers (2002).

11

The Art Direction

Everything is staged for filming. Art direction is a vast field of constructing huge to small sets, building big bridges to small statues and decorating interiors according to the need of the story. The epic film 'Ben Hur' needed 300 sets to capture the glory of Roman empire. The producers of 'Titanic' ordered a true replica of the Titanic ship that cost $ 90 million. The bridge in the film 'The Bridge on The River Kwai" took 9 months to be built. No film can start till the art work is ready and O.K.

Art direction is one of the most important aspect in the process of filmmaking. Art directors work according to the needs of the story. The director acts as a guide and supervisor. The complexities of the sets decide the time and money. A historical film may cost several thousands of dollars and take much time, space and energy. The art directors have to create the whole history. Tons of research works are needed including visits to the libraries, museums and meeting historians. The feel of the period is not easy to bring. Only creative art directors can do full justice to the historical story. They work long and hard to bring those days of the past back onto the screen.

Looking at the enormous cost of creating sets, many filmmakers prefer real locations. But the shooting is more easy inside the sets. It is always controlled and peaceful. As soon as the art director and set designer get the script, they read it, meet the filmmaker and develop a map and drawings. That decide the budget. Then the carpenters and other workers are hired to start the work of wood and bricks. Most of the art directors are degree or diploma holder in the study of art direction or set designing. Though many legendary art directors are unqualified genius, who have learned their craft by experience.

Many things are required for building sets and interior decoration. There are several art shops that give items on hire. The period of the film decide the props. If it is the time of World War II, the art director has to collect telephones, watches and all other goods that have the look of that time. An art director should travel much and be a good searcher. He should have an idea of the places from where he can get the required goods on hire or purchase. It is a passionate job.

Today almost every film needs some shots of special effects. So there is another category of visual effects art directors. They work closely with special effects supervisors. Totally different things are needed to film special shots that could be put on computers and new shots can be generated. It is more complex job. In Ronald Emmerich's 'Universal Soldier', a scene has a truck crashing into the Grand Canyon. The visual effects art director got a model truck and pushed it down a small slope near the Grand Canyon. Later the shot was mixed with CGI (Computer Generated Shot) and the effect was so real. In Vilsmaier's film 'Schlafes Bruder' (Sleep's Brother) a village in the mountain was supposed to burn down in winter. The problem was that the same village needed to feature in later spring time scene. So the filmmaker could not afford to destroy the original. A special effects art director built 18 houses made of card board and painted them black. The roofs made of cheap wooden blinds were ignited and fire was filmed. Technicians then copied the pictures of the original village into the scene to make it look as if the whole village was on fire. In Ronald Emmerich's 'Independence Day' a spectacular effect was the destruction of White House by a gigantic space ship. Under the special effects art directors supervision, a dozen carpenters made a plaster model of the White House just four paces wide. Then they put in the glass windows, covered miniatures with furnitures and sewed tiny curtains, then the scene was shot with seven cameras in the night and three months of an art work was destroyed in seconds. And it became one of the most shown scenes of the film.

The art and craft of the art direction is perfected over the years. Continuous learning, reading, searching and travelling make an art director perfect in his art. It is a highly creative job that demands physical labour too. An art director should have an aesthetic sense as well as common sense. An all rounder director never underestimates the power of the wood and bricks. He can guide his art director and get the desired outputs. The reality factor is the most important thing for the art director. The interiors and walls should look real on screen.

Some examples of the best art direction

Ben Hur	(1959)
Gladiator	(2000)
Titanic	(1997)
English Patient	(1996)
Schindler's List	(1993)
Crouching Tiger Hidden Dragon	(2000)
Harry Potter films	(2001)
Shakespeare In Love	(1998)
Ten Commandments	(1956)
Gandhi	(1982)
Mughal-E-Azam	(1960/India)
Howards End	(1992)
Sleeply Hollow	(1999)
The Last Emperor	(1987)
Amadeus	(1984)
Fanny & Alexander	(1983)
Raiders of the Lost Ark	(1981)
Star Wars	(1977)
The Godfather II	(1974)
Patton	(1970)
Chicago	(2002)

12

The Costume

The costume gives meaning to the story. It tells the time of the story and suggests its genre. The perfect and the beautiful costumes decorate the actors and they decorate the screen. Thirty-two thousand costumes were used in 'Quo Vadis' (1951), Madonna changed her costumes eighty-five times and wore a total of thirty-nine hats in 'Evita' (1996). Hong Kong director Yon Fan lavished $ 100,000 on costumes for his film 'Peony Pavilion' (2001). All these facts suggest nothing but the importance and need of the costumes and their designers.

Like the art direction, the story decides the type of the costumes, its design and fabric. If it is historical or costume drama, the dress designer's job becomes tough and challenging. He has to do lots of research works about the colour, fabrics and designs of that period. Each and every character has to be given due importance according to their shape of body and character. The costumes of the king, queen, soldiers and ministers should take the viewers in the past. Though dress designers have liberty in dealing with the past. This liberty gives the dress designers the freedom to be different. The imagination, creation and vision coupled with hardwork make a dress designer different from others. A good costume designer is always in demand. The director should give freedom to his designer for optimum results. No creative person can perform well under pressure.

A good designer knows his job very well. If he is preparing the uniforms for World War II soldiers, he knows that they should be worn out, weary and dirty. The colours and fabrics are very important for showing the regal splendour of the Roman empire. A costume helps an actor to feel his character and perform well. And the viewers feel the psychology of the characters. No auteur can start his film unless he is satisfied with the costumes of the film.

Costume continuity is another aspect to be looked upon. Continuity girls and boys have to write down all details about the colours, of the costumes wore by actors while shooting. Any fault will result in continuity jerk. Still photographs of the shots definitely help in avoiding continuity faults.

Once the director finalises the costumes of the film, dress designer starts his work. He hires tailors, embroiders to get the costumes ready. It is a very difficult and artful job. Devoted filmmakers and designers roam around the different parts of the world to buy desired clothes. Historical, religious, supernatural and fantasy films are more demanding for a particular kind of clothes and patterns. Nothing can be compromised. If the need is of worn out clothes, the designer has to stress them and that requires loads of work. They are put in boilers, bleached, go through razors and graters, even sometimes assistants have to jump on them out of frustration to give them the bloody worn outlook.

Few examples of the best films in costume designing

Ben Hur	(1959)
Braveheart	(1995)
Titanic	(1997)
Saving Private Ryan	(1998)
The Untouchables	(1987)
The Ten Commandments	(1956)
Gladiator	(2000)
Moulin Rouge	(2001)
Shakespeare In Love	(1998)
Last Man Standing	(1996)
Elizabeth	(1998)
Amistaad	(1997)
The Wings Of the Dove	(1997)
All About Eve	(1950)

Gandhi	(1982)
Henry V	(1989)
The Last Emperor	(1987)
Amadeus	(1984)
Fanny And Alexander	(1983)
Chicago	(2002)

13

The Make-Up

In documentary and non-fiction films, make-up is avoided to maintain the realism. But for fiction films, make-up is an integral part. And the shots are not canned till the make-up is perfect. Religious, fantasy, sci-fi, war and horror movies heavily depend on make-up. The characters, created and visualized by the writer can become alive only with the help of the make-up. A normal actor without make up cannot play Dracula or an alien. The specialities and technicalities are becoming more complex day by day. Special types of make-up are required to create different characters. Make-up is another art like several other arts to help films made.

John Travolta has to sit for hours to get ready with make-up for his role in 'Battlefield Earth'. Turning a human actor into Dracula or an alien takes much time, energy and demands a certain type of creativity. Imagination rules the world of make-up. We cannot forget Christopher Lee playing Dracula, but did we know, how much creativity and labour were spent on giving life to the characters like that. It is the wonder of make-up that turned humans into apes in 'Planet of the Apes'.

Every film demands different applications of the make-up. In a war film, soldier's faces are smeared with black powder and dry blood. False teeth and nails are joined to give the look of the ghost in horror films. Sometimes it becomes difficult to recognize the actor behind the make-up. All dramas, plays and films can never underestimate the value, and the power of the great make-up. It gives reality to the films.

Few best make-up films

The Lord of The Rings (Trilogy)	(2001, 2002, 2003)
English Patient	(1996)
Men In Black I & II	(1997-2002)
Planet of The Apes	(2001)
Elizabeth	(1998)
The Nutty Professor	(1996)
Mrs. Doubt Fire	(1993)
Topsy Turvy	(1999)
Driving Miss Daisy	(1989)
The Fly	(1985)
Amadeus	(1984)
Quest For Fire	(1982)
Frida	(2002)

14

The Music

Music is the third dimension. It is older to films. It soothes humans, fills ears with ecstasy, even entertains animals. All living organisms love music. There is no world without it. It gives you feeling of an ideal world, brotherhood, humanity, love, affection and takes you close to the spiritualism. It is pure and always blowing with the wind. It connects to your hearts and all your emotions rise up, you begin to feel.

Films are basically story telling. All filmmakers are story tellers. A story gathers more affecting power if it is supported with the magic of music. There are different tunes for different emotions. Music enhances the power of the films. Even in silent movie era, music had tremendous role to play as there was no dialogue in those films. Since ancient age, humans had invented so many kinds of musical instruments to entertain themselves. Today a disc may contain several thousands tunes and pieces, but in earlier times, a music director had to sit with his artists to compose the entire music of the film.

Director Ridley Scott had used few snatches of wailing chants by the Senegal Vocalist Baba Maal along with the main background score in his war film 'Black Hawk Down' (2001). The effect is that the horror of war becomes almost palpable. The magical background score by James Horner for the film, 'Titanic' (1997) had enthralled the viewers around the globe. Music tremendously conveys the message told by the writer.

There are four elements of a film — visuals, dialogue, music and effect. Dialogues and effects can be removed but visuals and music are the integral parts of a film. Music adds the extra dimension to the story. It is a creator of the mood and emotions. It makes viewers involve in the story. Mental condition of the actor can be clearly expressed with the help of music.

Once the film is edited, a VHS or CD is given to the music director. He takes it to his house, watches many times and visualizes the music pieces, write down the correct ones for different scenes. The director listens those pieces, makes changes if necessary. After his approval music director records the whole background score with the help of composer and recordists. The creation of the music is the job of highly innovative and imaginative persons.

In 1897, when Lumiere Brothers began showing their films, they hired saxophone quartlet to play along. In the early days of cinema projection, cinema halls used to hire orchestra to play along with the silent films. They were paid for providing live music. In those days distributors had to supply a set of band parts along with cans of films. Around 1931, the two most talented music directors, landed in Hollywood. Max Steiner and Wolfgang Korngold joined RKO and Warner Bros. They wrote excellent musics for several films. Though their music was little distracting but it laid the basic foundation in the field of music writing.

A right piece of the music always carries an impact. Though the power of silence cannot be ignored. Some scenes, when kept silent, make more impressions. It is not always better to fill the music all over the scenes. Music should never distract the viewers from the main visuals. Most of the dialogues should have no music at all. Try to explore the silence within the dialogues. Use pauses. General background music must be in keeping with the overall tenor of the film. Anything with a strong local style should be avoided until it relates specifically to the setting. Each piece of the music must be in harmony with the visuals.

When the music director creates all pieces, they were timed and marked. The next step is to compile a cue-sheet indicating where the musical changes are to take place. It is the aesthetic sense of the director that guides the music director how and when to begin the music and where to end on a particular scene. As long as the players are talking there should be no music. The moment one exits and walks or drives away music should begin and end on next scene. Where there is no dialogue, there is music or silence. Normally the music ends with an abrupt effect like the opening sound of the door, bell or stopping the car.

The primary purpose of all music is to tell the character's mood and emotion. A war scene can be beautifully shown with greater effect when there is only fighting, killing and shooting, the sound effects stop and music takes over. And after sometime it ends with the start of the sound. This effect can be seen in Fellowship Of the Ring (2001) and Saving Private Ryan (1998).

The location of the film decides the content of the music. A film set in Africa may have local tunes along with the main background score. Tragic, comic and romantic scenes have to be dealt differently. A mating or sexual scene can be emphasized by the music of drum's light beats. And a chase sequence can be given more power with large drum beats. The violin and mouthorgan are always used for showing grim and tragic stories. A director must have a deep sense of various types of music and the idea of start and end.

Few examples of the Best Dramatic Scores

Crouching Tiger Hidden Dragon (2000), English Patient (1996), Schindler's List (1993), Titanic (1997), American Beauty (1999), Traffic (2000), The Fellowship of The Rings (2001), Life Is Beautiful (1998), The Cider House Rules (1999), L.A. Confidential (1997), Goodwill Hunting (1997), Amistad (1997), Dances with the Wolves (1990), Il Postino (1995), The Red Violin (1999), The Godfather II (1974).

Few examples of the Best Musical Score

Shakespeare In Love (1998), The Full Monty (1997), Moulin Rouge (2001), As Good As It Gets (1997), Frida (2002).

15

The Special Effects

Since the very early days of cinema, filmmakers and other technicians had been continuously searching the ways to overwhelm the viewers, to make the magical films with the help of on shooting tricks, and studio gimmics. As the cinema progressed, new inventions and technologies came into practice. These technologies gave shape to the maker's imaginations.

The real age of CGI (Computer Generated Shots) started with 'Star Wars' in 1977. George Lucus, the father of the special effects, started the trend of real special effects into the films.

Just see 'Dinosaur' and you will soon forget that it is animated. Did anyone know that James Cameron had used 550 computer generated shots, that looked so real and so natural in his film 'Titanic' (1997). ILM (Industrial Lights And Magic) is the mother of all special effects. Stär Wars, Aliens, Abyss, Titanic, Twister and the list is endless. It was impossible to make films like Twister and Jurassic Park without the help of special effects.

For more than twenty years, George Lucus and the technical wizards at ILM have literally changed the face of the movie making with their stunning, often unbelievable visual effects. During this period ILM virtually redefined visual effects and blazed a trail into the digital realm, weaving together the intricate crafts model making and compositingly creating models and optical effects. ILM focused on technical innovations and had remarkably clear vision of leaving nothing to one's imagination.

On an average, American studios today invest $ 53 million in the production of a film. Around one-third of it goes towards

VFX. The special effects have become essential for almost all major Hollywood films. It is the power of special effects that make the Hollywood films different and crowd pullers around the world. The art lies in perfectly integrating these special effects so as to leave the viewers wondering about what he saw. All visual effects wizards try to explore all the possibilities available to a scene. They develop different logistic programme to be used for many films.

The optical bank in the copying workshop has been constantly replenished with digital processing for the last many years. Even pro-technicians responsible for explosions and fire on the sets have to keep up with the competition from digital effect. The best example for the highly competitive computer artist was the comic film 'Spawn'. The story was based on the agents from hell and abounded with fire, breathtaking morphing, expensive digital effects, animatronics and digitally composed, futuristic backgrounds. The hero wore a costume that stuck to his body like a second skin. His computer generated armour consisted of trillions of nerve contacts that converted his thoughts immediately into actions.

The most frequent tasks for digital work in film production are not spectacular effects, but the touch up work removing disturbing picture elements, correcting colour and light or merging synthetic picture elements with photo chemical directed scenes. For historical scenes, this would mean replacing modern street lamps or advertising banners on the screen. Similarly we can place together real camera shots with computer generated shots by using the technique of overlapping points; picture for picture.

Not only does VFX influence the aesthetics of the film; it also changes the entire production process considerably thus demanding the special knowledge and equipment. Once the storyboard is complete, it has to be decided whether a computer generated model will be more economical than actually creating and working with a miniature model; you require a lot of light, a relatively large team on the set, and a studio to direct scenes with models. For VFX productions, the locations are measured in advance and set replicated on computer accordingly. All actors are then filmed in front of a blue screen. But for explosions, real models are used to give more realistic results.

In Hollywood miniatures are no longer used for spaceships, background scenarios, aliens or unusual objects. Computer graphics are increasingly being used for this purpose. The movie director resorts to animatronics only when a close shot is required for details and high resolutions. However, for wide range camera settings, the effects specialists often prefer computer variants so that the size of the objects can be changed easily.

Planning and transplantation of visual effects can still be risky. There is always the danger that the spectator will detect the 'cover-up'. Ninety per cent of the visual effects are not perfect, but that is something only specialists can detect. Often it is lack of time or poor strategizing that let a digital effect escape perfection. Which is why VFX scenes should be used only when they can be executed perfectly.

The movement of the camera is very revolutionary in VFX films. In 'Godzilla' the effects specialists figured out how they could place the iguana in the scene of Brooklyn Bridge, so that the size ratios would match; they had an extra team solely to observe and check for precise laser measurements, right from the width of a zebra crossing stipe to the garbage van. Later they fed this data into the computer to create space-specified so that Godzilla did not run amok through the buildings.

The sinking of the Titanic : Sitting on the edge of their seats, millions of wide-eyed people watched actors skid on the decks, slide down ropes and in despair, jump off the ship from a height of 15 metres into ice-cold waters, a body hitting one of the masts jutting out of the deck as the Titanic tilted. Everything seemed so real. Director James Cameron made several real actors dressed in different costumes, act in different positions, some of them boxing each other, some jumping off a pile of cartons. These movements were simultaneously recorded using Motion Capture. Each digital actor could then be directed individually on the computer. This led to an achieved of several well directed virtual people, each acting differently. To show thousand people for each scene Cameron had used crowd control. Simply you do not pay virtual actors. In 'Titanic' atmospheric effects and lighting were digitally edited to augment the impression of the Arctic chill after the ship sinks.

Visual effects today bring more than defects. And the requirement of the date is : To make (non-virtual) filmed scenes seem even more real. In other words, to 'perfect' existing reality. Intelligent digital actors are a rage today. Now a computer animated young woman can walk up and down on a catwalk. Syntheticised animation is the future. The fundamental idea during programme development is the synergy of two new techniques movement synthesis in authenticity, based on movement algorithms.

From robotics and dynamic behavioural programming of the events at the other end, and with the advances in hardware and software technology, this technique can also be used for producing feature films. All a director has to do is change a situation and subsequently the digital actors will start walking, talking and moving independently. But George Lucus, the creator of the greatest number of digital actors, has denied the danger of digital actors taking place of human actors. Spielberg has termed it as a non-issue. Though in some cases virtual actors can be fitted, along with human actors. The wizards at ILM studio showed Tom Hanks meeting president John F. Kennedy (handshake and all) in 1994 film 'Forrest Gump'. In this film the computer graphics technology was harnessed to blend old footage with new films.

The technology is also a blessing for avid movie fans, the impossible is now made possible, on film. As more producers adopt new CGI techniques, we will see scenes that would have been impossible to enact in real life. The realism factor is the most important issue. The viewers are bored with video game like tons of special effect in star wars films. Film producers have to understand that there should be a balance between drama and visual effects and directors should do justice to both without sacrificing one for another. 'Jurassic Park' and 'Titanic' are the great examples of drama and visual effects.

CGI Techniques

Animatronics : The creation and use of computer controlled hydraulic dolls in movies.

Blue screen : A technique of first filming the character's motion in front of a blue background, and the scene later being filled in digitally.

CGI (Computer generated imaging) : Expression used for the process of editing and generating pictures digitally.

- **Crowd control :** You do not really need to shoot an extra individually in front of a background that will not be used in the film to fit in the miniature model later. The person is digitally duplicated. In short, you need only a hundred people to show ten thousand people.
- **Digital compositing :** Merges together optically filmed frames and scenes generated on the computer.
- **Motion capture :** The process of capturing movements using sensors. Natural movements flows are recorded on a computer and can then be transferred to computer created artificial figures in this way.
- **Morphing :** The process of merging forms or pictures (even those produced on PC).
- **Storyboard :** The term for an illustrated script, where the description of each scene involves hand made drawings.
- **Special effects :** (SFX) Today SFX broadly stands for tricks produced directly on the set, can deal with sound, light, props et al.
- **VFX :** Visual special effects, created exclusively on a computer.
- **Wire frames :** A mesh created on a computer, forming the basis for generating an artificial character which can be textured; its movements controlled on this mesh.

Milestones in Digital Film Effects

- **Hunger (1974) :** First fully animated figurative film ever made using morphing technique.

- **Star Wars (1977, Dir : George Lucus) :** The first movie to use vast amount of special effects, heralding the need for a new category in the Academy Awards, which it won for Death Star simulation.
- **Star Trek II : Wraths of Khan (1982) :** The first all digital computer generated image sequence for a motion picture.
- **Young Sherock Holmes (1985) :** Stained glass knight sequence. First computer generated character in a feature film.
- **Willow (1988) :** First feature film to use digital morphing technology.
- **Indiana Jones and The Last Crusade (1989, Dir : Steven Spielberg) :** First all digital composite for a feature film.
- **Terminator II : Judgment Day (1991, Dir : James Cameron) :** An otherwise boring Arnold Schwarznegger battles the T-1000, a robot formed from liquid metal right before your eyes.
- **Jurassic Park (1993, Dir : Steven Spielberg) :** One of the most successful films of all time, thanks to computer controlled hydraulic dinosaur dolls and computer generated lizards.
- **Forrest Gump (1994, Dir : Robert Zemeckis) :** Invisible 3D and 2D digital effects, blended new footage with old and removed an actor's leg.
- **Toy Story (1995) :** The first fully computer generated animation feature film to incorporate realistic 3D computer modelling.
- **Twister (1996) :** The first nature catastrophe film to make massive use of visual effects.
- **Titanic (1997, Dir : James Cameron) :** Large scale use of motion capture and 3D digital crowd for extras.

Oscar for the Special Visual Effects

- 1976 King Kong And Logan's Run
- 1975 The Hindenburg
- 1974 Earthquake

- 1972 The Poseidon Adventure
- 1971 Bed Knobs And Broomsticks
- 1970 Tora! Tora! Tora!
- 1969 Marooned
- 1968 2001 : A Space Odyssey
- 1967 Doctor Do Little
- 1966 Fantastic Voyage
- 1965 Thunder Ball
- 1964 Marry Poppins
- 1963 Cleopatra

OSCAR Winners for the 'Best Visual Effects'

- 1977 Star Wars
- 1978 Superman
- 1979 Alien
- 1980 The Empire Strikes Back
- 1981 Raiders of The Lost Ark
- 1982 E.T. The Extra Terrestrial
- 1983 Return of the Jedi
- 1984 Indiana Jones And The Temple Of Doom
- 1985 Cocoon
- 1986 Aliens
- 1987 Inner Space
- 1988 Who Framed Roger Rabbit?
- 1989 The Abyss
- 1990 Total Recall
- 1991 Terminator II : Judgment Day
- 1992 Death Becomes Her
- 1993 Jurassic Park
- 1994 Forrest Gump
- 1995 Babe
- 1996 Independence Day
- 1997 Titanic

- 1998 What Dreams May Come
- 1999 Matrix
- 2000 Gladiator
- 2001 Fellowship Of The Ring (The Lord of the Rings)
- 2002 The Lord of The Rings : The Two Towers.

16

THE STUNTS

Films are about motion and emotion. Without motion it becomes a play. It is the thrill of action, punches, crashing, chase, bullets and gravity defying stunts that enthralls the viewers not dialogues. Dynamism is the key of all filmings. And stunts are the instruments of the dynamism. People will never loose interest in action films. Though all films contain few scenes of actions, but many films exclusively belong to this genre.

Filming Action

The Choreography of action is the toughest and the highest risky job in the process of filmmaking. It consumes too much time, money, energy and injuries. The film director has to rely heavily on his action manager and stunt co-ordinator for filming action sequences. Too much rehearsals are needed for the perfect final shot. Filming of action is the job of so many specialists. There is always a danger of lives getting lost. Major actors are not supposed to do their own stunts. Duplicates are used. Many famous action sequences were directed by world famous action directors. The most memorable chariot race sequence of 'Ben Hur' was directed by veteran stuntman Yakima Kanut.

Chase

Every director confronts with chase. It may be a chase of men, vehicles or helicopters. The well choreographed chase sequences always captivate the viewer's minds. To make the chase more exciting, director should have a great sense of geography. Chase towards the camera is always more enthralling. The screen direction should be maintained, but it is not mandatory. Ben Hur has the best chariot race and

Matrix Reloaded has the best car chase in the history of motion picture.

Stunts

Film stars' lives cannot be put on danger. Though they may tempt to do their own actions, but it is not a good signal, stunts must be performed by the specialists. They know their jobs very well. Crashing, chasing, falling from the horses, jumping off the bikes are better done by the stuntmen. All the stunts demand skilled professionals, rehearsals, meticulous preparation and utmost safety and security measures. Any mistake can kill. All stuntmen are insured. They are highly paid for putting their lives at risk. Six stuntmen broke their ribs while jumping off the tilted Titanic in 'Titanic'. And many stuntmen died while filming other major action films. Many doctors remain on the sets while shooting. Jackie Chan, who performs his own stunts is the most injured actor around. Bruce Lee's son was accidentally shot dead while filming his last movie after 'The Crow'.

Stunts are charged according to the complexities of the danger. Stuntmen charge per take. That is why even rehearsals are recorded. There is no second chance of filming action shots. The burnt sets cannot be rebuilt. Many cameras are used for the recordings of the blast, falling cars and even chase. All takes must be kept safe for the editor's purpose.

The ground breaking moment in the history of action filmings was noticed when the director David Russel used a real corpse to be shot. He filmed a bullet going through the real dead body in his film 'Three Kings' (1999). The preview audience liked the close up of a man's innards being destroyed by gunfire. They said it was fascinating. Today the visual effects wizards are trying to develop the stunts prototype, so that one day virtual stunt artists can replace their flesh and blood counterparts in performing otherwise deadly feats.

Few Best Action films

All James Bond Films, Die Hard (1988) El CID (1961), Indiana Jones Films, Top Gun (1986), The Towering Inferno (1974), Con-air (1997), The Rock (1996), Last Man Standing (1997), Desperado (1995), Terminator II (1991), Terminator 3

(2003), Face Off (1997), Universal Soldier (1994), Speed (1995), The Fugitive (1993), Lethal Weapon (1998), True Lies (1995), Matrix Films (1999), Crouching Tiger Hidden Dragon (2000), Unforgiven (1960), Mission Impossible II (2000), Rambo III, Ben Hur (1959), Saving Private Ryan (1998), Pearl Harbor (2001).

17

THE PLAY AND THE FILM

The play celebrates the joys and fears of humanity. Theatre artists perform on behalf of their community. While films make you feel at the middle of your life. They too reflect the society and its culture. They mirror the society. With the invention of the medium called cinema, the eternal charm of the theatre started diminishing. Films became more approachable, likeable and life-like. The audience once loyal to the theatre, became loyal to the new medium. Cinema halls became the shrines of their worship. The protagonist of the films caused viewers to identify themselves with him. The first time seeing something moving on dead screen captivated their minds. It was a magical invention. Theatre has nothing but the actors, lines and a music, while films contained talents and technology. It was more life-like. That is why it came, it saw and it won. And it is still reigning. Can we still not call it an art. In reality it is above all arts. Because it combines all arts of the past and presents.

But both the film and the theatre, deal with the tragedy and the comedy. That are the basic two conditions of human life. Tragedy concerns the situation of a man naked and alone against the backcloth of universal eternity while comedy concerns a man's situation fully clothed in company against a back cloth of his society, domestic, local or national. The play is talent while the film is the result of the talent and technology, film's aesthetic and artistic importance rests in what the viewers see, what they hear is underscoring. A play is words and exaggerated physical actings, while a film is moving images and restrained performances.

The other differences :

- The play demands several rehearsals as there is no place for retakes while in films as many retakes are possible as the directors or the cameraman wants.
- You can cheat the live audience with a wrong look. But you cannot cheat the camera with same.
- Play is words. Film is movement.
- Play is loud because the audience watch it in master shot only, while the film has an arsenal of close-ups. Even a raised eyebrow is suggestive in films.
- Play cannot be preserved and needs to be staged every time it is shown to the live audience. Films are made once and can be shown in any number of time and places simultaneously.

But even today many people love the play more than films. Particularly actors, who come from theatres, always love the challenge of performing before live audience. Their first love is always theatre. The greatest contribution of theatre to the film is the supply of great actors. Theatre actors are more confident, know different schools of actings and take up their characters to greater heights. But one thing they have to understand and practice is the difference between screen acting and stage acting. Once they adapt themselves to this difference, they can become greats. The theatre has supplied actors like Marlon Brando, Al Pacino, Ben Kingsley and Robert De Niro. They know the difference between screen and stage acting and are now acknowledged as great actors.

The play is primarily written for stage. They can be better enjoyed on stage. But many plays including Shakespeare's have found place on screen. The translation of plays into films is tough and a writer always fails to do that. The play is meant to be read or staged not to be filmed. Few translations are great, others are unjust. Victor Hugo's Les Miserable has been staged for nearly a thousands times over the years and around the globe. It was also made into films, but it cannot match the live performance.

18

THE DOCUMENTARY

Documentary is the documentation of facts. Films are fiction, documentaries give us informations about people and places, animals, earth, science and all facts of our life and the world. The visuals in the documentary are supported by music and voice over. It has a fix goal and a message.

The process : Unlike film, documentary does not need any false staging or choreography of scenes. It records the real happenings and actions. The whole purpose is to teach the viewers about certain thing. There is no unreal things in documentary.

Idea and research : Once you get an idea that can teach as well as entertain, you start research works. And extensive research includes meeting people, recording their voice, writing down facts, travelling to the locations, looking for the best shots, getting permissions for shooting.

Budget : The content decides the budget. And the maker has to work according to the decided budget. All the possible expenditures are chalked out and a great planning on the stage of pre-production always help to save money and time. If the director is the producer of his own programme, he will certainly have more creative freedom.

Goal : The goal must be very clear. Who are your target audience, what are you going to teach and how will you do that. Everything should never be confusing. Remember, if you are trying to reach all, you will reach none.

Treatment : A tentative narration is written as soon as the research is complete. The makers should have a great sense of how to treat his subject in an interesting and informative manner. The beginning, middle and the end are very carefully planned. Dry things in the beginning can kill the viewer's interest. The same way a bad end will never inspire repeat watching. If the visuals are boring, no interest will take place. Even words however good they are can never lift bad and boring visuals.

Shooting : If you want to preserve your programme for years, use 16 mm or 8 mm films. Some heavy budget documentaries use 35 mm film. The quality of picture, its resolution and aging depend on films you use. 35 mm is the best film. Try to get the best shots, use psychological angling and place the camera on right positions. The psychological effects must be achieved, but only few makers succeed in achieving this effect. If you are making a documentary on war-torn country, take long reaction close ups of the aged people, children and even empty stomach animals. The deserted and bombed buildings provide a meaningful background. The shots of the rising smokes, hopeless faces and dry breads are the powerful images which nobody can afford not to see. Extreme close-ups of trembling hands and tears will have equal impact. Avoid verete (just point and shoot).

As the shooting ends, you have to check the footage, classify OK/NG shots, rewrite the narration, choose graphics and titles, record the narration (hire best voice-over artists), edit, record music and have final mix.

Music and Narration : Narration is the backbone of a documentary. It gives meaning to the visuals. But it is not better to have too much of talk and less visuals. Anything that bores, should be avoided. Sometimes visuals say everything. It is good to use pauses. Narration by a good artist will always help the content. He knows where to give power to the words and the ups and downs. Many documentaries are made without the narration, but their visuals and music are so powerful that nobody looses interest and can understand everything without the words. A Francis Ford Coppola produced documentary 'Kaonikowatsi' (life out of balance) has no narration. It has just visuals and a background music. It is one of the most expensive documentaries ever made. The visuals are so powerful and the music is so magical that it makes us spellbound. It tells the story of the U.S. gone out of balance. A right piece of music always emphasizes the images. A tiger chasing a deer can be given more power by the music of drumbeats. But the music should remain supportive only, it must not weaken the power of images.

Subjects : Everything is a subject for the documentary. There are political issues, news and current affairs, sports, education, information, corporates, biographies, mythological, tourism, philosophy, music, sales, and promotions, wild-life subjects that can be made into documentaries.

Few Noteworthy Documentaries

- Man with a Movie Camera (Dziga Vertov 1928)
- Coalface (Alberto Cavalcanti 1935)
- High School (Frederick Wiseman 1968)
- Roger and Me (Michael Moore 1989)
- The Thin Blue Line (Errol Morris 1988)
- Kaonikowatsi (Francis Ford Cappola)
- Aftermath : The Remnants of War (Daniel Sekulick 2001)
- Murder on A Sunday Morning (2001)
- I am a Promise : The Children of Stanton (1993)
- The Last Days (1998)
- The Long Way Home (1997)
- Bowling for Columbine (2002)

Importance of Films Over Video tape

Film can reproduce feeling better than video. Film is less literal than video tape. It has much more of visceral quality to it. It enables you to get deeper into the people and the place. As a producer, shooting on film today makes the greatest amount of sense because it makes the best archival medium. You can scan film upto 4000 lines of resolution per frame. Try to have the greatest amount of compressed content resolution that we can capture, as we cannot anticipate what the future is going to bring.

19

Films on Mental Illness

All actors wish to play mentally challenged characters. Thus they win Oscars. Tom Hanks did that, Jack Nicholson did that and all others want to do too. In 'Forrest Gump' Tom Hanks is mentally challenged but he braved a slow mind and defective spine to emerge as a campus athlete, Vietnam war-hero, ping pong champion and even a multi millionaire who breeds shrimps. 'Forrest Gump' is a wonderful film but does it depict the life real way. It makes you believe in the impossible. Hollywood is famous for its unreal portrayal of mental illness. But it can make only something that can sell, not bore.

Apart from a few films like 'Rain Man' and 'Girl interrupted' which treat mental illness sensitively and portray it like it is, the majority do more damage than good. Roughly, one in every 20 films has a character with some sort of mental illness, but very few directors bother to consult professionals to ensure that the portrayal is authentic. Most film use dramatic licence to the detriment of authenticity. Given that the average person's understanding of, and attitude to mental illness is derived almost entirely from Hollywood's offerings and not from psychology, journals, the role of cinema as a disseminator assumes almost frightening importance. If anybody hears about OCD (Obsessive Compulsive Disorder) he immediately thinks Jack Nicholson in 'As Good As It Gets', which fortunately was an authentic portrayal.

On the other hand the word psycho brings to mind images of violence, blood and murder as shown in Hitchcock's 'Psycho'. It may be an excellent film, but psychologically it is flawed. Because it makes the connection that mental illness is dangerous which is a sweeping generalization. Another film

'Nightmare On Elm Street', which is a representative of a whole genre of slasher films, perpetrates the same mass murderer myth. Easily the most abused one is that mental illness results from some terrible childhood trauma or because of abusive parents. This allows directors the luxury of flashback. Childhood trauma could cause mental instability but not psychopathology.

'One Flew Over The Cuckoo's Nest' is a classic of this genre. In which Jack Nicholson plays an inmate of a mental asylum. He had to play a man faking madness except was his character really a mad man faking normal, Nicholson's performance brilliantly suggested both, giving the role the complexity author Ken Kensey intended in his book. So far, Jack Nicholson had played two mentally challenged characters and won Oscars for both his films.

In 'The Fisher King', the Schizophrenic protagonist has visual hallucinations of a white stallion charging down on him when, in fact schizophrenics have only auditory hallucinations known as voices in the head. White stallions may make for effective cinema but psychologically it is skewed. Despite its drawbacks and false portrayals, cinema serves as a social register that documents the ways in which mental illness has been treated down the decades from the horrific electric shocks and lobotomy days shown in 'Cuckoo's Nest' to the misuse of behaviours modification techniques in the violent film "A Clockwork Orange". In this cult film Stanely Kubrick shows how the protagonist Alex, who is addicted to violence, is sought to be cured of his addiction, by the method of reverse association he is repeatedly shown a video clip dripping with violence and is simultaneously injected to induce a feeling of severe nausea. It is an attempt to reprogramme him and neutralize his personality.

There are, of course, the flukes out of Hollywood's nest the few well researched films like Rain Man where autism in an adult is sensitively portrayed (He is not crazy and he is not retarded). In Natural Born Killers, the thorny issue of culpability whether or not a mentally disturbed person has the cognitive capacity to distinguish between right and wrong — is powerfully dealt with. The amoral perspective of the two serial killers is brought out in the chilling lines —

"Insane, no psychotic, yes. Mickey and Mallary know the difference between right and wrong. They just do not give a damn."

Equally chilling though in a heart breaking way, are the lines from the Henry and Jane Fonda classic 'On Golden Pond', which is stalked by Alzhiemer's disease, easily one of the most brutal illness to affect the brain. Sometime a single line in the film is more insightful than two hours of the film. The tragedy of fading memory is brought out in the following dialogue : 'You want my number? What for? Oh to call me. Well I don't know, it got 'one' in it somewhere'. Russel Crow played Schizophrenic John Nash who is a nobel Prize Winner in 'A Beautiful Mind'. The emotionally handled screenplay and a remarkably restrained performance by Crowe and Ron Howard's great execution won 4 Academy Awards including the Best Picture and the Best Director in 2001. In one scene, he is shown holding his child in his arms. The kid is crying and Crowe is not affected, he continues to sit like a dummy without stopping the kid to cry. That makes an impression on the viewers. All aspects of the disease are brought out beautifully by the Crowe's performance.

The Best Illness Films

- Rain Man (1988)
- One Flew Over The Cuckoo's Nest (1975)
- A Beautiful Mind (2001)
- Forrest Gump (1994)
- As Good As It Gets (1997)
- On Golden Pond (1981)
- A Clockwork Orange (1971)
- The Fisher King (1991)
- Psycho 1960)
- Girl Interrupted (1999)
- Natural Born Killers (1995)

20

THE MOST UNDERRATED FILMS

Some films are made by the deep people for the deep people. General viewers will never like those films. If given the choice, he will prefer 'Godzilla' instead of 'The Thin Red Line'. But then there are few filmmakers, who like to make only those movies, which they believe in. They satisfy their creative instincts instead of satisfying the producers and the general viewers. One who is a real cinephile, can watch their films. Others may ignore the list. But one generation's oversight is bound to be another generation's discovery. Real good movies never loose their smell.

Here, there is a list of the films. Some are underrated. Some are overlooked. Some unsung. All crying for rediscovery. Commercial success is not the criteria for selection. We have seen that while real gems pass by, we make song and dance about mediocre to downright bad movies. There are some overrated films — 'Life Is Beautiful', 'Saving Private Ryan', 'As Good As It Gets', 'Unforgiven', etc. though they are very good but they are certainly overrated too.

Underrated Films

"The Thin Red Line" (U.S.)
Dir : Terance Mallick
Year : 1998
Cast : George Clooney, Sean Pen, John Travolta

A group of soldiers change, suffer and ultimately make essential discoveries about themselves during the fierce World War II battle of Guadal canal. The story is dark and depressing. Nominated for 8 Academy Awards but lost all.

"Caligula" (Italy)
Dir : Tinto Brass
Year : 1980
Cast : Peter O'Toole, John Gielgud, Hellen Mirren

Caligula is more than a glorified porn film. It is a story about Roman Emperor Caligula. It has sexual mixture including incest, homosexuality, bestiality and sadomasochism. Apart from the sex, Caligula is a cinematic underlining of the statement that power corrupts and absolute power corrupts absolutely.

"Truly, Madly, Deeply" (UK)
Dir : Anthony Minghella
Year : 1991
Cast : Juliet Stevenson, Alan Rickman

It is an unusual love story. The movie is as good as the title. Romantic, poetic, funny, whimsical, original and passionate. This film is directed by one of the most poetic auteur of romance and tragedy. 'The English Patient' director Anthony Minghella handled the delicate sense of fatal, obsessive romanticism. The dialogues are totally wet in romance.

"Heavenly Creatures"
Dir : Peter Jackson
Year : 1994
Cast : Kate Winslet, Melanie Lynkey

'Heavenly Creatures' delves on a dark fantasy of two teenage girls. The two girls meet in a school, create a secret fantasy world and become obsessive about it and each other.

The Quick And The Dead
Dir : Sam Raimi
Cast : Russel Crowe, Gene Hackman

The most underrated eastern movie. It is about a mean town, ruled by Gene Hackman who makes money by shooting contests. He is unbeaten as a Shooter till a gang of five reaches to the town.

"Cape Fear"
Dir : Martin Scorsese
Year : 1991
Cast : Robert De Niro

The most neglected film of Martin Scorsese, 'Cape Fear' deals with a criminal who feels he has been shortchanged by the lawyer who put him in jail and is out to seek revenge on him and his family.

"Batman 2"
Dir : Tim Burton
Year : 1992
Cast : Michael Keaton, Jack Nicholson, Danny De vito

'Batman 2' is the film, where Burton's craft is in full development. Jack Nicholson plays the joker. In 'Batman 2' there is always an undercurrent of sorrow. The Penguin played by Danny is one of the bad guys. Burton evokes the feeling of loneliness and pain.

"Clueless"
Dir : Amy Heckerling
Year : 1995
Cast : Alicia Silverstone

Heckerling's savvy, astute, witty, deft social observations of teenage school girls are remarkably accurate. Alicia plays super-rich Beverly Hills School girl who is totally 'Clued in'. The movie is full of 90s pop cultural references. It is a popular, critically appreciated film but dismissed by the majority as a light film.

'Bullet In The Head" (Hong Kong)
Dir : John Woo
Year : 1990
Cast : Tony Leong

John Woo directed 'Bullet In the Head' before making action blockbusters like 'Broken Arrow', MI-2, Face Off and 'Hard Target'. It is a Vietnam War movie. The year is 1967 and three small time scamsters, led by Tony Leong, get into trouble with the mob in Hong Kong. Soon they are put through a series of harrowing experiences as the Vietnam conflict starts. They have to choose between their lives and their friendship.

"The Color Purple"
Dir : Steven Spielberg
Year : 1985
Cast : Whoopi Goldberg, Danny Glover

The Eleven Oscar nominated and without winning any of them, 'Color Purple' remains one of the most underrated films. It is a cinematic adaptation of Alice Walker's Pulitzer Prize winning novel. Whoopy Goldberg, an African-American woman, who grows up in the rural south, was made pregnant by her own father, gets married to a cruel man. She looses both children and ability to bear children. And yet this woman endures, and in the end, prevails.

"Vive L'Amour" (Taiwan)
Dir : Tsai Ming Liang
Year : 1994
Cast : Lee Kang Shey, Yang Kuei-Mei

The film deals with urban mayhem, sexual frustration masturbation and depression. Lee Kang sells funeral urns, Yang, a woman who is a real estate broker and Chen is a vendor of street clothes. The three characters somehow rendezvous in an apartment that is put up for sale. The film examines their feelings of loneliness and functional existence.

"Babette's Feast" (Denmark)
Dir : Gabriel Axel
Year : 1987 (Oscar for the Best Foreign Picture)
Cast : Martine, Filippa

It is a spiritual parable. It is not easy to fathom the actions, thoughts and motives of the two beautiful, gifted devout sisters when they give up love, fame and money for god. Even their powerful suitors, at the end, feel that it is they who are lonely and unfortunate and the girls are still loved by the masses. The most memorable film by Axel.

"La Petite Lisa" / Little Lisa (France)
Dir : Jean Gremillon
Year : 1930
Cast : Nodia Sibirskaia

It is one of the finest examples of poetic realism. But it remains grossly underrated, even among the cognoscenti. This unconventional, psychologically charged melodrama has achieved its cult status among the connoisseurs of ghettoized cinemas. Inspired by D.W. Griffith's silent classic 'Broken Blossoms' (1919), the film revolves around a vulnerable young girl Nadia whose attempt to rise out of her deprived and impoverished origin, culminates in a tragedy.

"Girl on The Bridge" (France)
Dir : Patrice Leconte
Year : 1998
Cast : Chanteuse, Vanessa Paradis

It is a tribute a Fellini's 'La Strada'. The girl is a model. She is standing on a titular bridge ready to jump into the Seine when fate intervenes in the form of a knife thrower Daniel Auteuil. His exhortations fail and she jumps anyway. So does he, to save her. And thus begins a very strange relationship. She becomes his target. They find that anything they do together is touched by magic and turns wonderful.

"Destiny" (Egypt)
Dir : Youssef Chahine
Year : 1997

It is all about the true Islam of tolerance, freedom of expression and ideas. When Chahine's earlier work 'L' émigré' was banned, he immediately thought of 12th century Andalusia, where Muslims, Christians and Jews lived together. And put all his thoughts in this film, which is about Islam's Golden Age, about Andalusia Islam, the true Islam of tolerance.

"The Browning Version" (U.S.)
Dir : Mike Figgis
Year : 1994
Cast : Albert Finney

It is an adaptation of Terrence Rattigan's play about a failed schoolteacher. The film is highly honest, restrained and finally wrenching. It is a perfect antidote to the overrated 'Dead Poet's Society'. Albert Finney plays a schoolteacher of Latin and Greek who discovers in his last year, that he has failed to inspire his students. His terrific and highly restrained performance leaves us spellbound.

"Ecstasy of Angels" (Japan)
Dir : Kaji Waka Matsu
Year : 1972

The film deals with a group of young radical extremists, all of whom are known by names of days like Monday, Friday etc., who are betrayed by some of their group while raiding an US arms base. It also deals with how the ruling powers try to neutralise marginal elements who could destabilize society. There are enough of sex and violence.

"Saint Jack" (Singapore)
Dir : Peter Bogdanovich
Year : 1979
Cast : Jack Flowers (Ben Gazzara)

It is a memorable film on a bygone, spicy Singapore. The movie was released and promptly banned by the shocked Singaporeans. Thus the little film was lost to the general public. Jack is a pimp, he is a cynical American, who runs a small whorehouse. The customers and his women like him. But soon he is forced to close his shop. That is until the Vietnam War starts.

Other underrated films : Girls Meets Boy, The Changeling, Invasion of the Body Snatchers, Peeping Tom, Mission Impossible, Kharij, Kundun, The Russia House, Dead Ringers, Little Buddha, Secrets and Lies, Les Mistons (France, Dir : Francois Truffaut 1957), Eva (UK, 1962, Dir : Joseph Losey), Existenz (Dir : David Cronenberg, 1999), Six Degrees of Separation, Love and Death on Long Island (U.K., 1997, Dir : Richard Lwietniowski), Tokyo Drifter (Japan, 1966) 12 Storeys (Singapre, 1997, Dir : Eric Khoo), L'Atlante (Dir : Jean Vigo 1934), Flirting (Dir : John Duigan 1990), Babe 2 (1998), Within Our Gates (1919, Dir : Oscar Micheaux), Nang Nak (1999, Dir : Nonzee Nimibutr, Thailand), El Dorado (Dir : Howard Hawks 1967), Paras Pathar/Philosopher's Stone (India, Dir : Satyajit Ray 1957).

21
THE BOLLYWOOD

India produces the greatest number of films in the world. But qualitatively it is not up to the mark. Mumbai, unfortunately called Bollywood, is the city of films and business. All the Hindi films are made in this city. That constitutes of more than 30 per cent of the all films produced in India. Others are regional films and not watched by all Indians. Only Hindi films are watched nationally.

An Indian film is like a vegetarian dish that has a little of everything. There is no genre film. Tragedy, comedy, action and drama — all are mixed in one film to provide full entertainment to the visually illiterate masses. Intellectuals and high taste people separate themselves by watching Hollywood films. A commercial Hindi film is replete with romance, music, action, emotion, drama and dance. When all these ingredients are in balanced proportions, the film can keep the viewers (mostly college students, who like picnic type of film) engaged for three hours.

In Mumbai film industry, all directors, actors and producers are insecure and remain in the grip of fear of box office failure. They do not know about the fate of their films. 'Chalta Hai attitude' (Anything can Work) rules this film world. It is not organized. There is a situation of a fish market. You have to bargain, bribe and use approach to get your film made. If you have money and approach, you can do anything. Producers propose and stars dispose. The films are more like a picnic, full of many dances and songs. Indian filmmakers are scientists in making false movies. Bollywood films are more dangerous than narcotic drugs. They are very sentimental — you cry for every little thing. Sentimentalism makes people think less and cover up filmmaker's shortcomings and weaknesses.

> The whole film industry is in chaos. Nobody has an idea of the film in totality. The scriptwriter writes dialogues on the sets, actors never do their home works, they are not given scripts in advance, because there is no complete script. Once a film becomes a major hit, more than a dozen films are made like that. There is a rat race. Like Indian consumers, filmmakers and producers have also a sheep-like mentality. One succeeds others follow his footsteps. No one wants to be different. There is no chance of risk. Songs kill the narration, but they are not allowed to make films without them. Different locations of the world are used for filming songs. They provide a romantic escape to the depressed and never smiling Indian viewers. Inferiority complex causes these viewers to identify with the stars of the films. Here, viewers do not like real movies. They want a romantic escape.

Even until ten years ago, identification with the common man and his struggle for survival was alive in the films of Yash Chopra, Subhash Ghai, Prakash Mehra and Manmohan Desai. And then came Amitabh Bachchan (BBC has voted him as the star of the Millenium), the omnipresent angry young man, who lent a context as well as his powerful voice to the invisible mass. And then in 1990s came the new generation of stars. It was a projection period. Suddenly the film industry started enjoying its new found favour with the elite. Bollywood films are star's medium. Except few filmmakers like Ram Gopal Verma and Mani Ratnam, no director has the power of creative freedom or difference. The stars rule the industry. They care more about their clothes, appearances, glamour, glitz, and make-up, pomp and show than their performances. Shahrukh Khan killed legendary character of emperor Ashoka in 'Asoka'. Dress designers, stylists, journalists and personal trainers are gaining significance, along with the emergence of designer directors like Karan Johar. Characterization takes on a completely different meaning. It is more about designing a look rather than conceiving a character. It is more about élan than emotions. It is more about sensationalism than sensibilities. Bollywood stars, except Amir Khan, do not think. They have no view, no opinions, and no point of view. That is the star system of Bollywood!

Ninety-five per cent films flop over here. Nobody takes the responsibility. Is the giant entertainment industry grinding towards a halt? Everybody says that films flop because of lack of good writers. Hollywood films are adapted from novels and plays, which have won awards like Pulitzer, Booker or Nobel. That is why they are great and worth watching. There is no budget constraint in Hollywood. The talent and technology are superb. There is a perfect combination of art and entertainment. But in Bollywood, art never meets entertainment and *vice versa*. Art films have its own directors like Shyam Benegal and Govind Nihlani. They do not enter entertainment. The same way formula entertainment director David Dhawan would never risk making an art film. It is true that Bollywood suffers from acute shortage of fine writers. There are not much novelists over here. That is the reason, Bollywood filmmakers copy the Hollywood films. They Indianise it. Coppola's 'Godfather' has been copied into at least seven Hindi films. Many directors copy Hollywood films shot by shot.

Formula films mean play safe and perish. The overseas market (U.S./U.K. and Europe) is an all time low. The audio market is not good too. Nobody knows what to do. Distributors shy away from picking up new films. The average budget of a Bollywood film is around $ 4 million. Though it is difficult to be different. But when formulas are not working, then what to do. Today audiences are very sharp and visually literate too. Now these are a time for sensible and meaningful entertainment. Audiences are bored with love triangles and songs filmed in Switzerland.

Just as a person must keep redefining himself, so must a fraternity. As time progresses, sensibilities change. But the biggest problem of Bollywood is the total paucity of good scripts. There is no writer of the calibre of those who were with Bimal Roy, Guru Dutt and Raj Kapur. Their ideology nurtured literature, theatre and cinema of 1950s and 60s. since then only a stray Salim-Javed have brought in slickness in their scripts. But the scriptwriters are poorest people in Bollywood. They are paid very less, very late. How can minds work when the stomachs are empty?

The technology is also poor in Bollywood. Directors do not know their job. They do not know except master, close and OS shots. Only few cinematographers, like Ashok Mehta, have a sense of lighting. Others give flat pictures. There is no creativity among technicians. No director can be called an auteur. There is no Bimal Roy or Satyajit Ray. Sound quality is not upto the international mark. Actions do not look real. Extras never perform well. The shots never look real and natural. Special effects are not perfect. Make-up is not advanced. Like the nation, Bollywood is also in developing condition. Though Amir Khan's "Lagaan" has opened the eyes of Bollywood to rise to the occasion and become international. But whether others improve or not, we have to wait and watch.

The Biggest Box office Grossers of Bollywood (Mumbai)

- Kismat / Destiny
- Ratan
- Mother India (1957) "Oscar Nominated"
- Mughal-e-Azam / Akbar The Great (1960)
- Sholey / Embers (1975)
- Jai Santoshi Maa (1975)
- Maine Pyar Kiya (1989)
- Aankhen / Eyes (1968)
- Hum Aapke Hain Kaun....! (1993)
- DDLJ (Dilwale Dulhania Le Jayenge) (1995)
- Raja Hindustani (1996)
- Kuch Kuch Hota Hai (1998)
- Kaho Na Pyar Hai (2000)
- Gadar-Ek Prem Katha (2001)
- Lagaan (2001) "Oscar Nominated"

22

THE BOX OFFICE

All film's judgments are made at the box office. Each week a new film replaces the previous one. Everybody is affected by the storm or the silence of the box office. It forces filmmakers to change themselves, to produce something that can bring the storms of the viewers. The box office is as ruthless as ever. It does not respect your creative freedom. It has no emotion, no mercy just numbers!

The box office factor caused the makers of 'Pearl Harbor' to have a love story against the backdrop of Japanese attack otherwise there was not too much love at the time of World War II. 'Titanic', without the love story, is nothing but a sinking ship. The formulae of a love story against the backdrop of something big and tragic always works wonder at the box-office. A filmmaker gets more creative freedom, if he has given few major hits. All box-office gods are always in demand. Only the successful directors are allowed to take risks and experiments. Others have to follow the formulae.

Then there is another group of auteurs, who have the power of gravity. They bring audience to the cinema halls by their names only. A Steven Spielberg film can initially be a big crowd puller. The films like Harry Potter and Spider Man were first offered to Spielberg, but he rejected them saying that though the words like big grosser are nice to hear but it is not creative stimulating to do all those movies any more. Spielberg never succumbed to the pressure of formulae, otherwise he might have to do a love story against the backdrop of World War II in 'Saving Private Ryan' or Jews Holocaust in 'Schindler's List'. Other crowd pullers are Francis Ford Coppola, James Cameron, Oliver Stone and Michael Mann.

The stars also affect the collection at the box-office. The audience first see the stars in the posters of the films, then they decide to watch or not to watch. All have their own favourite stars. If girls like Tom Cruise, boys may like Tom Hanks. The star pulls the crowd by the power of his persona. But ultimately it is the story and its execution, that is the real crowd puller. A good story compellingly told always attracts the audience. Special effects loaded big budget films also prove to be crowd pullers.

Nobody can predict the fate of a film. It has been seen that while the big budget films like 'Water World' and 'Postman' flopped, smaller films became a huge hit. It was only 'Titanic' that was the most expensive film as well as the highest earner in the history of cinema. Any film that does not get audience is unsuccessful. Good films belong to all and bad films belong to the maker only. Different awards given in the field of cinema are other box-office boosters. Once a film gets an Oscar nomination, audience prefer to watch that film. There is a definite growth in the ticket sale. Right kind of promotion may help initially but over exposure has its own side effects. People watch too much of promos of the forthcoming films. They decide after watching promos. 'Godzilla' makers had spent $ 50 million on promotion only. But if the makers have full confidence on their product, promotion is not better. Over exposure on televisions always kills the curiosity that is associated with the film.

Box Office terms

Circuit : The area for which a distributor buys the distribution rights for a film for a period of 5, 7 or 10 years.

Ratio : The price for which a film is sold for a particular circuit.

Flop : If a film cannot even recover its investment, it is termed a flop.

Average : If a film manages to simply recover its cost, it is an average film.

Commission Earner : When a film recovers the investment and, over and above that, gets in revenues of 20 per cent more, it is termed a Commission earner.

Overflow : When a film crosses the Commission mark, the revenues thereafter are to be shared between the producer and distributor.

Semi Hit : A film that does a business of double the investment in it, it is termed a Semi-hit. The producer gets a handsome overflow from the distributor.

Hit : If a film more than doubles its investment in the distributors hands. It is termed a hit.

Super Hit : If the returns on a film are much more than double the investment, it is termed a super hit.

Block Buster : Block Busters were the names of the bombs that Hitler used against the Allies. Now they are used as the terms for the success of a film. In this, returns are almost triple the investment or even more.

23

MOVIES REWRITING HISTORY

Dramatics have long sacrificed fact in pursuit of art, and much of time it can be shrugged off, like geography teachers patiently explaining that the Volcano Krakotoa is, unlike the erroneous title of the 1969 adventure movie, west rather than east of Java. But there is a growing concern that in a post literate society, where children get more informations from films and television than books, the routine distortion of history in Hollywood films is becoming pernicious. Films are no longer more entertainments; they are a prime source of information for many young minds.

Lord Puttnam, whose 1981 film 'Chariots Of Fire' was praised for accurately recapturing the social tensions behind the 1924 Olympics, became the first cinematic heavy weight to rail against distortion in Hollywood films and warn of its long term damage.

History is ruthlessly violated in the films like 'Patriot' in which a peaceful former Benjamin Martin (Mel Gibson) was dragged into the American War of Independence. The film portrayed British history in a wrong way. Look at Disney's 'Dinosaur'. It is cute, but the film does not explain why the dinosaurs are no longer around. It is compelling in terms of imagery, but in terms of education it misleads children. Mel Gibson had done many false history films. He made his name in the film 'Gallipoli', in which the Australian troops were depicted as the main victims of a First World War campaign in which in fact, many more British than Australian troops died. He played the lead in one more anti-English epic 'Braveheart'.

For 'The Patriot', makers have gone to unusual lengths to assure the public, it is historically accurate, even hiring experts from the Smithsonian, the American equivalent of the British Museum, to cast an eye over the 38 scripts, written by Robert Rodat who also wrote 'Saving Private Ryan' that also marginalized the British. But the Hollywood experts say that they have to simplify few things, both to save the budget and to explain the bigger picture. Sometimes this act of simplification becomes an act of distortion. All the battles shown in 'The Patriot' and 'Braveheart' were, in reality, won by the British. But in contrast, films show them loose all the battles.

The film 'Gandhi' might have rekindled anti-British feelings. But in the film, Richard Attenborough had restaged the 1919 massacre at Amritsar in which British soldiers killed 379 demonstrating Sikhs. At least that massacre was historically correct. It will be an uphill struggle against a global tide of historical ignorance, however, especially among teenagers, who are the prime cinema going audience. Once a poll was conducted just before the release of the Spielberg film 'Schindler's List' and it was found that fourth out of five American children had not heard of Auschwitz. Similarly polls have found that the majority of American students believe that the Second World War leader in Russia was Lenin rather than Stalin and some believed his first name was John.

Judith Mackinlay, who teaches history at City College, Manchester, said that the Hollywood funded "Michael Collins" had directly caused confusion. One student reproduced whole dialogue almost verbatim for the film in support of an argument in her essay. Even undergraduate students would rather watch movies than wade through a textbook, without realizing that the directors are twisting the historical facts. Hollywood leaves behind powerful images. Some Britons believed that there is something of a deliberate agenda. It is more that just dramatic or commercial considerations : the great liberal establishment of Hollywood does all it can to blacken the western, imperial Colonial past, probably because the Americans largely missed out on the spoils.

James Bowman, an American historian, believed that Steven Spielberg was responsible for some of the most powerful Hollywood fakery, not only in 'Saving Private Ryan', but also

'Amistad', his antislavery epic. The deeper sin is to make every historical character from Merchant Ivory's Jefferson in Paris to 'Elizabeth I' as played by Cate Blanchett, sound like a modern liberal. In another war movie, 'U-571', starring Harvey Keital and pop star John Bon Jovi, it is shown how the US navy recovered an Enigma Nazi Code machine and changed the course of the war. In reality, although the US navy captured a cipher machine off West Africa in 1944, the original was seized in an equally daring and costly mission by HMS Bulldog three years earlier when America was not even in the war. It took parliamentary protest by Dr. Julian Lewis, conservative MP for New Forest East, before the filmmaker added a dedication to Bulldog at the end of the film.

The problem is that people so very easily confuse films with history. Where will it all end? Sheri Bearlstorm, the LA based author of Hollywood and History, once "said there was a simple morality at work in Hollywood. We are the top nation and we need history to explain how we got here. If that means stealing your history and heroes to do it, then Hollywood will think it is a small price to pay for the success at the box-office."

24

Film Piracy

Piracy is the biggest threat to the film as well as music. It is a nightmare that all film producers and distributors have to endure. VHS, VCD, laser discs can be easily copied. The piracy is in all fields. Softwares worth thousands of dollars can be purchased in not more than a hundred dollar in black market. And the cheap pirated copies of films; music and computer softwares flood the market and walk away with a major chunk of the monetary shares.

While piracy has become a major cause of concern for the film industry, a proper solution to curb the same is still awaited. There is a severe loss of revenue, not only for the creative people, but also for the government. Pirated VCDs generally arrive in other countries from Malaysia, Pakistan, Singapore, Hong Kong and the Middle East. The pirated copies reach other countries as soon as the international CD-DVD rights are sold. They make a master copy there and then smuggle it to the rest of the world, where more copies are made from the master one. Each country receives one smuggled master pirated copy. With technological advancement copying a CD has become a very easy and cheap job. A master copy of a CD is generally sold in two thousand to 20 thousand US dollars depending on the film. Then pirates further purchase the second print for one hundred to two hundred US dollar.

Cable operators show the films that have been just released. There is a huge public demand for new films. The competition is so fierce that the cable operators keep a watch on their rivals and often complain whenever they screen pirated films. While the theatre owners and film industry personalities feel that the government and police are not doing enough to curb piracy, the police have their own opinion of cooperation and mutual agreement.

The cable operators must be registered in all countries to curb piracy of films. The government can give them licence, which can be cancelled whenever they show pirated films. The pirated copies have poor quality of picture and sound. General public should be encouraged not to see pirated version. Digital Versatile Discs (DVD) are the latest discs, and along with their many advantages they cannot be copied. DVD has a built in lock system called Scrambling Device which prevents recording even by professionals. If one tries to copy then the picture on the reproduced copy will shake continuously. But computer programmes that decrypt DVD so that a movie can be copied from the disc to a PC are available on the internet, though they are illegal in the United States.

Movie piracy hitting mainstream cinemas has caused Hollywood lament. In the U.S. people use free software called 'Morpheus' to download new movies and T.V. shows without paying anything to anybody. Internet has caused severe revenue loss in the market of music and films. Everything can be downloaded for free. Now you can download nonstop with your cable modem while you are sleeping or at work. The other bonus of this kind of piracy is absence of commercials. People are trading movies today the way they were doing MP3s four years back.

Secretive pirate groups still compete to be the first to "release" a film or TV show on the internet with the optical balance of file size and video quality, and any commercials edited out. Now 40 gigabyte hard drives can store about 50 movies. Many PCs now also come with CD burners, which can be used to archive video files. Internet has created a global chain of serious and casual pirates causing a rapid expansion of illicit Video-on-Demand service.

Inexpensive Television Tuner Cards that can be installed on PCs, enable users to record anything shown on Television directly onto a hard drive. Digital video cameras equipped with fire wire, a technology that allows material to be transferred directly from the camera to a computer at high speeds, have made it easier to share the results of smuggling a camera into a theatre.

Piracy is a nuisance, menace, threat and loss for films and music. Nobody is trying to curb it. People get to hear the songs and see the films for free. So who is going to bother? None.

25

IMAX Films and Theatre

Today all old cinema halls are turning into multiplexes. An audience does not need to roam around the city for his favourites. He can watch many latest hits in one building. Equipped with the advanced projector, screen and DTS, the new cinema halls provide a totally different experience. But beyond the routine cinema halls there are a few ones, which are totally different in shape and size of everything. They are called IMAX theatres.

It has a jumbo screen whose sheer size and images provide a being there experience. A car zooming across the screen will have you ducking for cover. A tidal wave roaring across will engulf you in fear. The largest IMAX dome in the world is in Mumbai, India. It is 30 meters wide in diameter.

Facts

- The IMAX experience is a 15/70 mm film frame. That is ten times the size of a conventional 35 mm movie and five times that of a standard 70 mm frame.
- The screen is built of a specially diffused matte white vinyl perforated with thousands of tiny holes for acoustical transparency.
- Each IMAX film is about 45-60 minutes long.
- There are more than 130 educational and entertaining films in the large format movie library. They include T Rex : Back to The Cretaceous, Everest And Rolling Stone : At The Max, The Living Sea.
- IMAX Corp, founded in 1967, headquartered in Mississauga, Canada, is the pioneer of giant screen entertainment.

- At present there are over 200 IMAX theatres in 26 countries with 70 of them with 3D technology.
- IMAX technology premiered at the Fuji Pavilion, Expo 70 in OSAKA, Japan. The first IMAX theatre was opened in Toronto in 1971.

26

War Films

War makes great cinema, especially WW II. It is big business in Hollywood. War is always in season. Be it in the trenches, in the air, in the water, or on the screen — big or small. It is humanity and heart of darkness, the black hole of the human race. Yesterday, War-legalized murder for revenge, aggrandizement, power — has historical sanction. But for the last 100 years we have begun to see it far the evil it is. Different films had have showcased the evils and horrors of war. Some glorified it, and some showed horrors more vividly than ever. The battles of World War II have inspired numerous films from the 'Longest Day' to 'Saving Private Ryan'.

From the idealized to the brutally real, studios have mined American's history for stories of courage, bravery and sometimes criminality. People are attracted to war films because they want to see the high stakes drama, because war is life and death. But all war films are not historically accurate. The facts are twisted for the sake of nationalism and entertainment. And while Hollywood gets the technical stuff right, it is the characters and the situations that seem unreal. There are so few that are true and faithful to real life. Lots of war films are just fake.

War films are not likely to go away anytime soon. As long as war survives, the genre will get new angles.

A List of War Films

Saving Private Ryan	(dir : Steven Spielberg, 1998, five Oscar winner)
The Thin Red Line	(dir : Terrance Malick, 1998, Eight Oscar nominated)

Enemy At The Gates	(dir : Jean Jacques Annaud, 2001)
Pearl Harbor	(dir : Michael Bay, 2001)
Tigerland	(dir : Joel Schumacher, 2000)
The Battle of The Bulge	(dir : Ken Annakin, 1965)
Close Combat : Battle of the Bulge	
Dirty Dozen	(dir : Robert Aldrich, 1977)
The Longest Day	(dir : Ken Annakin, 1962)
The Bridge on The River Kwai	(dir : David Lean, 1957, five Oscar winner)
Apocalypse Now	(dir : Francis Ford Coppola, 1979, Two Oscar winner)
Platoon	(dir : Oliver Stone, 1986, four Oscar winner)
Where Eagles Dare	(dir : Brain G. Hutton, 1968)
Kelly's Heroes	(dir : Brain G. Hutton, 1970)
Airforce	
Tarzan Triumphs	
The Invisible Agent	
They Were Expendable	
The Story of G.I. Joe	
Behind Enemy Lines	(dir : John Moore, 2001)
Black Hawk Down	(dir : Ridley Scott, 2001, two Oscar winner)
Patton	(dir : Franklin J. Schaffner, 1970)
A Bridge Too Far	(dir : Sir Richard Attenborough, 1977)
In Love And War	(dir : Sir Richard Attenborough, 1996)
Force Five	(1981)
All Quiet On the Western Front	(dir : Lewis Milestone, 1930)
Buck Privates	(1941)
The Guns of Navarone	(dir : John Lee Thompson, 1961)
Back To Bataan	(1945)
The Blue Max	(1966)
Blue Skies	(1946)
Bombardier	(1943)

The Boys In Company 'C'	(1978)
The Caine Mutiny	(1954)
Catch 22	(1970)
The Devil's Bridge	(1968)
The Eagle Has Landed	(1977)
Force 10 From Navarone	(1978)
The Hindenburg	(1975)
Tora! Tora! Tora!	(1970)
Victory	(1981)
Buffalo Soldiers	(2002)
Hurt's War	(dir : Gregory Hoblit, 2002)
We Were Soldiers	(dir : Randall Wallace, 2002)
The Great Raid	
U-571	(dir : Jonathan Mostow, 2000)
Stalingrad	(dir : Joseph Vilsmaier, 1993)
Wind talkers	(dir : John Woo, 2002)
Bullet In The Head	(dir : John Woo, 1990)
Deer Hunter	(dir : Michael Cimino, 1978)
The Saviour	(2000)
Uncommon Valour	(dir : Ted Kotcheff, 1983)
Zeppelin	(dir : Etienne Perier, 1971)
The Colditz Story	(1954)
Wings	(1928, Best Picture Oscar)
Mrs. Miniver	(dir : William Wyler, 1942)
The Best Years of Our Lives	(dir : William Wyler, 1946)
From Here To Eternity	(dir : Fred Zinnemann, 1953)
War Hunt	(1962)

Well-known War Documentaries

'Fires Were Started' (1943) and 'Target For Tonight' (1941) by Harrywatt, 'Why We Fight', 'Point of Order' (1964) and 'Prelude to War (1942) by Frank Capra, 'Aftermath : the Remnants of War' (2001) by Daniel Sekulich, 'Battle For San Pietro' (John Huston), 'December 7th' by John Ford and 'Memphis Belle' by William Wyler.

27

Still Photography

Exposure

To control exposures, so that you can take good pictures, you must control the amount of light reaching the film. In dim light film needs plenty of exposure for a good result. The amount of exposure given to the film depends on a combination of two things : the brightness of the light reaching the film and the time for which the film receives the light.

Aperture

An aperture is a hole of variable size inside a camera lens. The size of the aperture controls the brightness of light reaching the film. Apertures are also called F Stops, hence the term 'Stop Down' which means reducing the aperture. F22, the smallest aperture, lets through one unit of light. F16 would allow 2 units of light.

Aperture Scale

Aperture	F 1.4	F 2	F 2.8	F 4	F 5.6	F 8	F 11	F 16	F 22
Units of light passed	256	128	64	32	16	8	4	2	1

Shutter

The shutter inside the camera body is the second half of the exposure team. It controls the time for which the film is exposed to light. A slow shutter speed let plenty of light reach the film, while a fast shutter speed lets only a small amount of light.

Most 35 mm SLR (Single Lens Reflex) cameras have a shutter just in front of the film called a 'Focal Plane' shutter. It is made up of two blinds, which move over the film when you press the shutter release. Whatever speed you choose the blinds always move at the same speed. The time for which the film receives light is controlled by the width of the gap between the two shutter blinds. For a very slow speed the first blind completely uncovers the film to flood it with light all over. The second blind is held back for little while.

Shutter Speed Scale

Shutter Speed	¼	1/8	1/15	1/30	1/60	1/125	1/250	1/500	1/1000
Units of light passed	256	128	64	32	16	8	4	2	1

Controlling Exposure

The amount of exposure you give for any subject depends on the brightness of the light (aperture) and the length of time light reaches the film (through shutter speed). A big aperture and a fast shutter speed can be used to photograph a subject. The same way a small aperture and slow shutter speed can be used to photograph a subject. The same way a small aperture and slow shutter speed can be used to photograph the same subject. The result differs. With fast shutter speed you need to use bigger apertures than with slow shutter speeds and *vice versa.*

Bracketing

If, after taking a meter reading, you are not sure of the best exposure to use, you can take several shots as insurance. Taking several pictures at different exposures is called 'bracketing'. Though it is a waste of the film, so only be used in extreme conditions when the picture is important and unrepeatable.

Depth of Field

The aperture controls the depth of field. The 'field' in this case is a crispy focused zone or band in the photograph. The 'depth' is how deep into the subject the crisply focused band starts and ends. If you take a picture from close to the subject using a big aperture, this band of sharpness (depth of field) is very shallow. The foreground and background are fuzzy and out of focus while a narrow strip of the subject is clear and sharp. If you use a small aperture, the band of sharpness

(DOF) becomes much deeper, as long as you are not too close to the subject.

Experience helps you to predict the most suitable aperture to get the depth of field you want.

Depth of Field Preview

It is easier to compose and focus a picture with the lens at its widest aperture. You see a bright image in the viewfinder. Some cameras have a button or a lever, which closes the lens aperture down to whatever you have choosen on the aperture ring to give you a correct exposure. The viewfinder becomes much dimmer as you reduce the aperture. But you are then seeing in the viewfinder approximately the same image, as the lens will project onto the film. You therefore have a visual idea of how much of the subject will come out sharp.

Depth of Field Scale

Most lenses have a depth of field scale marked near the aperture ring to guide you. The depth of the field scale cannot work on its own, it relates to the aperture ring and to the focusing scale. You have to set the correct focusing distance for the subject by turning the focusing ring until the subject looks sharp in the viewfinder. If the depth of field is the most important aspect of your picture, choose the aperture you want to use. Use a big aperture to throw a confusing background out of focus. Use a small aperture if you want to show a detail in the whole of picture.

Camera Shake

If you are using a slow shutter speed and the camera moves during the exposure then the picture is spoiled. The amount of blurring caused depends on how much you move the camera and what shutter speed is used. In a 1/30 or slower speed, it is difficult to hold the camera steady enough to prevent shake. You should either avoid slow speeds altogether or steady the camera during the exposure. Keeping still holding your breath, standing firm and trying hard not to move while you squeeze the shutter release gently, helps prevent camera shake. You can also steady the camera by leaning again a solid wall or tree. Pistol grips and rifle stock attachment all help to steady the camera by using your own body as a stabilizer. The most reliable support is a sturdy tripod.

Panning

A sharp image against a blurred background gives a strong impression of movement. To achieve this move, the camera should in the same direction and at the same speed as the 'subject' while the shutter is open. This is called panning. The best results happen with fairly slow speeds like 1/60 or slower.

Exposure System

There are several types of exposure systems available in modern SLR cameras. Most of the cameras have a built-in light meter. The meter measures light from the subject directly through the lens (TTL). It is convenient and reliable.

- **Manual exposure cameras :** You can adjust the aperture ring to get whatever effect you want. A moving needle or a coloured lamp in the viewfinder signals whether or not you will get a good exposure with the combination you have chosen.
- **Automatic exposure cameras :** It gives slightly less control but enables, corrects exposures to happen much more quickly and easily. There are several automatic exposure systems :
  - (a) **Aperture priority :** The photographer chooses an aperture to control depth of field. The camera automatically provides the correct shutter speed. Many of these cameras can be turned into manual exposure cameras by moving a switch called 'Manual Override'.
  - (b) **Shutter priority :** The photographer sets an appropriate shutter speed to control movement blurs. The camera automatically sets an aperture to give a correct exposure.
  - (c) **Multi-mode cameras :** A few automatic cameras can be used as shutter priority and aperture priority as well as manual exposure cameras. There is often a programmed exposure setting too where

the photographer has no control at all. The camera sets the aperture and shutter speed according to the available light and film speed.

(d) **Film :** There are only three main types of film — colour negative, colour slide and black & white negative. Colour negative film or colour print film produces a negative image and is used to make colour prints. Colour slide films or colour reversal films produce a positive image in the form of colour transparencies used for projection and reversal type prints. Black & white negative film produces a negative image and is used to produce black & white prints.

- **Daylight and tungsten film :** Slide film is balanced for use in daylight and with electronic flash. Tungsten slide film should be used to give true colours with artificial (Tungsten) light and special photographic lamps.

Film Speeds

On an SLR camera you will notice a dial with 'ASA' and numbers, perhaps, between 12 and 1600, or the equivalent in DIN, with numbers 12 to 33. This dial has to be set so that the marker corresponds to the ASA/DIN number of the film you are using. All three types of film are made in a range of film speeds. The term 'Film speed' describes how sensitive a film is to light. A slow speed (25-50 ASA) is not very sensitive to light while a fast film (200-400 ASA) reacts much quicker to light. Each speed is appropriate for a different lighting condition and has different advantage and disadvantages as the speed affects a colour saturation, grain, image quality, etc.

Choosing the Right Film Speed

- Medium film speeds (64 to 125 ASA) : Medium film speeds are probably the most used and can cope with a great range of subjects and conditions, though they may not be the perfect choice for the job in the hand. They give good colour, fairly fine grain and have good latitude to exposure error. They are only inadequate in very dim lighting condition.

- Slow Films (25-40 ASA) : Being less sensitive to light require wider apertures or longer shutter speeds to give more exposure. They give the best sharpness and detail, the finest grain and are the most suitable for making enlargements. However, because of the increased exposure they require, there is more risk of camera shakes and less potential for action shots in poor light.
- Fast Film (200-400 ASA and above) : Pictures which cannot be taken with slow or medium film are often possible with fast film, which can be used in low lighting conditions. The fast shutter speeds used are good for stopping action. However fast films are more grainy. It is best for the modest print size.

Speeds and Film Type

Film Type	Speed					
	Slow		Medium		Fast	
	ASA	DIN	ASA	DIN	ASA	DIN
Black & White print	25	15	64	19	400	27
	32	16	100	21		
	50	18	125	22		
Colour Print			80	20	400	27
			100	21		
Colour Slide	25	15	64	19	200	24
	50	18	100	21	400	27

Lenses

One of the biggest advantages of SLR cameras is that you can change the lens to use the most suitable type for the subject and the effect you want to create.

- **Focal Length :** Focal length is the distance between the lens and the film when the lens is focused on infinity. But because modern lenses are so complex in the way light travels through them, a lens can be physically longer or shorter than its marked focal length suggests. Focal length is measured in millimeters (mm). The most important aspects of focal length are that it affects (a) The size or magnification of the image in the viewfinder and on film and (b) How much of a subject is included in the picture. A 400 mm lens produces a bigger image of a subject than a 135 mm lens. If the focal length is doubled, the magnification doubles too, and so does the size of the image.

- **Angle of view :** You cannot change the picture area produced on film by a 35 mm SLR camera, it is always 24 mm by 36 mm.

Lenses for a 35 mm SLR (except for fisheye lenses) all give an image which completely fills this picture area. Long focal lengths cut down the area you see around the subject and they therefore have a small 'angle of view'. Short focal length gives a wide view and is called 'wide angle'.

Speed

When you hear of a 'fast or slow' lens, this is a reference to its maximum light gathering power. A lens with a big maximum aperture is called a fast lens. A slow lens has a much smaller maximum aperture. The bigger the maximum aperture the more expensive is the lens. The longer the focal length the smaller the maximum aperture possible.

Depth of Field

Focal length also affects the depth of field. A short focal length (wide angle) lens gives much more depth of field than a long focal length (telephoto) lens. With some wide angles it is almost impossible to get foreground and background out of focus. With some telephoto lenses it is impossible to get a foreground or background into focus.

Minimum Aperture

Most lenses stop down to at least F16 or F22. Longer telephoto lenses may have F32 and F45 settings perhaps smaller. But because depth of field decreases as focal length increases, F32 in a 300 mm lens does not give more depth of field than F22 in a 50 mm lens with the same subject.

Focusing

All general purpose lenses focus on distant subject. This is called infinity and usually means 30 metres away and more. The closest possible focusing distance varies from lens to lens. 50 mm lenses can focus on 45 cm, a 24 mm lens may let you get to 20 cm from the subject and a 300 mm lens may stop you going any closer than 4 metres. If you go closer than the limit, picture will be unsharp.

Suitable Lenses

The standard lens focal length for 35 mm SLR cameras is 40 mm to 58 mm. With a standard lens the angle of view and image size you see in the view finder is normal. Standard lenses are not very expensive, are of good quality and versatile. There are a wide range of lenses.

(a) **Wide angle lenses :** Anything less than 40 mm in focal length (for a 35 mm camera) is a wide angle lens. The depth of field increases with wide angles. Everything remains in sharp focus.

(b) **Telephoto lenses :** Anything greater than 60 mm in focal length (for a 35 mm camera), is a long focus lens. As focal length increases, the image size produced gets bigger. The angle of view gets smaller. Such lenses are expensive and of limited uses.

(c) **Zoom lenses :** You can change the focal length of a zoom lens. A zoom always has a limited focal length range : from 24 to 38 mm or 100 to 300 mm for example. The obvious advantage is that you have many focal lengths in one lens. This can reduce cost and minimizes the number of items of equipment you carry around. They are extremely convenient. You can zoom in or out to suit the desired image. Disadvantages include extra bulk and weight of zooms over single lens. There is also some loss in quality of picture. It is expensive too.

Looking After Lenses

Lenses are very expensive and so must be handled with care. Keep the front element clean. A skylight or UV filter fitted permanently to all your lenses keeps out dust and moisture. It also prevents you from touching the delicate lens with dirty or greasy fingers. A filter is much easier to clean than a lens and much cheaper of replace in case of damage. Some other precautions are :

- Keep the lens cap on when not using the lens. If you are storing or carrying a lens off the camera, put rear lens cap on.
- Keep water off your lenses. It can cause damage.
- Do not drop it. Do not attempt to service it yourself and never oil moving parts.
- In warm and humid condition, fungus can grow on or inside the lens and it is difficult to remove. Keep a bag of silica gel inside the storage container if you would not be using a lens for a long time.
- Always use special cleaning materials. A soft brush, a lintfree cloth, lens tissues and lens cleaning fluid or distilted water. Never use a solvent liquid and do not rub or you may scratch glass.

Use the following Ratio

Focal lengths	Maximum Aperture	Uses
85 mm To 100 mm	F 1.2 To F 4	For Portraits
105 mm To 150 mm	F 2.5 To F 4	Candid Photography
200 mm To 300 mm	F 2.8 To F 4.5	Sports, wildlife
400 mm To 500 mm	F 4.5 To F 8	Sports, wildlife
600 mm To 1000 mm	F4 To F 8	Motor & water sports
15 mm To 21 mm	F 2.8 To F 4	Dramatic landscape
24 mm To 35 mm	F 2.8 To F 4	Travel, landscape
28 mm To 50 mm (Zoom)	F 3.5	Landscape, large fields
35 mm To 140 mm (Zoom)	F 2.8	General purpose lenses
70 mm To 300 mm (Zoom)	F 3.5 To F 5	Portraits, sports, wildlife

Composition : See Cinematography chapter.

Candid Photography : In candid photography, the subject is either unaware of or unconcerned with the presence of the camera, and the photographer exercises no direct control over events. Candid photographs are marked by spontaneity and often look journalistic. Good candid technique entails photographing quickly and unobtrusively. Automatic cameras that do not require much adjusting are an advantage.

Portraits and full length views : A portrait consisting of a Frame-filling face or head and shoulders view evokes a feeling of closeness and intimacy. Focus on the eyes. If they are sharp, the picture will be perceived as sharp.

Be careful not to get too close or you risk caricaturing facial features. Do not approach nearer than 3.5 feet.

Lighting people outdoors : When you photograph people outdoors observe the way they look in different light. A person's appearance changes depending on whether light is hard or soft and depending on the direction from which it comes. Hard, direct sunlight can work well when you are not too close to the subject or when you are photographing a group. People with rugged faces that have lots of character lines, may be given hard lights. But the diffused light of open shade or an overcast day is much kinder to most faces. Its soft, wraparound quality reveals facial forms tenderly, without high lighting blemishes.

Direction of light : Straight front lighting can make faces look a bit flat, but is a safe choice for active subjects because they will be fully lighted wherever they roam in front of the camera. Side lighting creates drama, but at the cost of shadow detail on the unlighted side of the subject. To lighting from the overhead sun casts unpleasant shadows in eye sockets, beneath the nose and under the chin. You can side step these problems by having the subject tilt his head upward. Back lighting creates a halo of light separating subject from background, but leaves the side of the subject facing the camera in shadow.

Lighting people indoors : By far the easiest way to photograph people indoors is with a built-in or accessory automatic flash unit. The flash is fast enough to stop action crisply and produces attractive colour rendition on popular daylight-type colour films. If your camera can make exposures at about 1/60 seconds, has a lens with a maximum aperture in the vicinity of F/2.8 or faster and can accept fast films with ISO speeds of 200 or higher, you can make good indoor people pictures in reasonably bright existing light without using a flash. You can place your subject in a chair next to a window without direct sunlight.

- Avoid taking pictures after 9.30 a.m. and before 3.30 p.m.

- Never take a picture with the sun just behind you.
- Leave the looking room. Never place the subject in the centre of the frame.
- Always shoot when the light is from the side or at an angle or from the back of the subject.

28

OSCAR TRIVIA

"OSCAR is the highest honour in the field of motion picture."

—*Kevin Spacey*

Vital Statistic of the Statuette

The Oscar statuette is 13½ inches tall, which comprises 10½ inches of statuette and 3 inches of base. It weighs 8½ pounds and the base is 5¼ inches in diameter.

How Oscar was Born

Oscar's birth took place at a Hollywood banquet hall on May 11, 1927. Exactly one week after the Academy of Motion Picture Arts and Sciences was organised. It came into being after the MGM president Louis B. Mayer urged the Academy to create a special film award. Cedric Gibbons, art director at the MGM studios, responded immediately. He quickly sketched the figure of a knight holding a crusader's sword standing atop a reel of film whose five spokes signified the five original branches of the Academy. The spokes signified actors, directors, producers, technicians and writers. The statuette was sculpted by George Stanley, a Los Angeles based sculptor, in 1928. Originally the statuette was hand cast in bronze with 24 karat gold plating. However, from 1930 onwards it has been cast in Britannia metal which is an alloy of tin, copper and antimony. Then it is plated with copper-nickel-silver and 24 karat gold. Each application is highly polished before the next one is applied.

Other Facts

- When Oscars were first given in 1927, the statuettes

were not numbered. The numbering began in 1949, with the arbitrary number 501.

- The first onwards ceremony was held at Hollywood's Roosevelt Hotel on May 16, 1929. The tickets cost $ 10 and the number of the people was 250. Since the awards were announced three months in advance, the presentation took just about five minutes.
- 'Wings' (1927-28) was the first and the only silent film to win the best picture Oscar.
- The statuettes are all manufactured by RS Owens in Chicago. The winners have to hand over their trophies to the Academy so that Owens can affix plates with their names on them to the statuettes.
- The first-ever tie in Academy history was in 1931-32 when both Wallace Berry (The Champ) and Fredric March (Dr. Jeckyll and Mr. Hyde) won the best Actor Award.
- In 1933-34, The great Depression devastated Hollywood as thousand of employees lost their jobs. The screen writer's guild was formed and its members formally withdrew from the Academy. There was no Oscar ceremony in 1933. It was postponed for the next year.
- Will Rogers became the first 'modern' emcee at the awards in 1934. Till then the master of ceremonies was always the Academy president.
- Walt Disney was the first recipient to call the statuette an Oscar of course, stories abound about how the name Oscars came about. One version says that Librarian Margaret Herrick noticed the statuette's resemblance to her uncle Oscar Piece. Another story asserts that columnist Sidney Skolsky first printed the name, when Bette Davis remarked that the statuette's back resembled that of her husband Harmon Oscar Nelson.
- The best supporting actor and actress categories were established in 1936. But the winners received plaques not Oscar.
- The number of films that could be nominated as best

picture was not restricted to five till 1944. In 1934, the number of the films nominated was 12.

- The Academy was so poor in 1937 that it charged its members $ 5 and guests $ 10 for attending the ceremony.
- In 1938, Alice Brady was in bed with a broken ankle. She was awarded the best supporting actress for her role in 'In Old Chicago'. A stranger accepted the award for her. She never saw the award. And the thief was never found.
- French director Jean Renoir's 'Grand Illusion' was the first foreign film to be nominated for best film in 1938.
- The first posthumous award went to Sidney Howard in 1939 for his screenplay of 'Gone With the Wind'.
- 'Gone With the Wind' (1939) is the first colour film to win the best picture award. It had 13 nominations and won eight Oscars, including the first (Best supporting Actress) for an Black-American actress Hattie Mc Daniel.
- Till 1940, the awards were announced before hand. But in 1940, it was decided that the winner's name would be sealed, to be disclosed only when the envelope is opened at the presentation.
- In 1941 and for the next three years plaster Oscars were handed out due to the rationing of metal. It was a war time.
- Bob Hope hosted the Oscars for the first time in 1941. He went on to record 20 appearances as host or co-host.
- Orson Welles is the only person to be nominated in the best film, best directors, best actor and best screen writer category in the same year for 'Citizen Kane' (1941).
- The longest acceptance speech was given by Green Garsons in 1942. Winner of the best actress award for 'Mrs. Miniver', she went on with her thank-you for a full seven minutes.

- Ironically, Charlie Chaplin's silent comedy 'The Gold Rush' reissued in 1942 was nominated for the Best Sound Recording.
- The Oscars were relayed live via radio and even broadcast to the US Army overseas for the first time in 1943.
- Barry Fitzgerald is the only actor to be nominated in both lead and supporting categories for the same role in 'Going My Way' in 1944. He won the supporting Oscar.
- Until 1944, the Academy Awards were presented at a private dinner. The presentation ceremony was started in 1945. Since World War II was in full swing, tickets were sold to aid the war. Because of the black-outs, Bette Davis, the then Academy president, proposed that the ceremony be held in a theatre.
- In 1946 the Academy Awards were opened to the general public. They could buy tickets. But the practice was soon stopped.
- The First Foreign language film Award was given to the Italian film 'Shoeshine' in 1947.
- Laurence Olivier's 'Hamlet' (1948) a U.K. production was the first non-Hollywood film to win the 'Best Picture' Award.
- The costume design award was added to the categories in 1948. Costume designer Edith Head was nominated every year from 1948 to 1966. She won eight awards in all.
- The Academy awards ceremony was televised for the first time in 1952. NBC-TV and Radio broadcast the awards live from the venue.
- In 1956, people thought to have communist leanings were barred from the ceremony. But 'Friendly Persuasion' written by Michael Wilson, who was accused of being "red", made it to the nominations. The rule was revoked in 1958.
- In 1956, 'The Red Balloons', a 34 minute foreign film

with no dialogue won the award for the best original screenplay.

- Seven emcees including Bob Hope, Jerry Lewis and Laurence Olivier shared the stage in 1958, that year 'Gigi' won all the nine Oscars it was nominated for.
- The only time two people won the best director trophy was in 1961. Robert Wise and Jerome Robbins got it for 'West Side Story'.
- Sophia Loren was the first foreign actress to win the Best Actress Award for her role in the Italian film 'Two Women' in 1961.
- Patty Duke, 16, was the first minor to win a competitive Oscar in 1962. She won the Best supporting for 'The Miracle Worker'.
- Walt Disney is the all time winner with 26 Academy Awards to his credit. And he also holds the records with 64 nominations.
- Sidney Poiter was the first Afro American to win the Best Actor Award for 'Lillies of the Field' in 1963. Denzel Washington became the second for 'Training Day' (2001).
- Halle Berry is the first Afro-American to win the Best Actress Award for 'Monster's Ball' (2001).
- In 1968, the Academy Award were delayed by two days following the assassination of Martin Luther King Jr. in Memphis. Katherine Hepburn (The Lion In the Winter) and Barbara Streisand (Funny Girl) tied for the Best Actress that year.
- George C. Scott, a staunch critic of the Academy Award refused his Best Actor Award for 'Patton' in 1970. Producer Frank McCarthy accepted the award.
- Marlon Brando refused his Best Actor Award for 'The Godfather' in 1972 because he objected to the film industry's treatment of Native Americans. He sent an American Indian actress Maria Cruz to the stage. She read out an indictment against the industry's treatment of the Native Americans.

- Charlie Chaplin received an honorary Oscar in 1971. When the 83-year-old legend took the stage to receive the award, he put on the 'Little Tramp' bowler hat and said 'Words seem so futile, so feeble'.
- Tatum O' Neal at ten became the youngest actor to receive the award in a competitive category for 'Paper Moon' in 1973. It was the Best Supporting Actror Award.
- The 'Godfather II' is the only sequel to win the Best Picture award in 1974.
- Italian Lina Wertmuller (Seven Beauties) was the first woman director to be nominated for Oscar in 1976.
- Richard Drey Fuss at 29, was the youngest actor to win the Best Actor award for 'The Goodbye Girl' (1977).
- Marlee Matlin, 21, was the youngest actress to win the Best Actress award for 'Children of A Lesser God' (1986).
- Maggie Smith won the Best Supporting Actress Award for playing an Oscar loser in 'California Suite' (1978).
- Hitchcock was nominated for the Best Director five times for 'Rebecca' (1940), 'Lifeboat' (1944), 'Spell Bound' (1945), 'Rear Window' (1954), and 'Psycho' (1960). But he never won it.
- Woody Allen's contempt for the awards is well-known. In 1978 despite winning the Best Actor, the Best Director and the Best Original Screenplay Awards for 'Annie Hall', he did not attend the Oscars. Instead he was spotted playing the clarinet at Michael's Pub in Manhattan.
- Richard Pryor was the first black American to co-host the show in 1982.
- The 1983 Oscar show was the longest ever, clocking three hours and 42 minutes.
- Uruguayan film entry 'A Place In The Wind' was withdrawn in 1992 after being nominated, on account of a technical Snafu : It was supposed to have Argentinean origins.

- Jane Compion is only the second woman to get a Best Director nomination for 'The Piano' in 1993. The first woman was Lina Wertmulker (Seven Beauties, 1976).
- Whoopi Goldberg was the First black American woman to host the Awards in 1994.
- Mel Gibson (Braveheart), Kevin Costner (Dances with The Wolves) and Clint Eastwood (Unforgiven) are the only actors-turned directors to win both the Best Picture and the Best Director Awards.
- John Ford is the most honoured director with four awards; for 'The Informer' (1935), 'The Grapes of Wrath' (1940), 'How Green was My Valley' (1941), and 'The Quiet Man' (1952).
- William Wyler is the most Best Director nominated person. He was nominated for a record 12 times between 1936 to 1965 and won the award three times, for 'Mrs. Miniver' (1942), 'The Best Years of Our Lives' (1946), and 'Ben Hur' (1959).
- 'All About Eve' (1950) and 'Titanic' (1997) share the record for winning the maximum number of awards, 11 each.
- Only three films have won all the five major awards (Best Picture, Best Director, Best Actor, Best Actress, Best Screenplay); they are : 'It Happened One Night' (1934), 'One Flew Over The Cuckoo's Nest' (1975), and 'The Silence of The Lambs' (1991).
- 'Ben Hur' (1959) won 11 Oscars out of its 12 nominations.
- 'West Side Story' (1961) has won 10 awards of its 11 nominations.
- 'Gigi' (1958) and 'The Last Emperor' (1987) got nine out of nine, while 'The English Patient' (1996) won nine out of 10 nominations.
- 'Cabaret' (1972) has the record for winning the most Oscars (eight) without winning, the Best Picture Award.
- 'The Turning Point' (1977) and 'The Color Purple'

(1985) share the dubious distinction of receiving 11 nomination each without winning a single award.

- Richard Burton and Peter O'Toole both have been nominated seven times without winning an Oscar. Burton was nominated for 'My Cousin Rachel' (1952), 'The Robe' (1953), 'Beckett' (1964), 'The Spy Who Came in From the Cold' (1965), 'Who Is Afraid of Virginia Wolf?' (1966), 'Anne of The Thousand Days' (1970), and 'Equus' (1977). Peter O'Tool was nominated for 'Lawrence of Arabia' (1962), 'Beckett' (1964), 'The Lion in The Winter' (1968), 'Goodbye Mr. Chips' (1969), 'The Ruling Class' (1969), 'The Stuntman' (1980), and 'My Favourite Year' (1982).
- Among the actresses, Katherine Hepburn and Meryl Streep have received the most number of nominations, 12 each. Meryl Streep won two Best Actress Oscar for 'Kramer Vs. Kramer' (1979) and 'Sophie's Choice' (1982).
- Katherine Hepburn holds the record for the maximum number of Oscars. She won four awards for 'Morning Glory' (1932-33), 'Guess Who is Coming To Dinner' (1967), 'The Lion in the Winter' (1968), and 'On Golden Pond' (1981). She also had the longest award-winning career (1932 to 1981).
- Among the actors Jack Nicholson holds the record for maximum nominations and awards. He won three awards out of his 12 nominations.
- Italy's 'Life Is Beautiful' (1998) is the only second film to compete as both Best Picture and the Best Foreign Language film in the same year after "Z" in 1969.
- 'Crouching Tiger Hidden Dragon' (2000) is the most nominated (10) foreign film. 'Life is Beautiful' (1998) was nominated for 7 awards while 'Das Boot' and 'Fanny And Alexander' won 6 nominations each.
- John Williams was nominated for the 39th time for his score in 'Catch Me If You Can' (2002).

- Alfred Newman is the most Oscar Nominated (45) living person.
- The only westerner that have won the Best Picture Award are 'Cimarron' (1931), 'Dances With The Wolves' (1960) and 'Unforgiven' (1992).
- The only actors to win 'Consecutive' Oscars are :
  - (a) Luise Rainer — for 'The Great Ziegfeld' (1936) and 'The Good Earth' (1937) for the Best Actress.
  - (b) Spencer Tracy — for 'Captain Courageous' (1937) and 'Boys Town' (1938) for the Best Actor.
  - (c) Katherine Hepburn — for 'Guess Who's Coming For Dinner' (1967) and 'The Lion in Winter' (1968) for the Best Actress.
  - (d) Jason Robard — For 'All The President's Men' (1976) and 'Julia' (1977) for the 'Best Supporting Actor.'
  - (e) Tom Hanks — for 'Philadelphia' (1993) and 'Forrest Gump (94) for the Best Actor.
- The only two Films to win three Oscars for acting are 'A Street Car Named Desire' (1951) and 'Network' (1976).
- No film to date has won all the four Oscars for acting.
- The 76-year-old Henry Fonda is the oldest winner of the Best Actor Oscar for his role in 'On Golden Pond' (1981). And Jessica Tandy at 80 was the oldest actress to win the Best Actress Oscar for her role in 'Driving Miss Daisy' (1989).
- Walter Brennan won the most Best supporting Actor Oscar for 'Come And Get It' (1936), Kentucky (1938), and 'The Westerner' (1940).
- Shelley Winters and Dianne Wiest won the most Best supporting Actress Awards. Shelley won for 'The Diary of Anne Frank' (1959), and 'A Patch of Blue' (1965). Dianne won for 'Hannah and Her Sisters' (1986) and 'Bullets Over Broadway' (1994).
- Seven people have won the Best Actor Oscar twice. They are :

(1) Spencer Tracy — For 'Captain Courageous' (1937) and 'Boys Town' (1938).

(2) Fredric March — For 'Dr. Jeckyll and Mr. Hyde' (1932) and 'The Best Years of Our Lives' (1946).

(3) Gary Cooper — for 'Sergeant York' (1941), and 'High Noon' (52).

(4) Marlon Brando — For 'On The Water Front' (1954) and 'The Godfather' (1972 — award declined).

(5) Jack Nicholson — For 'One Flew Over The Cuckoo's Nest' (1975) and 'As Good As It Gets' (1997).

(6) Dustin Hoffman — For 'Kramer Vs Kramer' (1979), and 'Rain Man' (1988).

(7) Tom Hanks — For 'Philadelphia' (1993) and 'The Forrest Gump'.

- Shirley Temple was awarded an honorary Oscar at the age of five in 1934.
- Italy has won 13 Oscars for the Best Foreign Language Film the most recent being 'Life is Beautiful' (1998). It is a record.

Consecutive Directing wins :

- John Ford — For 'The Grapes of Wrath' (1940) and 'How Green Was My Valley' (1941).
- Joseph L. Mankiewicz — For 'A Letter To Three Wives' (1949) and 'All About Eve' (1950).
- 'Midnight Cowboy' (1969) is the only X-Rated film to win the Best Picture Oscar.
- George Burns (80) was the oldest actor, who had won the Best Supporting Actor Oscar for 'The Sunshine Boys' (1975).
- Roberto Benigni (Life is Beautiful), Orson Welles (Citizen Kane), Warren Beatty (Heaven Can Wait, Reds) and Woody Allen (Annie Hall) are a triple contender, not only for directing but as a nominee for the Best Actor and Best Screenplay Oscars.
- Randy Newman was nominated for three Oscars in the same year for his scores of 'A Bug's Life',

'Pleasantville' and for his song from "Babe, Pig in the City".

OSCAR AWARDS

1927-28

The Best Picture : Wings

The Best Director : Frank Borzage (Seventh Heaven), Lewis Milestone (Two Arabian Knights)

The Best Actor : Emil Jannings (The Last Command and The Ways of All Flesh)

The Best Actress : Janet Gaynor (Seventh Heaven, Street Angel and Sunrise)

1928-29

The Best Picture : The Broadway Melody

The Best Director : Frank Llyod (The Divine Lady)

The Best Actor : Warner Baxter (Old Arizona)

The Best Actress : Mary Pickford (Coquette)

1929-30

The Best Picture : All Quiet On The Western Front

The Best Director : Lewis Milestone (All Quiet on The Western Front)

The Best Actor : George Arliss (Disraeli)

The Best Actress : Norma Shearer (The Divorce)

1930-31

The Best Picture : Cimarron

The Best Director : Norman Taurog (Skippy)

The Best Actor : Lionel Barrymore (A Free Soul)

The Best Actress : Marie Dressler (Min And Bill)

1931-32

The Best Picture : Grand Hotel

The Best Director : Frank Borzage (Bad Girl)

The Best Actor : Fredric March (Dr. Jeckyll and Mr. Hyde) and Wallace Berry (The Champ)

The Best Actress : Helen Hayes (The Sin of Malelon Claudet)

1932-33

The Best Picture : Cavalcade

The Best Director : Frank Lloyd (Cavalcade)

The Best Actor : Charles Laughton (The Private Life Of Henry VIII)

The Best Actress : Katherine Hepburn (Morning Glory)

1934

The Best Picture : It Happened One Night

The Best Director : Frank Capra (It Happened One Night)

The Best Actor : Clark Gable (It Happened One Night)

The Best Actress : Caludette Colbert (It Happened One Night)

1935

The Best Picture : Mutiny on The Bounty

The Best Director : John Ford (The Informer)

The Best Actor : Victor McLaglen (The Informer)

The Best Actress : Bette Davis (Dangerous)

1936

The Best Picture : The Great Ziegfeld

The Best Director : Frank Capra (Mr. Deeds Goes To Town)

The Best Actor : Paul Muni (The Story of Louis Pasteur)

The Best Actress : Luise Rainer (The Great Ziegfeld)

1937

The Best Picture : The Life of Emile Zola

The Best Director : Leo Mc Carey (The Awful Truth)

The Best Actor : Spencer Tracy (Captain Courageous)

The Best Actress : Luise Rainer (The Good Earth)

1938

The Best Picture : You Can't Take It With You

The Best Director : Frank Capra (You Can't Take It With You)

The Best Actor : Spencer Tracy (Boys Town)
The Best Actress : Bette Davis (Jezebel)

1939

The Best Picture : Gone With The Wind
The Best Director : Victor Fleming (Gone With the Wind)
The Best Actor : Robert Donat (Goodbye Mr. Chips)
The Best Actress : Vivien Leigh (Gone With the Wind)

1940

The Best Picture : Rebecca
The Best Director : John Ford (The Grapes of Wrath)
The Best Actor : James Stewart (The Philadelphia Story)
The Best Actress : Ginger Rogers (Kitty Foyle)

1941

The Best Picture : How Green Was My Valley
The Best Director : John Ford (How Green Was My Valley)
The Best Actor : Gary Cooper (Sergeant York)
The Best Actress : Joan Fontaine (Suspicion)

1942

The Best Picture : Mrs. Miniver
The Best Director : William Wyler (Mrs. Miniver)
The Best Actor : James Cagney (Yankee Doondle Dandy)
The Best Actress : Green Garson (Mrs. Miniver)

1943

The Best Picture : Casablanca
The Best Director : Michael Curtiz (Casablanca)
The Best Actor : Paul Lukas (Watch on the Rhine)
The Best Actress : Jennifer Jones (The Song of Bernadette)

1944

The Best Picture : Going My Way
The Best Director : Leo MacCarey (Going My Way)
The Best Actor : Bing Crossby (Going My Way)
The Best Actress : Ingrid Bergman (Gaslight)

1945

The Best Picture : The Last Weekend
The Best Director : Billy Wilder (The Last Weekend)
The Best Actor : Ray Milland (The Last Weekend)
The Best Actress : Joan Crawford (Mildred Pierce)

1946

The Best Picture : The Best Years of Our Lives
The Best Director : William Wyler (The Best Years of Our Lives)
The Best Actor : Fredric March (The Best Years of Our Lives)
The Best Actress : Olivia De Havilland (To Each His Own)

1947

The Best Picture : Gentleman's Agreement
The Best Director : Elia Kazan (Gentleman's Agreement)
The Best Actor : Ronald Colman (A Double Life)
The Best Actress : Loretta Young (The Farmer's Daughter)

1948

The Best Picture : Hamlet
The Best Director : John Huston (The Treasure of Sierre Madre)
The Best Actor : Laurence Olivier (Hamlet)
The Best Actress : Jane Wyman (Jhonny Belinda)

1949

The Best Picture : All The King's Men
The Best Director : Joseph L. Mankiewicz (A Letter to Three Wives)
The Best Actor : Broderick Crawford (All the King's Men)
The Best Actress : Olivia De Havilland (The Heiress)

1950

The Best Picture : All About Eve
The Best Director : Joseph L. Mankiewicz (All About Eve)
The Best Actor : Jose Ferrer (Cyrano de Bergerace)

The Best Actress : Judy Holliday (Born Yesterday)

1951

The Best Picture : An American In Paris
The Best Director : George Stevens (A Place in the Sun)
The Best Actor : Humphrey Bogart (The African Queen)
The Best Actress : Vivien Leigh (A Street Car Named Desire)

1952

The Best Picture : The Greatest Show On Earth
The Best Director : John Ford (The Quiet Man)
The Best Actor : Gary Cooper (High Noon)
The Best Actress : Shirley Booth (Come Back Little Sheba)

1953

The Best Picture : From Here To Eternity
The Best Director : Fred Zinnemann (From Here To Eternity)
The Best Actor : William Holden (Stalag 17)
The Best Actress : Audrey Hepburn (Roman Holiday)

1954

The Best Picture : On The Waterfront
The Best Director : Elia Kazan (On The Waterfront)
The Best Actor : Marlon Brando (On The Waterfront)
The Best Actress : Grace Kelly (The Country Girl)

1955

The Best Picture : Marty
The Best Director : Delbert Mann (Marty)
The Best Actor : Ernest Borgnine (Marty)
The Best Actress : Anna Magnani (The Rose Tattoo)

1956

The Best Picture : Around The World In 80 Days
The Best Director : George Stevens (Giant)
The Best Actor : Yul Brynner (The King And I)
The Best Actress : Ingrid Bergman (Anastasia)

1957

The Best Picture : The Bridge On The River Kwai
The Best Director : David Lean (The Bridge On The River Kwai)
The Best Actor : Alec Guinness (The Bridge On The River Kwai)
The Best Actress : Joanne Woodward (The Three Faces Of Eve)

1958

The Best Picture : Gigi
The Best Director : Vincente Minnelli (Gigi)
The Best Actor : David Niven (Separate Tables)
The Best Actress : Susan Hayward (I Want to Live)

1959

The Best Picture : Ben Hur
The Best Director : William Wyler (Ben Hur)
The Best Actor : Charlton Heston (Ben Hur)
The Best Actress : Simone Signoret (Room At The Top)

1960

The Best Picture : The Apartment
The Best Director : Billy Wilder (The Apartment)
The Best Actor : Burt Lancaster (Elmer Gantry)
The Best Actress : Elizabeth Taylor (Butterfield 8)

1961

The Best Picture : West Side Story
The Best Director : Jerome Robbins and Robertwise (West Side Story)
The Best Actor : Maximilian Schell (Judgment At Nuremberg)
The Best Actress : Sophia Loren (Two Woman)

1962

The Best Picture : Lawrence of Arabia
The Best Director : David Lean (Lawrence of Arabia)

The Best Actor : Gregory Peck (To Kill A Mocking Bird)
The Best Actress : Anne Bancroft (The Miracle Worker)

1963

The Best Picture : Tom Jones
The Best Director : Tony Richardson (Tom Jones)
The Best Actor : Sidney Poitier (Lillies of The Field)
The Best Actress : Patrica Neal (Hud)

1964

The Best Picture : My Fair Lady
The Best Director : George Cukor (My Fair Lady)
The Best Actor : Rex Harrison (My Fair Lady)
The Best Actress : Julie Andrews (Mary Pappins)

1965

The Best Picture : The Sound Of Music
The Best Director : Robert Wise (The Sound Of Music)
The Best Actor : Lee Marwin (Cal Ballou)
The Best Actress : Julie Christie (Darling)

1966

The Best Picture : A Man For All Seasons
The Best Director : Fred Zinnemann (A Man For All Seasons)
The Best Actor : Paul Scofield (A Man For All Seasons)
The Best Actress : Elizabeth Taylor (Who is Afraid of Virginia Wolf?)

1967

The Best Picture : In the Heat of the Night
The Best Director : Mike Nichols (The Graduate)
The Best Actor : Rod Steiger (In the Heat of The Night)
The Best Actress : Katherine Hepburn (Guess Who's Coming To Dinner)

1968

The Best Picture : Oliver!
The Best Director : Carol Reed (Oliver)

The Best Actor : Cliff Robertson (Charly)
The Best Actress : Katherine Hepburn (The Lion In Winter) Barbara Streisand (Funny Girl)

1969

The Best Picture : Midnight Cowboy
The Best Director : John Schlesinger (Midnight Cowboy)
The Best Actor : John Wayne (True Girl)
The Best Actress : Maggie Smith (The Prime of Miss Jean Brodler)

1970

The Best Picture : Patton
The Best Director : Franklin J. Schaffner (Patton)
The Best Actor : George C. Scott (Patton)
The Best Actress : Glenda Jackson (Women In Love)

1971

The Best Picture : The French Connection
The Best Director : William Fredkin (The French Connection)
The Best Actor : Gene Hackman (The French Connection)
The Best Actress : Jane Fonda (Klute)

1972

The Best Picture : The Godfather
The Best Director : Bob Fosse (Cabaret)
The Best Actor : Marlon Brando (The Godfather)
The Best Actress : Glenda Jackson (A Touch Of Class)

1973

The Best Picture : The Sting
The Best Director : George Roy Hill (The Sting)
The Best Actor : Jack Lemmon (Save The Tiger)
The Best Actress : Glenda Jackson (A Touch Of Class)

1974

The Best Picture : The Godfather Part-II
The Best Director : Francis Ford Coppola (The Godfather Part-II)

The Best Actor : Art Corney (Harry And Tonto)

The Best Actress : Ellen Burstyn (Alice Doesn't Live Here Anymore)

1975

The Best Picture : One Flew Over The Cuckoo's Nest

The Best Director : Milos Forman (One Flew Over The Cuckoo's Nest)

The Best Actor : Jack Nicholson (One Flew Over The Cuckoo's Nest)

The Best Actress : Louise Fletcher (One Flew Over The Cuckoo's Nest)

1976

The Best Picture : Rocky

The Best Director : John G. Avildsen (Rocky)

The Best Actor : Peter Finch (Network)

The Best Actress : Faye Dunaway (Network)

1977

The Best Picture : Annie Hall

The Best Director : Woody Allen (Annie Hall)

The Best Actor : Richard Drey Fuss (The Goodbye Girl)

The Best Actress : Diane Keaton (Annie Hall)

1978

The Best Picture : The Deer Hunter

The Best Director : Michael Cimino (The Deer Hunter)

The Best Actor : John Voight (Coming Home)

The Best Actress : Jane Fonda (Coming Home)

1979

The Best Picture : Kramer Vs Kramer

The Best Director : Robert Benton (Kramer Vs Kramer)

The Best Actor : Dustin Hoffman (Kramer Vs Kramer)

The Best Actress : Sally Field (Norma Rae)

1980

The Best Picture : Ordinary People

The Best Director : Robert Redford (Ordinary People)
The Best Actor : Robert De Niro (Raging Bull)
The Best Actress : Sissy Spacek (Coal Miner's Daughter)

1981

The Best Picture : Chariots Of Fire
The Best Director : Warren Beatty (Reds)
The Best Actor : Henry Fonda (On Golden Pond)
The Best Actress : Katherine Hepburn (On Golden Pond)

1982

The Best Picture : Gandhi
The Best Director : Sir Richard Attenborough (Gandhi)
The Best Actor : Ben Kingsley (Gandhi)
The Best Actress : Meryl Streep (Sophie's Choice)

1983

The Best Picture : Terms Of Endearment
The Best Director : James L. Brooks (Terms of Endearment)
The Best Actor : Robert Duvall (Tender Mercies)
The Best Actress : Shirley Maclaine (Terms of Endearment)

1984

The Best Picture : Amadeus
The Best Director : Milos Forman (Amadeus)
The Best Actor : F. Murray Abraham (Amadeus)
The Best Actress : Sally Field (Place In the Heart)

1985

The Best Picture : Out Of Africa
The Best Director : Sydney Pollock (Out Of Africa)
The Best Actor : Willian Hurt (The Kiss of The Spider Woman)
The Best Actress : Geraldine Page (The Trip To Bountiful)

1986

The Best Picture : Platoon
The Best Director : Oliver Stone (Platoon)

The Best Actor : Paul New Man (The Colour of Money)
The Best Actress : Marlee Matlin (Children of A Lesser God)

1987

The Best Picture : The Last Emperor
The Best Director : Bernardo Bertolucci (The Last Emperor)
The Best Actor : Michael Douglas (Wall Street)
The Best Actress : Cher (Moonstruck)

1988

The Best Picture : Rain Man
The Best Director : Barry Levinson (Rain Man)
The Best Actor : Dustin Hoffman (Rain Man)
The Best Actress : Jodie Foster (The Accused)

1989

The Best Picture : Driving Miss Daisy
The Best Director : Oliver Stone (Born On The Fourth Of July)
The Best Actor : Daniel Day-Lewis (My Left Foot)
The Best Actress : Jessica Tandy (Driving Miss Daisy)

1990

The Best Picture : Dances With The Wolves
The Best Director : Kevin Costner (Dances With The Wolves)
The Best Actor : Jeremy Irons (Reversal Of Fortune)
The Best Actress : Kathy Bates (Misery)

1991

The Best Picture : The Silence of The Lambs
The Best Director : Jonathan Demme (The Silence of The Lambs)
The Best Actor : Anthony Hopkins (The Silence of The Lambs)
The Best Actress : Jodie Foster (The Silence of The Lambs)

1992

The Best Picture : Unforgiven

The Best Director : Client Eastwood (Unforgiven)
The Best Actor : Al Pacino (Scent of A Woman)
The Best Actress : Emma Thompson (Howard's End)

1993

The Best Picture : Schindler's List
The Best Director : Steven Spielberg (Schindler's List)
The Best Actor : Tom Hanks (Philadelphia)
The Best Actress : Holly Hunter (The Piano)

1994

The Best Picture : Forrest Gump
The Best Director : Robert Zemeckis (Forrest Gump)
The Best Actor : Tom Hanks (Forrest Gump)
The Best Actress : Jessica Lang (Blue Sky)

1995

The Best Picture : Braveheart
The Best Director : Mel Gibson (Braveheart)
The Best Actor : Nicholas Cage (Leaving Los Vegas)
The Best Actress : Susan Saradon (Dead Man Walking)

1996

The Best Picture : The English Patient
The Best Director : Anthony Minghella (The English Patient)
The Best Actor : Geoffrey Rush (Shine)
The Best Actress : Frances McDormand (Fargo)

1997

The Best Picture : Titanic
The Best Director : James Cameron (Titanic)
The Best Actor : Jack Nicholson (As Good As It Gets)
The Best Actress : Helen Hunt (As Good As It Gets)

1998

The Best Picture : Shakespeare In Love
The Best Director : Steven Spielberg (Saving Private Ryan)
The Best Actor : Roberto Benigni (Life is Beautiful)

The Best Actress : Gwyneth Paltrow (Shakespeare In Love)

1999

The Best Picture : American Beauty

The Best Director : Sam Mendes (American Beauty)

The Best Actor : Kevin Spacey (American Beauty)

The Best Actress : Hilary Swank (Boys Don't Cry)

2000

The Best Picture : Gladiator

The Best Director : Steven Soderbergh (Traffic)

The Best Actor : Russel Crowe (Gladiator)

The Best Actress : Julia Robert (Erin Brockovich)

2001

The Best Picture : A Beautiful Mind

The Best Director : Ron Howard (A Beautiful Mind)

The Best Actor : Denzel Washington (Training Day)

The Best Actress : Halle Berry (Monster's Ball)

2002

The Best Picture : Chicago

The Best Director : Roman Polanski (The Pianist)

The Best Actor : Adrien Brody (The Pianist)

The Best Actress : Nicole Kidman (The Hours)

OSCAR FOR THE BEST FOREIGN LANGUAGE FILM

1947

Shoeshine (Italy)

1948

Monsieur Vincent (France)

1949

The Bicycle Thief (Italy)

1950

The Walls of Malapaga (France/Italy)

1951

Rashomon (Japan)

1952

Forbidden Games (France)

1954

Gate of Hell (Japan)

1955

Samurai, The Legends of Musashi (Japan)

1956

LA Strada (Italy)

1957

The Nights of Cabiria (Italy)

1958

My Uncle (France)

1959

Black Orpheus (France)

1960

The Virgin Spring (Sweden)

1961

Through A Glass Darkly (Sweden)

1962

Sundays And Cybelle (France)

1963

Eight And A Half (Italy)

1964

Yesterday, Today And Tomorrow (Italy)

1965

The Shop On The Main Street (Czechoslovakia)

1966

A Man And A Woman (France)

1967

Closely Watched Trains (Czechoslovakia)

1968

War And Peace (USSR)

1969

"Z" (Algeria)

1970

Investigation of a Citizen Above Suspicion (Italy)

1971

The Garden of The Finzi Continis (Italy)

1972

The Discreet Charm Of The Bourgeoisie (France)

1973

Day For Night (France)

1974

Amarcord (Italy)

1975

Dersu Uzala (USSR)

1976

Black And White In Color (Ivory Coast)

1977

Madam Rosa (France)

1978

Get Out Your Handkerchief (France)

1979

The Tin Drum (Germany)

1980

Moscow Doesn't Believe In Tears (USSR)

1981

Mephisto (Hungary)

1982

Volver A Empezar (Spain)

1983

Fanny And Alexander (Sweden)

1984

Dangerous Move (Switzerland)

1985

The Official Story (Argentina)

1986

The Assault (The Netherland)

1987

Babette's Feast (Denmark)

1988

Pelle, The Conqueror (Denmark)

1989

Cinema Paradiso (Italy)

1990

Journey of Hope (Switzerland)

1991

Mediterraneo (Italy)

1992

Indochine (France)

1993

Belle Epoque (Spain)

1994

Burnt By The Sun (Russia)

1995

Antonia's Line (The Netherlands)

1996

Kolya (Czech Republic)

1997

Character (The Netherlands)

1998

Life Is Beautiful (Italy)

1999

All About My Mother (Spain)

2000

Crouching Tiger, Hidden Dragon (Taiwan)

2001

No Man's Land (Bosnia And Herzegovina)

2002

Nowhere in Africa (Germany)

29

THE INTERESTING LITTLE FACTS

- **The Most Expensive Films :**

Titanic (1997)	-	$	250 million
Waterworld (1995)	-	$	175 million
Armageddon (1998)	-	$	174 million
Pearl Harbor (2001)	-	$	150 million
Cleopatra (1963)	-	$	44 million

- **Highest Grossing Films :**

Titanic	-	Grossed around $ 1800 million
Gone with The Wind	-	around $ 200 million
Star Wars	-	around $ 1000 million
Independence Day	-	around $ 811 million

- *The Biggest loss* :
  - MGM's 'Cut throat Island' (1995) cost more than $ 100 million, but it could earn back only $ 11 million.
  - 'Waterworld' (1995) is another big loss.
- The most expensive film Rights — The highest price ever paid for film rights was $ 9.5 million for the Broadway musical 'Annie' (1982). Columbia Pictures bought the rights in 1978.
- Most filmed author : A total of 350 films based on plays by Shakespeare have been made to date. 75 films were made on only "Hamlet" and 51 on "Romeo And Juliet".
- Most filmed horror author — Stephen King remains the most filmed horror author with at least 20 films made on his novels. Films are : Carrie (1976), The

Shining (1980), Misery (1990), and Shawshank Redemption etc.

- The most filmed story — 'Cindrella', a classic fairy tale, is the most filmed story. 95 films were based on this story.
- Most frequently portrayed character — The French Emperor Napolean Bonaparte has been the subject of more than 175 films since 1897.
- The fictional character most frequently portrayed on the big screen is Sherlock Homes, the detective created by Sir Arthur Conan Doyle. He has been portrayed by 75 actors in more than 211 films since 1900.
- The longest Film : The 85 hour 'Cure for Insomnia' (1987), which was directed by Henry Timmis IV, consists of Groban reading his own 4,080 page poem, interspersed with scenes of a rock and band and some X-rated footage.
- Most Costumes in One Film : A record of 32,000 costumes were worn in Quo Vadis (1951).
- Oldest Hollywood director — George Cukor (1899-1983). Made his final film 'Rich And Famous', in 1981 at the age of 81.
- Youngest Hollywood Producer — Steven Paul was 20 years old when he produced and directed 'Falling In Love Again' in 1980.
- Largest Film studio complex — Universal City in Los Angeles, California, USA, covers 170 ha (420 Acres) and has 561 Buildings and 34 Sound Stages.
- Most profitable Film Series — The 21 Bond movies, based on the novels by Ian Fleming and largely produced by Cubby Broccoli, have grossed more than $ 1000 million world-wide. It is estimated that over 50% of the world population have seen at least one Bond Film.
- Highest grossing horror films are : Scream (all 3 parts), The Exorcist.
- Highest-grossing Comedy film is 'Austin Powers : The Spy Who Shagged Me' (1999).

- Most versatile award winner actress/singer/director is Barbra Streisand. She had won two Oscars, five Emmys, Seven Grammys, Seven Golden Globes and Special Tony Award in 1970 as Broadway Actress of The Decade.
- The highest paid female star is Julia Roberts. Her fee is $ 20 million per film.
- Most weight loss and gain — The record-holder is Robert De Niro, who gaind 27 kg. for his role as Jake La Motta in Martin Scorsese's Raging Bull (1980). Jennifer Jason Leigh went down to a weight of 39 kg. for her role as an anorexic Teenager in 'The Best Little Girl in The World' (1981). Gary Oldman lost 13 kg. to play punk star Sid vicious in 'Sid And Nancy' (1986) and ended up in hospital suffering from malnutrition. Tom Hanks lost 20 kg. in 'Cast Away' (2000). Will Smith gained 20 kg. of extra weight to play boxer Muhammad Ali in Michael Mann's Ali (2001).
- Alee Guinness played eight members of the ill fated d'Ascoyne family in 'Kind Hearts and Coronets' (1949).
- Dustin Hoffman was 33 when he played the role of Jack Crabb in 'Little Big Man' (1970). In the course of the film his character ages from 17 to 121.
- Most devoted Method Actors — Daniel Day Lewis is reputed to have spent many nights without sleep in a mock jail cell in order to prepare for his role in 'In The Name Of The Father' (1993), while for 'Last of the Mohicans' (1992) he went to a survival Camp to learn to track and kill animals and make canoes and trees.
- Nicholas Cage had two teeth removed without painkillers for his part in 'Vampire's Kiss' (1988). He also ate few live cockroaches to make the scene really shock.
- Dustin Hoffman had deliberately not slept for a couple of days and not eaten anything to prepare for a scene in 'Marathon Man'.
- The husky voiced actress Mercedes Mc Cambridge swallowed 18 raw eggs with a pulpy apple to produce her violent gaggling sounds in 'The Exorcist'.
- Robert De Niro, in his typical, almost masochistic quest

for realism, trained with boxer Jake La Motta each day for a full year before production of 'Raging Bull' began. He blackened his eyes, broken his upper teeth caps and damaged his chin. Scorsese halted the production for four months so that De Niro could gain weight.

- Highest paid child performer — Macaulay Culkin was paid $ 1 million for 'My Girl' (1991) when he was 11 years old. He subsequently earned $ 5 million plus 5% gross for 'Home Alone – II : Lost in New York' (1992) and a reputed $ 8 million for 'Richie Rich' (1994).
- Shirley Temple was 7 years old when she became the youngest No. 1 Star at the US box Office in 1935.
- Warner Brother's 'Lights of New York' (1928) was the first all talking film of the world.
- Stan Laurel and Oliver Hardy acted together in more than 50 comedy films between 1927 to 1940. They first appeared together in 'Lucky Dogs' (1917). Their 'Music Box' won an Oscar for the Best short film. Their was the longest comedy partnership.
- The longest screen partnership belongs to the pair of Indian Stars Prem Nazir and Sheela. They starred together in 130 movies till 1975.
- The longest Hollywood partnership was 15 films together by Charles Bronson and Jill Ireland from 1968 to 1986.
- The longest screen career belongs to Curt Bois. He made his debut in 'Der Fidele Bauer' (Germany, 1908) at the age of eight. His final film appearance was 80 years later in Wim Wender's Wings of Desire' (Germany 1988).
- John Wayne did the most leading roles. He acted in 153 films, starting with 'The Drop Kick' (1927) and ending with 'The Shootist' (1976). He played the lead in 142 films.
- Walt Disney's 'Jungle Book' (1967) is the highest grossing animated film ever made, with $ 205 million.
- 'The Lion King' (1994, Disney) grossed a record of $ 766 million in over 60 countries. The film took 600 animators three years to make. Its song 'Can You Feel

The Love Tonight', was awarded an Oscar for the 'Best Original Song'.

- Disney's 'Snow White' (1937), which has taken $ 175 million would top the list of the highest grosser if inflation were taken into account.
- Japan's highest grossing animated film is 'Princess Mononok' (1997). It grossed $ 156 million in Japan only.
- 'The Simpson', an animated film featured the voices of 228 celebrities.
- Dream works 'The Prince of Egypt' (1998) is the most expensive animated film. It cost $ 60 million and was in production for four years, worked on by 350 artists and animators. The 4 minute Red-Sea Sequence alone took 3500 hours to complete.
- The character of Zorro is the most filmed Comic Character. He has been portrayed in 69 films. The character was invented by Johnston Mc Culley in 1929.
- 22 Godzilla films were made by Japan between 1954 and 1995.
- Al Pacino turned down many films that include 'Kramer Vs Kramer', 'Born on The Fourth Of July,' 'Apocalypse Now,' 'Star Wars,' 'Pretty Woman,' 'Crimson Tide'.
- Actors who played James Bond —

(i) Sir Sean Connery : 1. Dr. No. (1962)
2. From Russia With Love (1963)
3. Goldfinger (1964)
4. Thunder Ball (1965)
5. You Only Live Twice (1967)
6. Diamonds Are Forever (1971)
7. Never Say Never Again (1983)

(ii) George Lazenby : 8. On Her Majesty's Secret Service (1969)

(iii) Roger Moore : 9. Live And Let Die (1973)
10. The Man with The Golden Gun (1974)

11. The Spy Who Loved Me (1977)
12. Moonraker (1979)
13. For Your Eyes Only (1981)
14. Octopussy (1983)
15. A View To A Kill (1985)

(iv) Timothy Dalton :
16. The Living Day Lights (1987)
17. Licence To Kill (1985)

(v) Pierce Brosnan :
18. Golden Eye (1995)
19. Tomorrow Never Dies (1997)
20. The World Is Not Enough (1999)
21. Die Another Day (2002)

- The film "Look Who's Talking' (1989) starring John Travolta was made at $ 7 million budget. It grossed $ 400 million.
- Band of Brothers (2001) was the most expensive ($ 120 million) T.V. Mini-series ever made. 10 hours mini-series were made by Steven Spielberg and Tom Hanks, which was aired on HBO. It tells the story of World War II.
- First movie in history to be officially banned by the Pope is 'Hail Mary' by Jean Luc Godard.
- Alfred Hitchcock, one of America's greatest filmmakers, never won an Oscar for Best Director. Saul Bass, not Hitchcock, Story boarded and directed the now notorious shower sequence in 'Psycho'.
- The famous chariot race of the film 'Ben Hur' (1959) was not directed by its director William Wyler. It was directed by Japanese Stuntman Yakima Kanut.
- Stanley Kubrick used K-Y jelly coating on the Alien Monster in '2001 : A Space Odyssey' (1968). Shredded condoms simulated its ghastly Jaw tendons. Real blood and entrails were shipped from a London Slaughter house, spurted plentifully on the sets, sometime inspiring real sickness and distress.
- The stunt director Yon Fan was responsible for the

gravity defying actions in Matrix Films, and 'Crouching Tiger Hidden Dragon' (2000).

- Finally Steven Spielberg earned the University degree in film and electronic arts in 2002. He was 55. Before his bachelor's degree, he already had five honorary doctorates.
- The outtake from Kubrick's 'Shining' was used as the end title sequence of Ridley Scott's 'Blade Runner'.
- ***Censor ratings :***
  - (a) G - Suitable for general audience.
  - (b) PG - Parental guidance needed for children under 17.
  - (c) R - Restricted for under 17.
  - (d) X - People under 17 is completely restricted (Porn Film).
  - (e) C - Children's Film.
- Mario Puzo, the author and Screenplay writer of 'Godfather' series, had also written screen plays for 'Superman' & 'Superman II'.
- The well-known comedians are : Charlie Chaplin, Buster Keaton, Harold Lloyd, Jerry Lewis, Stan Laurell, Oliver Hardy, and Jim Carry.
- Al Jalson was the first person to talk on the screen. The film was "Jazz Singer" (1927).

30

THE BEST GENRE FILMS

Romantic Comedies

1. When Harry Met Sally
2. Crossing Delencey (Joan Micklin Silver)
3. It happened One Night (Frank Capra)
4. Say Anything (Cameron Crowe)
5. Everyone Says I Love You (Woody Allen)

Cops and Robbers

1. Dirty Hary (Don Siegel)
2. Heat (Michael Mann)
3. Prince of the City (Sidney Lumet)
4. Serpico (Sidney Lumet)
5. The Untouchables (Brian De Palma)

Gangsters

1. Kiss of Death (Henry Hathaway)
2. The Long Good Friday (John Mackenzie)
3. Carlito's Way (Brian De Palma)
4. Donnie Brasco (Mike Newell)
5. Prizzi's Honour (John Huston)

Sci-fi Fantasy

1. Close Encounters of The Third Kind (Steven Spielberg)
2. Brazil (Terry Gilliam)
3. Excaliber (John Boorman)
4. Solaris (Andre Tarkovsky)

Romantic Drama

1. Truly, Madly, Deeply (Anthony Minghella)
2. Shadowlands (Sir Richard Attenborough)
3. 84, Charing Cross Road (David Jones)
4. Mr. North (Danny Huston)
5. Leaving Los Vegas (Mike Figgis)

Detective

1. The Maltese Falcon (John Huston)
2. The Name of The Rose (Jean Jacques Annand)
3. Devil in a Blue Dress (Carl Franklin)
4. Murder On The Orient Express (Sidney Lumet)
5. The Seven Percent Solution (Herbert Ross)

Funny

1. The General (Buster Keaton)
2. Duck Soup (The Marx Brothers)
3. A Fish Called Wanda (Charles Chrichton)
4. Take The Money And Run (Woody Allen)
5. Beetle Juice (Tim Burton)

Spoofs

1. High Anxiety (Mel Brooks)
2. M.A.S.H. (Robert Altman)
3. Life of Brian (Monty Python)
4. The Naked Gun (David Zucker)
5. Pink Panther (Blake Edwards)

Film Noir

1. Double Indemnity (Billy Wilder)
2. Kiss Me Deadly (Robert Aldrich)
3. Touch Of Evil (Orson Welles)
4. Red Rock West (John Dahl)
5. Coup De Torchon (Bertrand Tavernier)

Thrillers

1. The French Connection (William Friedkin)
2. Witness (Peter Weir)

3. Marathon Man (John Schlesinger)
4. Dead Again (Kenneth Branagh)
5. Clear And Present Danger (Philip Kaufman)

Horror

1. The Exorcist (William Friedkin)
2. The Shining (Stanley Kubrick)
3. The Innocents (Jack Clayton)
4. The Changeling (Peter Medak)
5. Suspiria (Dario Argento)

Religious

1. The Diary of A Country Priest (Robert Bresson)
2. Babbet's Feast (Gabriel Axel)
3. Kundun (Martin Scorsese)
4. The Mission (Roland Joffe)
5. Little Buddha (Bernardo Bertolucci)

Westerns

1. High Noon (Fred Zinnemann)
2. Once Upon A Time In The West (Sergio Leone)
3. The Wild Bunch (Sam Peckin Path)
4. The Searchers (John Ford)
5. The Quick And The Dead (Sam Raimi)
6. The Stagecoach (John Ford)
7. Unforgiven (Client Eastwood)

Weird

1. Picnic At Hanging Rock (Peter Weir)
2. Blue Velvet (David Lynch)
3. Dead Ringers (David Cronenberg)
4. The Stepford Wives (Bryan Forbes)
5. The Texes Chainsaw Massacre (Tobe Hopper)

Suspense

1. Hallo-ween (John Carpenter)
2. Rebecca (Alfred Hitchcock)

3. The Vanishing (George Sluizer)
4. Psycho II (Richard Franklin)
5. The Dead Zone (David Cronenberg)

Courtroom

1. Witness for the Prosecution (Billy Wilder)
2. Presumed Innocent (Alan Pakula)
3. The Verdict (Sidney Lumet)
4. A Few Good Men (Rob Reiner)
5. Breaker Morant (Bruce Beresford)

Movies About Movies

1. Cinema Paradiso (Giuseppe Tornatore)
2. The Purple Rose of Cairo (Woody Allen)
3. The Player (Robert Altman)
4. Sullivan's Travels (Preston Sterges)
5. Get Shorty (Barry Sonnenfeld)

Con Men

1. The Sting (George Roy Hill)
2. House of Games (David Mamet)
3. The Usual Suspects (Bryan Singer)
4. Sleuth (Joseph Mankiewicz)
5. Deathtrap (Sidney Lumet)

The Spy

1. The Ipcress File (Sidney Furie)
2. The Spy Who Came In from The Cold (Martin Rit)
3. Funeral In Berlin (Guy Hamilton)
4. The Russia House (Fred Schepisi)
5. The Little Drummer Girl (George Roy Hill)

The Fallen Women Films

1. Anna Karenina (Clarence Brown, 1935)
2. Ann Vickers (John Cromwell, 1933)
3. Camille (George Cukor 1937)
4. Back Street (Robert Stevenson 1941)
5. Blonde Venus (Sternberg 1932)

31

Pre-Production Works

Break-down Samples

Locationwise

	Jupiter Bunglow		Date :
	Settings	Scenes	Artists
1.	Girl's House	Sc # 1,2,2A, 2B, 2C	Tuhina, Alex + Two Jr. Artist
2.	Boy's Room	Sc # 8A, 9,10,12 A	Alex and Douglas

Requirement List

(Special props)			Date :
Date of Shooting	Actual Locations	Going to Cover	Props
1. 23-7-2002 (Tuesday)	Petrol Pump	Sc# 4 & 5	Files, Radio, Two Guns
2. 24-7-2002 (Wednesday)	XM Studio	Sc# 10, 10A	Bulletin Board, Map of Africa

Scene Order List

SC#1 – $\frac{\text{Girl's House/INT'Day}}{\text{Mother, Alex, Tuhina}}$ (2 July 2002)

SC#2 – $\frac{\text{Boy's House/INT/Night}}{\text{Alex, Mother, Servant}}$ (3 July 2002)

SC#3 – $\frac{\text{Garden/Ext./Day}}{\text{Alex, Tuhina}}$ (5 July 2002)

ARTIST SCHEDULE

Sl. No.	Artist & Phone	Character	Date & time	Remarks
1.	Ben/6339629	John	22 July 2002 10 A.M.	Bring Blue Tie
2.	Franklin/2553296	Caesar	23 July 2002 8 P.M.	X

BUDGET LIST

Sl. No.	Post	Fee	Remarks
1	2	3	4
1.	Director		
2.	Chief Assistant Director		
3.	1st Assistant director		
4.	2nd Assistant director		
5.	Cameraman		
6.	1st Assistant Cameraman		
7.	2nd Assistant Cameraman		
8.	3rd Assistant Cameraman		
9.	Editor		
10.	Assistant editors		
11.	Writers		
12.	Sound Recordist.		
13.	Assistant Recordist		
14.	Art Director		
15.	Assistant Art Director		
16.	Make-up Man		
17.	Assistant Dressman		
18.	Dress Designer.		
19.	Assistant Dressmen		
20.	Hair Dresser		
21.	P.R.O.		
22.	Still Photographer		
23.	Production Controller		

1	2	3	4
24.	Production Manager		
25.	Title Music		
26.	Boom Man		
27.	Background Score		
28.	Setting Boys		
29.	Camera Equipment		
30.	Camera Attendants		
31.	Lights		
32.	Light director		
33.	Light men		
34.	Spot Boys		
35.	Film Negative/type		
36.	Post Production		
37.	Costumes		
38.	Special props		
39.	Jr. Artist		
40.	Conveyance		
41.	Generator		
42.	Transport		
43.	Refreshment		
44.	Artist		
45.	Miscellaneous		
46.	Special effects		
47.	Special effects supervisor		
48.	Film Laboratory		
	GRAND TOTAL		

Notes : (A) Apart from these major categories, you also have to pay to assistants in every department, and for location visits, publicity and other unseen charges and expenses.

(B) Fees for every department and persons differ country to country and depends on the nature of story, production value, starcasts, locations etc.

32

GLOSSARY

- Imaginary Line : If shots from either side of an imaginary line connecting two subjects are intercut, the direction of the action and performer's positions laterally reversed.
- Asymmetrical Balance : A pictorial arrangement in which a larger object close to picture centre is balanced by smaller objects near the screen edge.
- Aspect Ratio : The proportions of the screen. For regular T.V. 4 : 3 (1 : 33 : 1). For super 16 mm TV film, 1 : 66 : 1, for HDTV, 16 : 9 (1 : 77 : 1). Some TV cameras can switch between the 4 : 3 and 16 : 9 standards.
- Barrel Distortion : A Form of distortion on a wide-angle lens, in which lines near the centre edges of the picture bulge outwards.
- Base Station : A central control unit for digital video cameras.
- Blocking : Working out performer's positions, moves and actions, relative to the setting and camera's position.
- Chroma key (colour separation overlay, CSO) : Electronic equipment for inserting a subject with a special colour background (usually blue) into any video 'background' to create a seamless composite.
- Electronic Cinematography Camera (ECC) : A video camera designed with mechanical and electronic features that provide performance similar to 35 mm cine camera, and produce typical 'Film look' picture quality.
- Floor Marking : Chalked, crayoned, or taped marks indicating the positions of cameras, talent, furniture, scenery.

- Picture Noise : A random speckling or 'Snow' pattern, due to electronic circuit noise.
- Polarizing Filter : A special plastic filter, which can differentiate between lights from different directions. It darkens blue skies, and kills reflections in glass, water, metal.
- Split Focus : A compromise focus setting when depth of field is limited and two subjects at different distances cannot both be sharply focused; both are left slightly soft focused.
- Whip Pan (Swiss pan, Blur pan, Zip pan) : A very rapid pan movement, showing the scene clearly at its start and finish but blurring all intermediate detail.
- Wild Track : Atmospheric or environmental sound, recorded (usually without picture), or potential background effects to be inserted into a programme.
- Anamorphic Lens : Lens attachment having different magnifications, horizontally or vertically, used in the taking and project of wide screen films such as cinemascope.
- Cinema Scope : First professional wide screen system using anamorphic lense on the camera to compress a wide (2 : 55 : 1) aspect ratio onto a normal 4 : 3 film frame. A similar lens on the projector restores correct appearance for presentation in the cinema.
- Double 8 mm Film : Length of film 16 mm wide, but with twice the usual number of perphorations along each edge. The film is run through the camera twice, images being recorded on half the width on the original run through and on the opposite half during the return passage. After process the film is slit down the middle and the two halves joined end to end, giving on 8 mm wide standard 8 film of twice the original length.
- Lens : Curved, Optically worked glass-sometimes a special plastic — capable of forming an image of a subject by the bending of light rays emanating from it. Practical movie lenses are made up of a combination of many elements which are designed to overcome faults in image formation.

- Montage : Semi-abstract, representational assembly of short scenes used to create a specific mood. Superimpositions and dissolves are frequently used in this technique.
- ND Filter (Neutral density filter) : A grey filter for reducing the amount of light passing through the lens without altering its colour.
- Projection Sync : The Synchronization of Picture and accompanying sound track for projection or printing. The method takes into account the displacement between the Picture gate and sound head in the projector, amounting to 18 frames (sound ahead) for super 8 magnetic, 22 frames for super 8 optical, 26 frames for 16 mm optical, 28 frames for 16 mm magnetic, and 56 frames for standard 8 magnetic.
- RMS (Root-Mean-Square) : Used mainly to measure the true continuous power output of an amplifier with a continuous sine-wave applied.
- Sky Light Filter : An extremely pale, straw ultra-violet absorbing filter, used to prevent excess blue in the rendering of distant scenes.
- Telecine : Equipment for scanning film for television, Converting the images into a TV signal.
- Turrets : Sliding or rotating mounts for several camera lenses, allowing rapid change of focal length. They have now been largely superseded by Zooms. Though 16 mm cameras still have them.
- UV Filter : Clear or pinkish Filter that stops the passage of U.V. (Ultra Voilet).
- Additive Colour : A method of mixing light where virtually any colour (except the pure spectrum colours) can be produced by adding various proportions of the primary colours — blue, green and red.
- Complementary Colours : These are pairs of colours which, when mixed together, give a grey (neutral). For example, a grey is formed when yellow and blue light are mixed together. Therefore yellow is complementary to blue and *vice versa*. Other complementary colours include green and magnetta, red and cyan.

- Parallax Error : The difference between the image seen through the viewfinder of a camera and the image seen by the lens, which results from the fact that the two view from slightly different positions. Parallax error occurs when cameras have separate viewfinder and taking lenses.
- Star Filter : When placed in front of the camera lens, a star filter gives a star like appearance to strong high lights.

33

Further Readings

- Professional Lighting Handbook
  By Carlson
  (A description and discussion of the general hardware of film lighting.)
- Motion Picture Camera and Lighting Equipment
  By Samuelson, David
  (Includes extremely useful data on film lighting equipment).
- "Making Meaning : Inference and Rhetoric in the Interpretation of Cinema."
  By David Bordwell
  (An in-depth study of film reviewing.)
- Film and Reform
  By Ian Aitken
  (On British documentary film movement.)
- The Art of Record
  By John Corner
  (A Very useful book for those who want to pursue documentary further.)
- Shades of Noir
  By Joon Copjec
  (About the re-emergence of film noir in contemporary Hollywood.)
- Hitchcock : The First Forty-four Films
  By Eric Rohmer and Claude Chabrol
  (Study of Hitchcock films.)

- Hitchcock

  By Francois Truffaut

  (The most famous book on Hitchcock.)
- The Classical Hollywood Cinema : Film Style and Mode of Production to 1966.

  By Bordwell, Janet Staigr and Kristin Thompson.

  (The undisputed, authoritative heavy weight study of Classical Hollywood cinema, covering the history of film, style, technology and mode of production.)
- A Short Guide to Writing About Films

  By Timothy

  (A concise and practical guide for students of script writing.)
- The Five C's of Cinematography

  By Joseph V. Mascelli, A.S.C.

  (A must read for all filmmakers and cinematographers.)
- The Home Movie Maker's Handbook.

  By Christopher Wordsworth

  (For amateur and serious students alike.)
- Film Studies

  By Warren Buckland

  (It talks about aesthetics, narrative, genres and documentary films.)
- The Practical Director

  By Mike Crisp

  (A useful book for all film students.)
- On Camera : How To Produce Film and Video

  By Harris Walts

  (From ideas to the post production are discussed in details.)
- The American War Films : History and Hollywood by Frank Mc Adams.

  (A detailed study about the war films.)

- Movies and Mental Illness

  By Danny Wedding

  (It deals about the movies made on human mental illness.)
- Bollywood : Popular Indian Cinema

  By Lalit Mohan Joshi

  (A new look on Bollywood Films and production.)
- "Complete Guide To American Films Schools and Cinema and Television Courses

  By Ernest Pintoff (Penguin Books)

  (For a comprehensive list of media courses in the U.S.)
- Media Courses UK (BFI)

  By Lavinia Orton

  (For a comprehensive list of media courses in U.K.)
- Directing Actors

  By Judith Weston
- Hollywood and History by Sheri Bearlstorm.
- 'Our Films, Their Films' by Satyajit Ray.
- 'Going To The Movies', 'Screenplay', 'The Screen Writer's Work book', 'Selling a Screenplay, Four Screenplays' and 'The Screen Writer's Problemsolver' by Syd Field.
- "Film Sense", "Film Forms" by Eisenstein.
- "The Movies" by Griffith and Mayer.

34

Film Schools, Museums and Websites

SCHOOLS

- American Film Institute
  John F. Kennedy Centre
  For the Performing Arts
  Washington D.C. 20566
  U.S.A.
  and
  P.O. Box 27999
  2021 North Westen Avenue
  Los Angeles CA 90027
  U.S.A.
- Australian Film Institute
  49, Eastern Road,
  South Melbourne,
  VIC 3205,
  Australia.
- British Film Institute (BFI)
  21, Stephen Street,
  London WVI 4 AY,
  England.
- Centre National de la
  Cinematographie
  12, Rue de Lubeck
  75116 Paris
  France.
- Cinemateque Francaise
  Musee du Cinema
  7 Avenue Albert-de-Mun
  75016 Paris
  France.
- Cineteca Italiana
  Via Palestro 16
  20121 Milan
  Italy.
- Deutsches Instit fur film
  kunde
  Schaumainkai 41
  60596 Frankfurt Main
  Germany.
- Sevenski Film Institutet
  Box 27126,
  Filmhuset,
  Borgvagen 1-5,
  S-102 52 Stock Holm,
  Sweden.
- Finnish Film Foundation
  Kanavakatu 12
  SF-00160 Helsinki
  Finland.

- Filmoteca Espanola
  Carretera de la Dehesa de la Villa
  S/n 28040 Madrid,
  Spain.
- Film and Television Institute of India (FTII)
  Law College Road,
  Pune,
  Maharashtra – 411004,
  India.
- Mass Comunication & Research Centre (MCRC)
  Jamia Milia University
  New Delhi, India.
- Dutch Film and Television Academy
  Lte Bocremastraat
  1054 PP Amsterdam
  The Netherlands
- European Academy for Film and Television
  Rue Verte 69
  1210 Brussels
  Belgium
- Film Institute of Ireland
  6, Eustace Street,
  Dublin 2
  Ireland.
- Hong Kong Film Academy
  P.O. Box 71311
  Kowloon
  Hong Kong.
- Hungarian Film Institute
  Budakeszi ut 5 1/B
  Budapest
  Hungary.
- Israel Film Institute
  5 Yelin Mor Street
  Tel Aviv 67058
  Israel.
- National Centre for Screen Studies
  Dronningens gt. 16
  N-0104 Oslo
  Norway.
- Society of Cinema Studies
  C/o University of Texas Press
  P.O. Box 7819,
  Austin, TX 78713-3819,
  U.S.A.

Museums

- Museum of the Moving Image
  (National Film Theatre)
  South Bank
  London SEI 8XT
  England.
- Netherland Film Museum
  Vondelpark 3
  1071 Amsterdam,
  The Netherlands.
- National Museum of Photography
  Film and Television
  Pictureville
  13 Rodford,
  BDI 1NQ
  England.
- Museo Nazionale del Cinema, Palazzo Chiablese,
  Piazza San Giovanni 2,
  10122 Turin,
  Italy.

- Film Museum Jacques Ledoux
  Rue Baron Hozta 9,
  1000 Brussels
  Belgium.
- Deutsches Film Museum
  Schaumainkai 41,
  60596 Frankfurt/Main
  Germany.
- Det Danske Film Museum
  Store Sondervoidstraede 4
  1419 Copenhagen K.
  Denmark.
- American Museum of the Moving Image
  35th Avenue, at 36th Street,
  A Storia Queens
  New York, U.S.A.

WEBSITES

1. www.livjm.ac.uk/-mccscubi/screenlinks.html
   For jobs, training, Hollywood studios, Script writing Academic Sites and television.
2. www.newshare.com/sb
   This site offers news items about the film entertainment.
3. www.vfxhq.com
   This site offers news and information on visual special effects.
4. www.tef.ua.edu/screen site/contents.htm
   It is a serious and scholarly website about film and television.
5. www.uk.imdb.com/search
   On this site you can get informations about 130,000 movies.
6. www.hollywood reporter.com
7. www.laig.com/law/entlaw/filmfes.html
   This site tells informations about film festivals around the world.
8. www.suntimes.com/ebert/ebert.html
   (For all the film reviews since 1985.)
9. www.kali.murdoch.edu.an/-entnuum/doco/links.html.
   Informations about documentary films.
10. www.variety.com
    The famous trade newspaper Daily, variety is available on this site.

11. www.corona.bc.ca/films/main.html
    This site gives you advance information about future film productions.
12. www.chireader.com /movies/index.html
    For film reviews.
13. www.labyrinth.net.au/-muffin/news-home_c.html.
    Talks about Hitchcock's films with an emphasis on serious scholarship.
14. www.cyberfilmschool.com
    Provides articles on Script writing, movie making and related topics.
15. www.cinemastudies.org